The Word of the Lord

7 Essential Principles
for Catholic
Scripture Study

The Word OF THE Lord

7 Essential Principles for Catholic Scripture Study

Steven C. Smith, Ph.D.

Our Sunday Visitor Publishing Division
Our Sunday Visitor, Inc.
Huntington, Indiana 46750

Nihil Obstat:
Msgr. Michael Heintz, Ph.D.
Censor Librorum

Imprimatur:
✠ Kevin C. Rhoades
Bishop of Fort Wayne-South Bend
March 27, 2012

The Scripture citations used in this work are taken from the *Catholic Edition of the Revised Standard Version of the Bible* (RSV), copyright © 1965 and 1966 by the Division of Christian Education of the National Council of the Churches of Christ in the United States of America. Used by permission. All rights reserved.

Excerpts from the *Catechism of the Catholic Church, Second Edition*, for use in the United States of America, copyright © 1994 and 1997, United States Catholic Conference — Libreria Editrice Vaticana. Used by permission. All rights reserved.

Every reasonable effort has been made to determine copyright holders of excerpted materials and to secure permissions as needed. If any copyrighted materials have been inadvertently used in this work without proper credit being given in one form or another, please notify Our Sunday Visitor in writing so that future printings of this work may be corrected accordingly.

ISBN: 978-1-61278-588-2 (Inventory No. T1284)
eISBN: 978-1-61278-246-1
LCCN: 2012939905

Interior design by M. Urgo
Cover design by Amanda Falk
Cover image by Shutterstock

PRINTED IN THE UNITED STATES OF AMERICA

The Word of the Lord presents the principles of Catholic Biblical exegesis drawn from Church documents. Readers of this book will gain an understanding of the many methods of scriptural interpretation from the Fathers of the Church to the present day. Through a discussion of *lectio divina*, Smith lays the foundation for scriptural prayer, which is a key component in the transformation of self that is integral to the interpretation of Scripture in the Church. This is a helpful book at a time when the relations between Scripture and Tradition and Scripture and Divine Revelation are background for many other conversations in the Church today.

— *Francis Cardinal George, O.M.I.*
Archbishop of Chicago

With numerous references to doctrinal texts, spiritual classics, and papal documents, the book is eminently scholarly, but consistently read-able, gently helping the reader move from the pages of this book to the pages of Holy Scripture. As a result of Dr. Smith's book, I believe there will be many Bibles that will be dusted off, read, and studied. Dr. Smith helps us to truly ponder the Word, and what it means for our lives; his suggestions for further study and his questions for reflection prompt us to take the Word to heart, and "fall in love," with Scripture all over again. We are encouraged to see how our lives continue to be touched and molded by the hand of God, and to appreciate how God's loving "fingerprints are on all the pages of our lives ... With *7 Principles*, we come to truly appreciate this, and to understand that a spiritual father, a man of the Word, nourishes us, too, with substance that will guide us on our way, and help us to grow as men and women of faith, equipped to nourish others. Dr. Smith has fed us well.

— *Dr. Dianne Traflet, Associate Dean and*
Assistant Professor, Pastoral Theology
Immaculate Conception Seminary
School of Theology, Seton Hall University

Dr. Steven Smith's new book, *The Word of the Lord*, is a perfect companion for those who wish to deepen their knowledge of Sacred Scripture during the Year of Faith proclaimed by Pope Benedict XVI. Dr. Smith, while always remaining faithful to the teachings of the Church, is able to breathe new life into our current perspectives on Scripture by the seven

LIST OF TABLES AND FIGURES

Tables

Figures

FOREWORD

As you read this book, you will join with me in saying, "Thanks be to God." The reason is simple. At Mass, we Catholics always hear "*The Word of the Lord*," and then respond, "*Thanks be to God*." Yet the readings that we hear throughout our lives at the Sunday Masses are but portions of the Bible. If we are ever to come to a deeper faith and knowledge of Jesus, *the Living Word*, we must become *students of the written Word of God* in its entirety. As St. Jerome reminds us, "Ignorance of Scripture is ignorance of Christ." An essential part of following Jesus — as a disciple — is to become a disciplined student of Scripture, both the Old Testament and the New. And for that we need good teachers, like Dr. Steven Smith.

In Acts 8, we read about an Ethiopian Eunuch who needed help to understand a hard text in Isaiah. God sent him Philip the Deacon to explain how the oracle pointed to Jesus. Likewise, we do well to have expert guidance in reading Scripture. In particular, we need teachers who are able to impart the wisdom that comes from the Holy Spirit through the authority and living tradition of the Church.

Above all, it is the Holy Spirit who guides the Church "into all truth," as Jesus promised (Jn. 15:13). Through the Church, then, we are guided in our reading and interpretation of Scripture. Along the way, we come to discover the principles and methods of Catholic Scripture study. And that is what makes this book so valuable. Whether it is the mystery of biblical inspiration and the divine authority and truth of Scripture, or how to make sense of the difficult parts of the Old Testament, you will get expert guidance from Dr. Steven Smith. In a clear and conversational style, he addresses a host of crucial questions: How was the biblical 'canon' gradually formed over the course of centuries? How is Scripture *directly related to* the Holy Eucharist? What are the different senses of Scripture? What is the role of Sacred Tradition in biblical interpretation?

Most importantly, readers are guided step by step through *seven principles of Catholic biblical interpretation* by a veteran teacher of Sacred Scripture at Mount St. Mary's Seminary, one of the oldest and most respected houses of formation in the United States. From years of experience in the classroom and parish, Dr. Smith is able to communicate clearly for a wide range of readers, from seminarians and clergy to young adults and professionals. No matter what your background, here you will find many practical examples and memorable illustrations to help digest each lesson. And that's why I predict that, when you are finished reading *The Word of the Lord*, you will say, *Thanks be to God.*

Scott Hahn, Ph.D. (Fr. Michael Scanlan Chair
of Biblical Theology and the New Evangelization)
Franciscan University of Steubenville

ACKNOWLEDGMENTS

Numerous persons should be thanked for their contributions in the completion of this book. To begin with, I wish to thank Monsignor Steven Rohlfs, Rector of Mount St. Mary's Seminary (Emmitsburg, MD), who has allowed me to use my gifts in the education and formation of Catholic seminarians. I pray that this project reflects "the Mount's" excellent reputation in training tomorrow's priests, which I am humbled to take part in every day.

Along these lines, I wish to express sincere thanks to all of the faculty at Mount St. Mary's Seminary, from whom I am continually inspired. In particular, I am especially grateful to Fr. Tommy Lane and Dr. William Bales — my two excellent colleagues and real gentlemen in the Scripture Department. Likewise, I wish to thank my friend and colleague, Deacon James Keating, of the Institute for Priestly Formation (Omaha, NB). The readers of this book will glean many more insights, in terms of integrating Scripture study with our life of prayer, because of Deacon Keating's input.

Additionally, I wish to express sincere thanks to all of my seminarians (past and present) for their devotion to Christ and His Church and for their feedback as this writing project unfolded before their eyes. In particular, I wish to express my thanks to all the seminarians of the class of 2013 and 2012, who contributed some of the questions at the end of each chapter. *Stare forte!*

Certainly, I owe a debt of gratitude to Bert Ghezzi and the entire team at Our Sunday Visitor. Their generosity and patience with me and their many smart and creative contributions to *The Word of the Lord* are too numerous to mention.

Finally, and on a more personal note, my deepest appreciation is reserved for my lovely and supportive wife and my best friend, Elizabeth. No one on earth will ever fully realize the sacrifices involved in teaching, speaking, and writing. This book would not have been possible without her own dedication to our marriage and family, and without her love for me. I am thankful beyond words for Elizabeth's gentleness and holiness, and her endless patience with me. My darling daughters, Isabelle and Olivia, you are blessed to have such a caring mother. Among her many other talents, Elizabeth is a fine editor and, were it possible to dust this copy for fingerprints, her hand would be detected in places too numerous to count. It is to you, Elizabeth, that I dedicate this book.

Seven Indispensable Principles for the Study of Scripture

Thou hast said, "Seek ye my face."
My heart says to thee,
"Thy face, LORD, do I seek."
Psalm 27:8

The book you are about to read was written for everyone who has ever asked, "What does a *Catholic* approach to Scripture study look like?" As a seminary professor of Sacred Scripture, I'm well aware that today's Catholic has an abundance of resources available for the study of God's Word — from biblical commentaries to apologetics to theological reflections on Scripture such as Pope Benedict's two magnificent volumes in the *Jesus of Nazareth* series.[1]

Despite this wealth of excellent biblical resources, I am continually struck by a recurrent question I am frequently asked. At some point or another, people from many different backgrounds have asked me if I know of a book that explains "the Catholic approach" to Scripture study. Additionally, I'm asked a more specific set of sub-questions, such as the following:

- "My brother who is a Protestant Christian gave me a book that his pastor wrote, and it's pretty good ... but there's no discussion of how the Bible came to be, or who determined the 'official list,' etc. And the book makes no mention of the 'extra books' we Catholics read. Can you recommend a book that explains these questions?"

- "I'm not a Scripture scholar, but I have started a Bible study group at our parish. I'd like to feel more prepared to help answer questions others ask — as well as my own — on a number of of the Magisterium of the Catholic Church and her most trusted and true biblical theologians.

Whatever your interests, it is hoped that you will not only "learn" how to study Scripture as a Catholic, but more importantly, fall in love with God's Word all over again, and the Savior within its pages. For in the pages of the Bible we meet the messiah of Israel and the Revealer of God to the world. We meet the One who reaches out to "Samaritans" of every age and background with Living Water. Come, meet the Man who can show us everything we've ever done (John 4:39) — and everything we're meant to become in the blessed Trinity. *"It is no longer because of your words that we believe, for we have heard for ourselves and we know that this is indeed the Savior of the world"* (John 4:42).

Steven C. Smith, Ph. D.
Holy Week, 2012

Notes

1   Joseph Ratzinger (Pope Benedict XVI), *Jesus of Nazareth. Vol. I. From the Baptism in the Jordan to the Transfiguration.* San Francisco: Ignatius Press, 2007; *Jesus of Nazareth. Vol. II. Holy Week: From the Entrance into Jerusalem to the Resurrection.* San Francisco: Ignatius Press, 2010.

2   This book can be used as a reference, i.e., to look up a particular topic for further clarity. Yet, in order to derive the most out of the study, and to understand the breadth of the Catholic approach presented here, it is recommended that the book be read a chapter at a time, from beginning to end. Afterward, use the book as a reference tool.

3   Pope Benedict XVI, *Verbum Domini* ("The Word of the Lord"). Post-Synodal Apostolic Exhortation on the Word of God in the Life and Mission of the Church. Promulgated Sept. 30, 2010. Available online at: http://www.vatican.va/holy_father/benedict_xvi/apost_exhortations/documents/hf_ben-xvi_exh_20100930_verbum-domini_en.html#INDEX. Reference will be made to *Verbum Domini* throughout . The document is discussed in more detail in Ch. 2 (below).

Principle 1
God's Word: Divine Words in Human Language

Principle #1: Catholic Biblical Interpretation is governed by the firm belief that Scripture is the inspired word of God, expressed in human language. God's Word was written under the direction and inspiration of the Holy Spirit and — at the same time — was written by true human authors with their intellectual capacities and limitations. The thought and the words belong both to God and to human beings in such a way that the whole Bible comes simultaneously from God and from the inspired human authors.

The Right Foundation

What makes the words in the Bible so unique, so powerful? The answer is clear: for Christians, it is because we believe the Bible is "inspired." Of all the ideas we will discuss, none is of greater magnitude or has more ripple effects in the pond of biblical interpretation than divine inspiration. One scholar rightly refers to it as the *foundational principle* in our approach to Sacred Scripture:

> Obviously, [this principle] is the most important of all. It is described as 'foundational' and it functions as the basis of all the others. It expresses the conviction of the Church's faith regarding the nature of the Bible: it is 'the word of God expressed in human language' and must, therefore, be interpreted as such.[4]

Scriptures led to their canonization. Yet, the first Christians did not anxiously await the finalization of the canon and only then pay attention to the Scriptures; from the beginning, they were prayed and read in the early liturgies: "All of Scripture is intrinsically liturgical. Liturgy is like a golden thread that runs through the many pearls of salvation history and holds them together."[12]

Justin Martyr, writing in the mid-second century, writes that when the Christians gathered to worship the Lord on "the day of the Sun," they gathered together and listened as the Scriptures were proclaimed: "For as long as there is time the *Memoirs of the Apostles* or the writings of the prophets are read."[13] In a word, the early Christians "prayed what they believed" and they "believed what they prayed." This notion is known as *lex orandi, lex credendi*:

> The Church's faith precedes the faith of the believer who is invited to adhere to it. When the Church celebrates the sacraments, she confesses the faith received from the apostles — whence the ancient saying: *lex orandi, lex credendi* … The law of prayer is the law of faith: the Church believes as she prays. *Liturgy is a constitutive element of the holy and living Tradition.*[14]

From the earliest liturgies of the Apostolic era, biblical inspiration was (and is) inextricably tied to this notion of *lex orandi, lex credendi.* The canonization process, which was a relatively long process, encompassing the better part of three centuries, was to be sure a decisive moment in the status of the Scriptures. The development of the canon distinguished the "inspired books" from those not accepted in the canon.

FOR REFLECTION | *To what extent is my prayer life informed by my reading of Scripture … and to what extent is my reading of Scripture a response to my life of prayer?*

Following the Apostles and Church fathers, the Church as a whole firmly held to the belief in the unique status of the Scriptures as "God's Word." In fact, inspiration did not face a serious challenge until the modern age (certainly not at least until the time of the Reformation). It is important to realize that until the modern age, the Church had no need to produce a document explaining biblical inspiration, since it had not been questioned.

Following the Protestant Reformation, the Catholic Church re-affirmed her absolute confidence in the Holy Scriptures. In 1546, the Council of Trent gave us our definitive canon of Scripture as an article of faith, but also addressed the divine authorship of the Bible, referring to Sacred Scripture (and Sacred Tradition) as "inspired."[15]

In the mid to late nineteenth century, with the rise of modern rationalism and skepticism, the Church saw the need to articulate its position on the matter. Vatican I, like the Council of Trent before it, referred to the Scriptures as "being written under the inspiration of the Holy Spirit," and "having God as their author."[16] Since the time of Vatican I, all of the Church's teaching documents on Scripture have focused on inspiration to a greater degree, and rightly place special emphasis on it as a "first principle" in reading and interpreting the Bible.[17]

The Mirror of God

Given the history of this doctrine, and its importance as a first and foundational principle, we need to understand well the concept of biblical inspiration. But our consideration of it should go beyond a mere "basic affirmation." As I tell my seminarians, "Inspiration is more than something we need to believe to 'avoid heresy!'" As Catholics, we certainly need to affirm the Church's authoritative teaching on the inspiration of Sacred Scripture. But then we should pause, and ask, *"How important is this to me as a follower of Jesus?" "Do I really live as if Scripture really is inspired?"*

Such reflective questions are necessary, because the inspiration of Scripture has profound implications in our lives as Christians. *Divino Afflante Spiritu*, Pius XII's landmark encyclical promoting a new era of biblical studies, referred to Sacred Scripture as a "heaven-sent treasure" and "the most precious source of doctrine on faith and morals."[18] Similarly, the *Catechism of the Catholic Church* reminds us that it is from the inspired Word of God that the Church continues to find her "nourishment and strength."[19]

As Jesus taught us, we cannot live on "bread alone" (Deut 8:3; Matt 4:4). We need to find our strength and nourishment in God, in the Word made flesh (John 1:14). When we look to the written Word, we encounter the Living Word, Jesus, who is love revealed. In *Verbum Domini*, Pope Benedict XVI reminded us that Jesus is "the one, definitive Word given to mankind" — just as in his second encyclical, *Caritas in Veritate,* he reminded us that all people "feel the impulse to love authentically."[20] Yet, this the term inspiration. We're all familiar with expressions like, "What an *inspiring* sunset!" or "She is an *inspired* actress!" In such instances, the term "inspiration" often refers to a natural beauty, a human talent — or an emotional response to such things, leaving us filled with wonder, delight, gratitude, or awe.

These are beautiful — and *natural* responses. Yet, they do not necessarily lead us closer to the meaning of "inspiration" as it concerns the books of Scripture. If we turn to the apostles themselves, we soon learn that when it comes to the origins of the Bible, to say that Scripture is "inspired" is to say that it is God-breathed, and of *supernatural* origins.

In fact, when we look carefully, we can observe that the language of "divine inspiration" is to be found in the Scriptures themselves. The Apostle Paul writes, "All Scripture is *inspired* by God and profitable for teaching, for reproof, for correction, and for training in righteousness, that the man of God may be complete, equipped for every good work" (2 Tim 3:16–17).[24] What does Paul mean by "inspired" in this context?

A closer look at his choice of words may help us understand his thought. In his letter to Timothy, Paul uses a particular term, which is typically translated "inspired." In the original Greek, the term is *theoneustos*, which means, quite literally, "God breathed" (*theos* = God, *pneustos* = breath). The word "inspiration" comes from the Latin term *inspirare*, "to breathe in." Thus, the Greek and Latin origins point us to a profound meaning of "inspiration."

In the Bible, God himself breathes forth His own life, pours forth His Spirit into these texts. God exerts a divine prerogative and initiates His supernatural presence upon the human authors of the books of Scripture. God guides these authors in order to assure that they faithfully convey — precisely and completely — all the truths He wished to communicate. He has done so that we might, like young Timothy, "lack nothing" we need to live the Christian life faithfully. He did so out of love for us — and to "equip" His Church — all of us, to do His works.

Paul's words are instrumental for our understanding of inspiration, yet the development of the doctrine was not all sewn up with just one verse of Scripture. In fact, if we search for some sort of explicit doctrine or definition of inspiration in Scripture, we may be disappointed, for our search would be in vain. Likewise, the Scriptures do not explicitly define God's "role" in the writing of the sacred books. However, all is not lost. In fact, if we delve deeper into the Scriptures, beginning in the Old Testament, we'll soon discover some fascinating patterns of "divinely inspired speech" that emerge. If we take our primary insight given to us from St. Paul in one hand, namely, that the Scriptures are truly *God breathed* — and couple that with the patterns we are about to look at from the pages of the Old Testament, we'll be a lot further along in understanding what our Church really teaches about the inspiration of God's Word.

Have you ever dreamed of being a spy, like James Bond, or a soldier behind enemy lines, listening in on an important conversation? If we turn to the book of Exodus, we find ourselves "eavesdropping" on a divine conversation. In Exodus, God speaks to Moses, and instructs him to compose the Torah, God's law, in written form: "*And the LORD said to Moses,* Write this for a memorial in a book, and rehearse it in the ears of Joshua …" (Exod 17:14).

On numerous other occasions throughout salvation history, we hear authoritative echoes of God's voice, for example, in the Hebrew phrase, *köh 'ämar yhwh 'ädönäy,* "*thus says the Lord,*"[25] and many more times in the expression, *dibre yhwh,* or "*the word of the Lord.*"[26]

Beyond such expressions, we can see specific criteria by which, for example, God speaks through various biblical prophets. For example, in the book of Deuteronomy:

> And the LORD said to me, "They have rightly said all that they have spoken. I will raise up for them a prophet like you from among their brethren; and I will put my words in his mouth, and he shall speak to them all that I command him. And whoever will not give heed to my words which he shall speak in my name, I myself will require it of him. But the prophet who presumes to speak a word in my name which I have not commanded him to speak, or who speaks in the name of other gods, that same prophet shall die." (Deut 18:17–20)

The most profound interpretation of Scripture comes precisely from those who let themselves be shaped by the Word of God through listening, reading and assiduous meditation.

— Pope Benedict XVI, *Verbum Domini* § 48

Notice in the passage from Deuteronomy, God declares to Moses three criteria of the true "prophet of God." These same three elements can help us understand the inspiration of Scripture more generally.

chute, he believed he now had a way of getting across the lake. Walking out onto the windy, frozen lake, Bear placed the parachute *in front of him*, grabbed the makeshift handle and held on for dear life! Soon, the chute had picked up a great gust of wind, lifted up off the frozen lake, and effectively pulled him along over the surface of the lake at a fairly high rate of speed.

What would have been an impossible task was now possible; Bear made it across the distance of lake in a little more than *twenty minutes*. It was an amazing thing to watch — but I imagine that it was much more exhilarating from his point of view! This arctic adventure illustrates our point well: what Bear was unable to accomplish in his own human capacities, was accomplished by the sheer power of the wind, literally carrying him over the surface of the frozen lake.

The divine Presence is no longer to be localized in a single place, the material tabernacle: henceforth, God will be in Jesus Christ, everywhere.

— Henri de Lubac, *Medieval Exegesis of Scripture*, Vol. I, p. 235

In Scripture, St. Peter uses a word that describes a similar phenomenon: the prophet is carried forward (*phero*) by the power of the Holy Spirit, much like a sail propels a boat forward by the power of the wind interacting within and commandeering the sail. This is how the Apostle wants us to conceive of the process of prophetic speech, as God's words really communicated through, or *carried forward* through the human person. He writes that it is not the person's own "impulse" that accomplished this, but rather, "men moved by the Holy Spirit spoke from God" (2 Pet 1:21).

In short, we have seen how the Scriptures themselves reveal a pattern, a paradigm, in which God speaks to us: 1) The Scriptures speak forth God's own words; 2) The Scriptures involve human authors and their capacities; and 3) The Scriptures "carry forward" precisely what God intends to say.

This "biblical pattern" is reflected, too, in the Church's teaching document on Sacred Scripture. Pope Benedict recently made the following statement:

"The Constitution *Dei Verbum* itself, after stating that God is the author of the Bible, reminds us that in Sacred Scripture God speaks to man in a human fashion and this divine-human synergy is very important: *God really speaks to men and women in a human way.*[30]

Now that we have considered the first crucial dimension of biblical inspiration carefully, i.e., its divine origins, let us turn our attention to the other equally important aspect, i.e., its human quality.

In Scripture, God speaks to man in a truly human way.[31]

As we have seen, the Church teaches and has always taught that all the books of Sacred Scripture and all of their contents "have God as their author."[32] Yet, in order to arrive at a truly Catholic understanding of "inspiration," it is crucial to see that the Scriptures are indeed "God's words," but they are simultaneously His words expressed in *human* language, *human* capacities as well as *human* limitations.

God really speaks to men and women in a human way.

— Pope Benedict XVI

In other words, Scripture is the result of God's divine action, coupled with human cooperation in the process. As the Church reminded us at Vatican II,

> Since God speaks in Sacred Scripture through men in human fashion, the interpreter of Sacred Scripture, in order to see clearly what God wanted to communicate to us, should carefully investigate *what meaning the sacred writers really intended, and what God wanted to manifest by means of their words.*[33]

Note how *Dei Verbum* describes all of this: God communicates in Scripture through human beings, *in a human fashion.* Therefore, if we really want to study Scripture well, it is not enough to say "God wrote it, I believe it."

This may come as a shock to some, but belief in the Bible as "God's words" is not enough. True, we cannot begin to comprehend the mysteries of Sacred Scripture unless we first embrace it as *God's own words.* Yet, unless we also approach the Bible as really a work of human beings as its "true authors,"[34] we will not discover the literal meaning of Scripture. As

7   *DV* §11. In reference to the phrase, "relying on the belief of the Apostles," *DV* includes the following Scripture citations: John 20:31; 2 Tim 3:16; 2 Pet 1:19-20, 3:15-16.

8   CCC 107; Cf. *DV* §11. We will deal with this concept of Scripture teaching "firmly, faithfully, and without error" those things God wanted written within it (i.e., biblical inerrancy) in more detail later in the chapter.

9   *DV*, 21.

10   The Church does not accept any theory of inspiration in which the Church's "approval" of the books of Scripture somehow imparts or bestows inspiration upon them.

11   Benedict XVI, *Jesus of Nazareth* (San Francisco: Ignatius Press, 2007), xi.

12   S. W. Hahn, *Letter and Spirit: From Written Text to Living Word in the Liturgy* (New York: Doubleday, 2005), 35. Hahn discusses how the unity that exists between Scripture and the Liturgy is both *material* and *formal*; "material" in the sense that much of Scripture itself is concerned with the liturgy, and "formal" in the sense that "Scripture took its final form ... for the sake of liturgy, and the canon itself derived from liturgical tradition" (34-35). On this crucial connection between Scripture and liturgy, see: James A. Sanders, *From Sacred Story to Sacred Text* (Philadelphia: Fortress Press, 1987); Andrew Brian McGowan, "Is There a Liturgical text in this Gospel? The Institutional Narratives and their Early Interpretative Communities," *Journal of Biblical Literature* 118 (1999), 73-87.

13   Justin Martyr, *First Apology*, 65.

14   CCC 1124 (emphasis added).

15   *Decretum de Canonicis Scripturis* ("Fourth Session of the Council of Trent," 1446). "The Council clearly perceived that this truth and rule are contained in the written books and unwritten traditions which have come down to us, having been received by the apostles from the mouth of Christ Himself, or from the apostles *by the dictation of the Holy Spirit, and have been transmitted as it were from hand to hand ... for God alone is the author of both* ... as coming from the mouth of Christ or being *inspired by the Holy Spirit* and preserved in continuous succession in the Catholic Church." This is the first time a magisterial document used the term "dictation" in discussing Scripture. Yet, its use should <u>not</u> be misunderstood and applied in a more stringent way. Here, the Council is emphasizing describing the Holy Spirit's authoritative guidance of the human authors. Vatican I's definition of inspiration omitted this term (see following note).

16   *DF*, Third Session of Vatican I, Ch. 2.

17   Cf. *PD* §41; *SP* §3; *DAS* § 1; *Dei Verbum* §11; *IBC*, I.A.a; III.d.2.c; I.A.4.f, etc. Note: The *IBC* document, which comes on the 100th anniversary of *PD* (1893) and the 50th anniversary of *DAS* (1943), did not articulate the doctrine anew; it simply affirms "inspiration" throughout.

18   Pius XII, *Divino Afflante Spiritu* §1. Encyclical letter, "On the Promotion of Biblical Studies" (1943). Available online at: www.vatican.va/holy_father/pius_xii/encyclicals/documents/hf_p-xii_enc_30091943_divino-afflante-spiritu_en.html

19   CCC 104.

20   Benedict XVI, *Caritas in Veritate* §1.

21   Benedict XVI, *Caritas in Veritate*, §34.

22   "In discerning the canon of Scripture, the Church was also discerning and defining her own identity. Henceforth Scripture was to function as a mirror in which the Church could continually rediscover her identity and assess, century after century, the way in which she constantly responds to the gospel and equips herself to be an apt vehicle of its transmission" (*IBC*, III.B.1.e).

23 CCC 105.

24 This passage is often cited by some Christians to attempt to prove that "Scripture alone" (i.e., *Sola scriptura)* is the one authoritative source for faith. Yet, such a notion is not biblical and cannot be demonstrated from this text or any text in Scripture. Rather, Sacred Scripture and Sacred Tradition form "one deposit of the word of God" (*DV* §10). We will deal with this more in Ch. 3 (below).

25 E.g., Exod 4:22, 5:1, 7:17; Josh 7:13; Isa 65:8; Jer 9:21; Ezek 3:11; Zech 1:3.

26 E.g., Gen 15:1, 4; Exod 9:21; Num 15:31; Deut 28:2; 1 Sam 3:1; 7, 21; 15:10; 2 Sam 7:4; 22:31; 24;11; 1 Ki 6:11; 12:24; 13:9, 17, 20, 32; 16:1, 7; 2 Ki 1:17; 3:12; 7:1; 9:26; 20:4, 16, 19; Isa 1:10; 2:3; 28:13, 14; 38:4; 39:5; 66:5; Jer 1:2, 4, 11, 13; 2:1, 4, 31; 3:1; 6:10; 7;2; 8:9; 14:1; 16:1; 21:11; 25:3; 32:26; 36:27; 46:1; Ezek 1:3; 3:16; 6:1, 3; 7:1; 11:14; 12:1, 8, 17, 21, 26; 20:2; 21:3, 6, 13, 23; 38:1; Hos 1:1; 4:1; Joel 1:1; Amos 7:16; 8:12; Mic 1:14; Zech 4:6, 8; 6:9; Ps 18:31; 33:4, 6; Dan 9:2; Ezr. 1:1; 1 Chr 11:3, 10; 12:24: 15:15; 2 Chr 34:21.

27 Cf. Aidan Nichols, *The Shape of Catholic Theology: An Introduction to its Sources, Principles and History* (San Francisco: Ignatius Press, 1991), 113.

28 See the website of Edward "Bear" Grylls for more biographical information: www.beargrylls.com.

29 Episodes of "Man vs. Wild" are periodically broadcast on the Discovery Channel: http://dsc.discovery.com/fansites/manvswild/manvswild.html.

30 Benedict XVI, Address to the Participants in the Plenary Assembly of the Pontifical Biblical Commission (April 23, 2009); cf. *DV* §13.

31 CCC 107.

32 *DV* §11, CCC 105.

33 *DV* §12 (emphasis added).

34 *DV* §11.

35 *DV* §12.

36 *Decretum de Canonicis Scripturis*, Fourth Session of the Council of Trent. The issue of the canon of Scripture will be dealt with in the Excursus at the end of Ch. 3 (below).

the Gospels. The Four Gospels may have "pride of place" but the wisdom books, or any other books of the biblical canon are not "more" or "less" inspired than other books. A book is either inspired or it isn't — and all the books within the canon of Scripture, as adjudicated by the Catholic Church are the inspired Word of God.

Q: *"Did God inspire some parts of Scripture and not others, or are some parts 'more inspired' than other parts?"*

No. To the contrary, all of the canonical texts, as originally written by the human authors *and all of their contents* are indeed inspired Scripture. As I like to remind my seminarians, various passages from the Old Testament, which may feel less relevant are nonetheless just as inspired as our favorite miracle stories from the Gospels.

Dei Verbum provides great clarity here: God worked through the human authors and "consigned to writing *whatever He wanted written, and no more.*"[40] God is indeed the ultimate author of Sacred Scripture and He guided the various human authors to write "whatever He wanted" written. This means for example, that the various genealogies in Scripture, or other difficult passages, are within the books that the Church enthusiastically embraces as God's inspired Word. You would do well to remember this point when reading Scripture. Do not quickly rush past the genealogies in the Book of Numbers (Ch. 1, 26) and in the Gospel of Matthew (Ch. 1), nor past the inscriptions above many of the Psalms, nor past the prologue to Sirach. *Slow down.* These passages and words are every bit of the inspired canon as the rest. They are there for a reason; we only need to discover what truths they hold. They instructed the original readers, and if we pay close attention, they will instruct us today as well. When studying Scripture, allow time to explore such intricacies in the biblical text. You might otherwise miss something important.

FOR REFLECTION | *Do I manage my time and schedule in such a way that allows for significantly "slowing down" when reading? Could I make a few modifications in my schedule to make this a reality? How might my knowledge of and devotion to Scripture change if I wasn't as "rushed," and simply moved through the text more attentively?*

It is equally important to realize that inspiration is much more than some sort of "negative protection" with respect to the work of the fallible, human authors. This is not because the Bible is "brimming with misinformation."[41] No, it is a result of the Lord's active involvement in the first place. God is the primary author of all that is within Scripture, *vitally directing all that is within* it; not merely safeguarding those things that He did not wish to be contained in Scripture.

Q: "Among the various approaches or 'models' of inspiration, which one is closest to the Church's understanding?"

It is true that there have been, historically speaking, various views on biblical inspiration.[42] Yet, (for better or worse), until the time of the Enlightenment, particular emphasis was placed on the divine Author, the Holy Spirit. While the ancient and medieval did not intentionally "downplay" the human dimension, God's role was of particular importance in any discussions of inspiration. The dynamic relationship between the two is, in some ways, more of a modern understanding. This is a good thing in many respects, as along the way, there have been models that have overemphasized either the Divine author or the human authors.

The Dictation Model. This theory, which was advanced in the sixteenth and seventeenth centuries argues that in Scripture, God communicates not only the ideas but also the *words and verbal expression to the human authors.* In essence, the role of the author was simply to be open to receive God's actions. This model of inspiration found some artistic resonance in Caravaggio's beautiful *Inspiration of Matthew.*[43]

In the following quote, the Spanish Dominican Melchior Cano (1509–1560) reflects the limitations of this model: "Not only the words *but even every comma* has been supplied by the Divine Spirit … falsity is excluded by the sacred authors … *everything great or small has been edited by the sacred authors at the dictation of the Holy Spirit.*"[44]

Such an approach is not compatible with the Catholic understanding of inspiration. The problems are clear: while holding to a high view of God's role in the process, it so diminishes the place of the human author to the extent of being meaningless in the process, a "stenographer" in the process. In fact, such a model is antithetical to the Incarnational nature of Christianity and is closer to the Islamic understanding of the giving of the Koran to the angel Gabriel and "recorded" in a series of ecstatic visions by Mohammed. Some fundamentalist Christians prefer this model, as it seems to alleviate any of the complexities of human authorship, but it does injustice to the rich, life-giving dynamic that actually occurred between the Holy Spirit and the (true) human authors.

FUNDAMENTALISM

Fundamentalism may be defined as an early 20th century movement among Protestants in response to liberal theology, and is often marked by strict adherence to the Bible alone and other creedal elements (e.g. "King James only," the rapture, excessive prophetic or apocalyptic interpretations). As liberal biblical scholarship blew across Europe and the United States, especially from Germany, more traditional Protestant Christians reacted against it, perhaps with good intentions, but often without the adequate tools or proper sophistication to engage such skepticism on an intellectual and academic level. As a result, it spread rapidly (especially through radio and television preaching), fostering poor habits of Scripture among many. Today, as a result of greater education, it is less pervasive but no less problematic where it exists. Three points to keep in mind about fundamentalism:

Most Protestants/Evangelicals do not hold a fundamentalist outlook. In fact, many are rather embarrassed by its vestiges today. Don't assign labels or condemn; get to know people, seek common ground.

However, fundamentalism is not completely eradicated, and it can be found among both Protestants and Catholics. Some poorly catechized Catholics find certain elements attractive and have fused its core tenants with Catholic beliefs. E.g. Those attempting to be "more Catholic than the Pope" in their view of Scripture, or those that hold to the "one true translation" (i.e., Douay-Rheims alone).

Fundamentalist views can be overcome with true history and true theology. Yet, in most instances, progress is not achieved through apologetically-dense conversations. Don't seek to simply win arguments: listen, show interest, be charitable in your answers (1 Pet 3:15). Most of all, pray for conversions.

For more on fundamentalism, see: **"National Conference of Catholic Bishops Ad Hoc Committee on Biblical Fundamentalism,"** available as a small brochure from USCCB Publishing; Ronald D. Witherup, *Biblical Fundamentalism: What Every Catholic Should Know* (Collegeville, MN: Liturgical Press, 2001).

The "Communal Inspiration" Model. At the other end of the spectrum from the Dictation model is the Communal Inspiration model. Whereas the former places too much emphasis on the Divine author, the latter overemphasizes the human authorship to the exclusion or diminishment of the Holy Spirit. In the mid-twentieth century, many scholars had developed theories of the formation of the Four Gospels, for example, in which the role of the "individual eyewitness" is de-emphasized — and the role of the "community" in which they ministered to is accentuated. Building on Karl Rahner's investigations into biblical inspiration,[45] individuals like R.A.F. McKenzie and others advanced theories of inspiration that placed excessive emphasis on the role of the "early communities."[46] Like the Dictation model, this model can err in that it risks de-emphasizing one aspect of authorship (in this case the role of the Divine) while exaggerating the role of the other — and again, not merely the human author, but the broader community" of the Apostles.

To be clear, the biblical authors were not "islands onto themselves" — everything they wrote they wrote for the "good of the Church." Nevertheless, the danger of this model is in viewing, for example, the Gospel of Matthew as less of a *recollection* or *remembering* of Jesus *by an individual eyewitness*, and more of a *response to Jesus,* by a community of the Apostle, or some deeply layered process of redaction. Often, the latter approach becomes a rather speculative endeavor (what did/didn't Jesus really say or do?), and the "role of the community" is heightened to the extent that we no longer "see" Matthew "seeing Jesus," but really a community in search of its identity, given its own struggles, needs, etc. In short, Matthew (Mark, Luke, John) are detached from the Gospel, and no longer of much consequence.

The Church has rightly cautioned us from seeing both of the above models as insufficient. While on the one hand the Dictation model emphasizes the divine element and diminishes (or eradicates) the human element, the "Communal" model does the opposite — it over-emphasizes the human element (not just the individual but the whole community) and diminishes the role of the Divine author.

With this in mind, we turn to the model that is closest to the understanding of the Catholic Church. While the Church does not "endorse" models of inspiration, it merely is a witness to the truth of the Word of God, this model clearly corresponds to what the Church affirms about the inspiration of Sacred Scripture, as a "cooperative" effort on the part of *both* the Divine author *and* the human authors.

The Plenary Model. In Latin, the term *plenus* means full; thus, the Plenary model of inspiration (or "Verbal model") asserts that <u>all</u> of the words of Scripture are equally inspired by God. Importantly, the model asserts that God the Holy Spirit is indeed the ultimate author and Source of Sacred Scripture. The Plenary model attests that the Divine author included all things within the Bible that He intended for humanity to know in written inspiration, and likewise excluded that which he did not want. It likewise asserts that the human authors were real authors, not mere instruments but genuine authors, who wrote from the full capacities of mind, heart and spirit (with personality, interests, etc.). What most distinguishes the Plenary model from other models is that it *fully affirms <u>both</u> the human <u>and</u> the Divine sources as authors — in a simultaneous and cooperative manner.* For these reasons, this particular approach is the one that is closest to the Church's understanding as articulated in *Dei Verbum* and other Magisterial texts. It is likewise the approach adhered to in this book.

Table 1: Relative Roles of the Divine and Human Author(s) in the Inspiration Process[47]		
Model of Inspiration	**Role of the Holy Spirit**	**Role of the Human Authors**
Dictation	+	−
Communal Inspiration	−	+
Plenary	+	+

Saint Jerome recalls that we can never read Scripture simply on our own. We come up against too many closed doors and we slip too easily into error. The Bible was written by the People of God for the People of God, under the inspiration of the Holy Spirit.

— Pope Benedict XVI, *Verbum Domini* § 29

FOR REFLECTION

> *Who are the people in my life that stru*
> *confused by, or outright reject the Bi*
> *Word"? What are the issues or experiences ㄴ..*
> *have shaped their view of Scripture? What are their*
> *present questions or obstacles? Finally, what are my*
> *hopes for them, and what might God want my role*
> *to be in their life?*

Q: *"What about errors in the Gospels; how does that effect inspiration?"*

Perhaps you have wondered about this, or have been asked questions of this sort. To begin to answer the question properly, it is worth noting that such questions may begin with a presumption; namely, that the Gospels are full of errors.

Whenever I am asked questions like this, I try to charitably, yet directly respond to the question with one of my own: "To which 'error' in the Gospels are you referring?" Often times, what many people call "errors" in the Four Gospels are not errors, but divergences among the Gospel narratives. These situations require attention as to their explanation or "cause," but apparent discrepancies in particular details between the Four Gospels may be pointed to as an indication that the Bible is deficient and untrustworthy.

For example, the Gospel of Mark records that Jesus healed Peter's mother-in-law: *And immediately he left the synagogue, and entered the house of Simon and Andrew, with James and John. Now Simon's mother-in-law lay sick with a fever, and immediately they told him of her.[31]And he came and took her by the hand and lifted her up, and the fever left her; and she served them.* (Mark 1:29–31). The Gospels of Matthew and Luke contain a version of this miracle (Matt 8:14–17, Luke 4:38–41), yet each of the three narratives contain particular details and emphasize (or omit) certain aspects of the healing by Jesus:

- For example, Luke records that Jesus entered "Simon's house" (Luke 4:38) whereas Matthew records it as "Peter's house" (Matt 8:14). Mark, for his part, says Jesus entered the house "of Simon and Andrew" (Mark 1:29). In these same verses, Mark alone states that "James and John" also went into the house with Jesus whereas the other Evangelists make no mention of who did or did not go into the house with Jesus.

- Mark and Matthew write that Peter's mother-in-law "lay sick with a fever" (Mark 1:30, Matt 8:14). Interestingly, Luke's version is unique in this regard. Luke, the Evangelist and companion of St. Paul, whom Paul refers to as "the beloved physician" (Col 4:14), adds a clinical remark, stating that the woman "was ill with a *high* fever" (Luke 4:39).

- In Mark's account, Jesus came and "took her by the hand and lifted her up" (Mark 1:31); whereas Matthew records only that Jesus "touched her hand and the fever left her" (Matt 8:15). Luke states that Jesus merely "stood over her … and it left her" (Luke 4:39), adding another clinical detail, stating that Jesus "rebuked" (ordered, took charge of) the fever.

These are just a few examples of how each Evangelist fashions his Gospel and specific accounts within them in a distinctive manner. As we noted, all three Gospel accounts describe the house in a particular way: the house of Peter, the house of Simon, the house of Simon and Andrew. All of these are correct. As we know, the disciple known first as "Simon" was re-named "Peter" by Jesus, when he confessed that Jesus is "the Christ, the Son of the living God" (Matt 16:16–18; cf. Mark 3:16; Luke 6:14; John 1:42). And, as we know, the disciple "Andrew" was Simon's/Peter's brother (Matt 4:18; Mark 1:16; Luke 6:14; John 1:40, etc.). Here, all of these accounts describe *the same location of the miracle using different terminology*.

Likewise, other differences were noted in the above miracle story. It was suggested that Luke's background might help explain his particular sensitivity to the ailment itself. Gospel scholars have offered various explanations as to the particular presentation of this miracle story in the other two accounts.

In light of these facts, it's difficult for me to understand, at least in the case of the three accounts of the healing of Peter's mother-in-law, why such distinctions would need to be labeled as "contradictions." In any event, even if someone insisted on labeling these as such, I would assert that the term "error" does not fit anywhere in the conversation.

To be fair, we may look elsewhere in the Gospel accounts (or elsewhere in the Scriptures), and find any number of puzzling passages, some that are "trickier" than this one. Agreed. Yet, we ought not over-reach and ascribe an "error" to the Bible, when in fact other explanations — quite reasonable ones, I might add, can be identified.

Additionally, in acknowledging a somewhat complex process in which the Four Gospels originally developed, from oral to written/final form, there are a number of considerations. For example, we just noted some of the differences between the three "Synoptic" (i.e., Matthew, Mark and Luke) Gospels, and how each highlights various details of the miracle story. Moreover, when we look more carefully at the Gospels side by side, what ought to strike us are not any discrepancies between them, but rather, the astonishing number of *similarities*, of the corroborating details between them.

To be clear — all three of the above accounts record that Jesus Christ entered the house of his disciple and healed Simon Peter's mother-in-law. That is remarkable. That all the Gospels, as individual and distinct portraits of Jesus, agree with one another in such a large number of broader and frankly, more important details about the life, death and resurrection of Jesus is quite remarkable.

Questions and concerns about "errors" in the Gospels often rest upon an expectation that they agree in every detail in order to be trustworthy and true. As we saw, this is not the case at all. Each of the Gospels is the work of a particular author who has a particular purpose in writing. This purpose, along with his background, recollection of Jesus, and the needs of the Gospel audience, as he understands it, all account for the "content" and "style" of his particular account. In this way, we see again that the inspired Word of God is an encounter with Jesus, given by God *in an authentically human and personal way, for the sake of the Church*. As the *Catechism* states,

The sacred authors, in writing the Four Gospels, selected certain of the many elements that had been handed on, either orally or already in written form; others they synthesized or explained with an eye to the situation of the churches, the while sustaining the form of preaching, but always in such a fashion that they have told us the honest truth about Jesus.[48]

There can never be any real discrepancy between the theologian and the physicist, as long as each confines himself within his own lines.

— Pope Leo XIII, *Providentissimus Deus* §18

The *Catechism* is raising a very important issue in the study of the Gospels, which we raised in an earlier discussion in this chapter; namely, that the human authors were genuine authors, "true" authors and not mere stenographers. So, there is a dynamic interplay between the Divine author and the human authors. (Recall what was said above about the "plenary model" of inspiration best representing the Catholic position.) As such, each Evangelist made use of all of his human potential in shaping and composing his Gospel:

> To search out the intention of the sacred writers, attention should be given, among other things, to *'literary forms.'* For truth is set forth and expressed differently in texts which are variously historical, prophetic, poetic, or of other forms of discourse. The interpreter must investigate *what meaning the sacred writer intended to express and actually expressed* in particular circumstances by using contemporary literary forms in accordance with the situation of his own time and culture.[49]

Later, we will discuss various means of uncovering meaning in Scripture, and how an understanding of "literary forms" can help us understand what a sacred writer "intended to express and actually expressed." For now, what is important to see is that God determined to present us the truth about Jesus in the Gospels in a distinctively *human fashion, in all of its complexity.*

Q: "Okay, I think I understand what you're saying about these 'diverse' accounts in the Four Gospels. But in general, does the Bible contain errors or doesn't it?"

Today, the answer of many, perhaps most secular academic scholars would be "Yes, the Bible contains errors." Yet, the Catholic Church (and many other Christian communities) holds that the Bible is "inerrant" ("free from error"). We can and indeed must trust the Bible, that what it teaches us is true.

In order to deal with this question, we first should be willing to acknowledge that on the surface, there do seem to be an array of biblical texts that seem to challenge our reason. Even setting aside the miracles of Jesus and the Gospels for the time being, we could look to the Creation accounts in Genesis 1 and 2 and ask questions about the presentation of God creating the world in six days. Some fundamentalists hold strictly to a "literal six days" of creation, and date the age of the earth at about four thousand years old. When presented with ample data from the scientific community as to the much, much older age of the earth, such persons often refuse to examine the scientific knowledge as "credible." Often in a knee-jerk fashion, it is batted away, as if it has no value. "*The Bible says* ..." they will say, and those Christians who dispute their interpretation are sometimes labeled as "unbelievers" — and worse is said of the scientists! What do we do with such challenges? Is it an *either*/or proposition? Must we either hold fast to what "the Bible says" in a strict, literalistic manner ... *or* side with the scientists and reject what the Bible has to say? Of course not — and those who construct the argument in such a way are making a false dichotomy between the truth of Scripture, and those truths that reverberate in nature and in other natural elements, discernible through human reason and intellect. In short, *truth does not contradict truth*.

Still, we ought to rightly acknowledge that the Scriptures do contain a number of apparent discrepancies with science and/or history. Various theologians have sought to deal with these discrepancies in various ways and much has been written about this issue in the late nineteenth and twentieth centuries.

Rather than describe the various approaches, we will describe two primary models of biblical inerrancy — both from the perspective of faith. The first major model of inerrancy is often referred to as the "**restricted view**" and the other model is known as the "**unrestricted view**."

(Note: As we discuss these, it will be apparent I adhere to the "unrestricted" model. I believe this is the approach held by the Church, and that this is clear when one sifts through all of the Scripture documents and takes that at face value. In fairness, Catholic scholars of good will hold to the "restricted" view — and some examine the Scripture documents and see an "evolution" from a "tighter" or restricted view a century ago to a "freer" and less restricted view at the time of Vatican II. I do not share this evolutionary perspective — no pun intended. In either case, what's most important are not matters of theological debate but understanding *what the Church teaches*. Therefore, I will indicate below what the Catholic Church teaches about inerrancy, i.e., "the truth of Scripture.")

Following this, we'll discuss a related topic — the secular challenge to the "reliability" of Scripture, especially as it relates to the "copies" of ancient biblical manuscripts.

Restricted View of Inerrancy. This approach begins with a 'hermeneutic of faith,' yet inerrancy is subjected to certain limitations. This approach seeks to deal with the question of inerrancy by more or less "distinguishing" between those portions of Scripture that are absolutely "necessary" for our salvation, such as Christ's Incarnation, the Resurrection, etc., from those portions of Scripture that are merely incidental to our faith, such as various historical places, persons or things mentioned in the Bible. In short, inerrancy is "restricted" to only those things necessary for our salvation. Those that adhere to this model generally believe the Bible is "free from error," provided that "free from error" refers to those "essential" elements of the Bible — and only those, that are necessary for salvation.

In other words, the remaining non-essential portions of Scripture may or may not be "without error" — and either way, their veracity does not impinge upon the claim that the Bible is inerrant. Now, some very faithful theologians have held this view, and have done so, it seems, out of reverence and conviction in those "necessary" truths that are non-negotiable (Incarnation, etc.) One such proponent of this view was Blessed John Henry Newman (1801–1890). Newman lived in a time when modern rationalism and skepticism were rampant, and he was interested in countering their claims that the Bible indeed contained errors and/or was altogether unreliable.

Yet, in affirming the inerrancy of Scripture, Newman distinguished those facts in Scripture that are necessary for our salvation and those that were not. He referred to the latter category as "obiter dicta," i.e., things recorded in Scripture "by the by" (historical details, etc.). Newman reasoned that such *obiter dicta* were irrelevant to the question of the Bible's inerrancy, inasmuch as they were incidental to the Bible's primary purposes and not necessary for "belief" either way.

Unrestricted View of Inerrancy. In contrast to the above approach, the unrestricted inerrancy model does not limit "free from error" to only those passages that are necessary for our salvation. In other words, the unrestricted view does divide the Word against itself, but accepts the whole of Scripture as "free from error."

This seems like a rather bold assertion. So we must ask, *Is this unrestricted model synonymous with Fundamentalist approaches?* Not necessarily.

It is true that some Fundamentalist approaches may rest upon an unrestricted view of inerrancy. Here again, we would do well to underscore that Fundamentalist approaches must be set aside as deficient and unacceptable. But — and this is an important clarification — merely embracing the inerrant nature of Scripture is not what makes Fundamentalist views problematic. The problems with Fundamentalist approaches to Scripture stem from its *rigid literalism*. As I tell my own students, I do not doubt the *faith* of Fundamentalist interpreters — but their conclusions often leave little room to see the amount of *reason* brought to the Sacred Page. Fundamentalist approaches are often faith-infused — but reason-deficient. Healthy biblical study always requires both faith and reason working together:

> The Church remains profoundly convinced that faith and reason "mutually support each other"; each influences the other, as they offer to each other a purifying critique and a stimulus to pursue the search for deeper understanding.[50]

Along these lines, it must be underscored that a more nuanced — and reasoned approach to unrestricted inerrancy, apart from such "literalistic" views, is not only *possible*. It is *embraced* by Pope Leo XIII in his encyclical *Providentissimus Deus*. Clearly, in the encyclical, he mitigates any "restricted" approach to biblical inerrancy:

> *There can never, indeed, be any real discrepancy between the theologian and the physicist*, as long as each confines himself within his own lines, and both are careful, as St. Augustine warns us, "not to make rash assertions, or to assert what is not known as known." If dissension should arise between them, here is the rule also laid down by St. Augustine, for the theologian: "Whatever they can really demonstrate to be true of physical nature, we must show to be capable of reconciliation with our Scriptures; and whatever they assert in their treatises which is contrary to these Scriptures of ours, that is to Catholic faith, we must either prove it as well as we can to be entirely false, or at all events we must, without the smallest hesitation, believe it to be so."
> "[The Holy Spirit] Who spoke by them, did not intend to teach men these things (that is to say, the essential nature of the things of the visible universe), things in no way profitable unto salvation." *Hence they did not seek to penetrate the secrets of nature, but rather described and dealt with things in more or less figurative language, or in terms which were commonly used at the time, and which in many instances are in daily use at this day, even by the most eminent men of sci-*

ence. Ordinary speech primarily and properly describes what comes under the senses; and somewhat in the same way the sacred writers — as the Angelic Doctor also reminds us — "went by what sensibly appeared," or put down what God, speaking to men, signified, in the way men could understand and were accustomed to.[51]

What Leo XIII is getting at here is that we cannot view Scripture as we would a "textbook" pertaining to science or history. The human authors expressed the theological truths of God, but they themselves understood science and history as did other human beings of their time. *In no way does this limit inerrancy.* Rather, it means, that we can trust that the Bible is true — all of it — and do so in the utmost degree, and with the most important thing of all — our salvation:

> The basic outlines of the empirical history of Israel, the life and death of Jesus of Nazareth, and the empty tomb, together with the foundings of His Church on the apostolic group, *all are salvifically relevant truth — even though such factual description does not fall under the rubric of faith and morals.*[52]

Unlike both the "restricted" and Fundamentalist approaches to inerrancy, the "Catholic — Unrestricted" view properly integrates *faith and reason*, and allows both to inform and challenge the biblical reader in a cooperative fashion. The essence of the principle is that God cannot lie. Since God is the ultimate author of Sacred Scripture, and since He cannot lie (Heb. 6:18), biblical inerrancy can in no way be restricted. God's divine authorship is irreconcilable with any notion of error in Scripture. As Leo XIII wrote, one cannot "narrow inspiration to only certain parts of Scripture or admit that the Sacred Author has erred" (*Prov. Deus* 20). This approach unhesitatingly affirms that "inspiration is not only incompatible with error, but rejects it as absolutely and necessarily as it is impossible that God Himself, the supreme truth, can utter that which is not true" (ibid). Yet, unlike the Fundamentalist approach, this view does not evade questions involving legitimate discrepancies. Such issues are faced with the fullness of reason and intellectual integrity. Working with appropriate tools of scientific and historical inquiry, the Catholic exegete searches for possible explanations. His search is *hopeful yet realistic*, knowing that some tensions may be legitimately resolved, while other difficulties will require additional data and/or more precise interpretation and may not be satisfactorily reconciled at present. In the meantime, the

Catholic exegete continues to express full and firm confidence in the inspired and inerrant Word of God.

Q: "I heard that the Church had 'loosened' its view a bit on inerrancy following Vatican II. Is this true?"

It is not at all clear that there is any change in thought from Pope Leo XIII's first Scripture encyclical (*Providentissimus Deus*) over a hundred years ago to Vatican II's *Dei Verbum*, right up to the present day with Pope Benedict XVI's *Verbum Domini*.

Rather, there is only continuity of thought and unanimity as to the fact that the Bible was and is inspired and free from error. Period.

The Catholic Church has taught, continues to teach and will always uphold the firm conviction that the Holy Scriptures simultaneously has God as its ultimate author and human persons as its true authors. We believe that the Bible was inspired by the Holy Spirit and that it is in fact inerrant. This teaching on the inerrancy of Scripture is well-summarized in *Dei Verbum*:

> Since therefore all that the inspired authors or sacred writers affirm should be regarded as affirmed by the Holy Spirit, we must acknowledge that the books of Scripture *firmly, faithfully, and without error teach that truth which God, for the sake of our salvation, wished to see confided to the Sacred Scriptures*.[53]

To understand the doctrine let us look at another quote that precedes and complements *Dei Verbum*; that of the encyclical *Providentissimus Deus*:

> For all the books which the Church receives as sacred and canonical, are written wholly and entirely, with all their parts ... and so far is it from being possible that any error can co-exist with inspiration, that inspiration not only is essentially incompatible with error, but excludes and rejects it as absolutely and necessarily as it is impossible that God Himself, the supreme Truth, can utter that which is not true.[54]

The history of the Church's teaching on inerrancy goes back, as does the doctrine of inspiration itself, to the crisis of modernist rationalism in the late nineteenth and early twentieth century. The central point to see in this quote is this: the first and foremost reason we hold firmly to inerrancy is that God, who is truth, cannot and does not lie.

Clearly, our Church's teaching on inspiration and inerrancy is obviously incompatible with secular academic approaches. As Catholics, we firmly hold that there is indeed one God and He is the ultimate author of Scripture: *it is not merely a human book*. And God cannot and does not, by His very nature, lie.

FOR REFLECTION

When have I encountered some Christian experience that could be described as "fundamentalist" in some way? How did it make me feel — how did it impact my walk with Christ? What ways, if any, have my views on fundamentalist approaches to Christianity changed — and what caused them to change? How do I feel about future encounters with such a worldview? Why?

At the same time, it must be understood that our Church's teaching does not go to the other extreme either, i.e., by adopting a view embraced by many Fundamentalist groups. As such, the Catholic position is not compatible with the understanding of inerrancy held by some other Christians. Some Protestants — and frankly, some Catholics too today — hold to what might be called an "extreme inerrancy" or "literalistic inerrancy" of the Bible, which does not take into account the concern for its literary forms or the intention of the biblical authors.

As such, the Bible is interpreted in a "literalistic" manner — without a proper accounting for the literary forms or genres that the biblical authors made use of, as discussed above. Given this oversight, such individuals arrive at conclusions that would seem to put the Bible "at odds" with science and/or history. Yet, we must "think better" about the authors of Scriptures. They were true human beings, not robots; they made genuine use of their natural capacities and relied upon their senses. For example, the biblical writers frequently employ figurative speech, e.g., *"the going down of the sun."* Understanding this is of first importance.

For, since the Bible is not written as a science textbook, it cannot (and should not) be accused of making "scientific errors." This does not "let the Bible off the hook" with respect to the historical matters in the Bible (names, dates, events, etc.), which do indeed fall under the mantle of inerrancy, since God reveals himself *in and through history*.

And it needs to be said that with regard to its "historicity," the Bible has indeed undergone an intense century and a half of scrutiny and been put to the test by many skeptics who have dismissed or sought to diminish its historicity. The integrity of the Bible — and its historical claims — has been vindicated again and again in the face of such critiques.

One example of this sort concerned the modern hypothesis (quite popular in the late nineteenth century) that the Gospels were composed in the mid to late second century, long after the death of the Apostles. Yet, many advances and archeological discoveries (such as the Rylands Fragment) have put to rest any notions that the Four Gospels originated any later than A.D. 100. To be sure, there are difficulties and anomalies that remain to be properly answered. But as biblical scholar N.T. Wright, a believing Anglican scholar is fond of saying, *"authentic Christianity has nothing to fear from history."*

Q: *"Doesn't* Dei Verbum *limit inerrancy to 'faith and morals'?"*

Behind such questions is a key passage in *Dei Verbum:*

> The inspired books teach the truth. Since therefore all that the in-spired authors or sacred writers affirm should be regarded as af-firmed by the Holy Spirit, we must acknowledge that the books of Scripture firmly, faithfully, and without error teach that truth which God, *for the sake of our salvation*, wished to see confided to the Sacred Scriptures.[55]

Those who would argue for a more limited scope of inerrancy sug-gest that *Dei Verbum* is "toning down" the strong rhetoric of *Providentis-simus Deus*. Such reasoning often includes the following: (a) That *Provi-dentissimus Deus* was written during a time of intense challenges from modern rationalism; and (b) that *Dei Verbum* seems to narrow the focus of inerrancy. Perhaps, this line of reasoning continues, Vatican II was up-dating and "limiting" inerrancy to faith and morals, in light of modern biblical criticism; as to discourage a sort of "Catholic fundamentalism."

On balance, I believe that such a position is mistaken. *Dei Verbum*, like all Church teaching, must be read in light of the continuous teaching of the Church on the matter. To be sure, as a document of the Council, it must be given its due importance. Yet, when one looks at the *deposit of faith* of the Church on the interpretation of Scripture, it is clear that Vatican II was in no way moving away from the classical understanding of inerrancy, as put forth in *Providentissimus Deus* (1893) and fifty years afterward, in *Divino Afflante Spiritu* (1943). Pope Leo referred to the unrestricted view of inerrancy described in *Providentissimus Deus* as the "ancient and unchanging faith of the Church." In no way should *Dei Verbum* be seen as presenting a "new" understanding of the teaching, but rather, it should be seen as presenting a fresh emphasis on the teaching and its importance with respect to our salvation.

Let us now move a bit beyond the realm of the question of inspiration and inerrancy of Scripture, and discuss a related but different set of questions that have to do with the reliability of the Bible, especially in regard to Bible translations.

Q: "Which Bible translations are 'inspired'?"

The Catholic Church teaches us that the inspiration of the Word of God is located in the "autographs" only, i.e., the original compositions written by the biblical authors themselves. The Church makes no such claims about "inspired translations." Once we move to beyond the original autographs that make up the canon, we are beyond the realm of inspiration and inerrancy. Our modern translations are based upon the original inspired biblical texts, but are not in themselves protected from human errors, e.g., as a result of scribes.

Accordingly, it is incorrect to speak of "inspired translations." (E.g., "Is the ABC translation 'more inspired' than the XYZ translation?") Certainly, we could speak of more (or less) *accurately rendered* translations. We might even describe Bible translations as "excellent," "good" or even "casual" when it comes to the translation work. Yet, such conclusions do not fall under the rubrics of inspiration or inerrancy.

Q: "Are the manuscript copies of the Bible reliable?"

Today more than ever, when many are questioning the truth of Scripture, it is important to understand why some hold very different views from the Church on the issue of the inerrancy of the Bible; and how, especially in light of such considerations, the Church continues to proclaim with confidence that the Bible is "without error" and, more generally, that it is a wholly reliable historical document.

Just as people of faith differ on the question of the Bible's inerrancy, it's important to recognize that secular individuals differ on such questions as well.

In general, those of a purely scientific or empirical approach would necessarily reject both biblical inspiration and inerrancy. In this sense, such views are characterized by an absence of faith and a bifurcated sense of reason. The text is examined on purely historiographic terms; 'supernatural phenomena' are set aside. The Bible is treated like any other work of antiquity and approached with considerable skepticism. As such, a biblical text may be found to portray historical subjects accurately, but is just as likely to contain errors.

Many secular academic scholars tend to accentuate the natural dimension and human authors of Scripture while ignoring or discounting the supernatural and divine author of Scripture. A good example is contemporary biblical scholar Bart Ehrman, a biblical scholar involved in textual criticism, and as such, someone concerned with the transmission of ancient biblical manuscripts over time.

> For me, though [the loss of the original manuscripts of the New Testament] was a compelling problem. It was the words of Scripture themselves that God had inspired. Surely we have to know what those words were if we want to know how he had communicated to us, since the very words were his words, and having some other words (those inadvertently or intentionally created by scribes) didn't help us much as we want to know *His* words. The Bible began to appear to me as a very human book … This was a human book from beginning to end. It was written by different human authors at different times and in different places to address different needs … Those of us [students] at Moody believed the Bible was absolutely inerrant in its very words.[56]

The context of the above quote concerns his views on the "corruption" of the text of Scripture, and why, through scribal error or invention, Jesus has been subsequently "misquoted."

Ehrman's analysis of the "problem" seems confused at best and misleading at worst. He speaks of our copies as "not helping us much" in knowing "God's words." This is an unfair assessment of both: a) The *overwhelming* number of biblical manuscripts we possess today; and b) the overall integrity of these manuscript copies.

A) Overwhelming number of biblical manuscripts

First, we should emphasize the sheer number of biblical copies. Many historical documents are preserved in only a few manuscripts copies.

Various texts from Greco-Roman literature are preserved in ten, twenty or at best, perhaps a hundred manuscript copies. Additionally, we

Today, Ehrman is just one of many biblical scholars who believe that it is not possible to speak of the Bible as inerrant in any meaningful way (if at all). Often times, such positions are related to the variants and discrepancies in Scripture itself. In certain instances, a malformed understanding of inerrancy or other forms of fundamentalism lead to such erroneous positions. To be fair, however, not all scholars who question the inerrancy of Scripture start out as "biblical fundamentalists" who abandoned their faith. Many arrive at such conclusions based upon genuine scholarly convictions. I often describe this later group as "secular academic" biblical scholars. Yet whatever the cause, such convictions tend to involve a discounting of the supernatural in the composition of Scripture. In the end, it is for such scholars *only a human book.*

Conclusion: A Treasure in Earthen Vessels

What has been accomplished in our review of this first principle? In this chapter, we have seen that our Church teaches that the Bible really is God's Word to us; it is trustworthy and true. The Bible was inspired by the Holy Spirit, who is the ultimate author of Sacred Scripture. At the same time, God employed human beings, along with all of their human capacities, to convey His word to us in the manner of human writing. As such, the Bible was indeed composed by *authentic human authors* and not courtroom stenographers. The Bible was simultaneously authored by human beings who cooperated with the Holy Spirit to communicate just what He wanted, and no more.

As a "foundational" principle, biblical inspiration has a number of significant implications. In this chapter, we discussed a number of questions that pertain to Principle #1 ("God's Word: Divine Words in Human Language"). We saw that all the books of the canon are "equally inspired" and all their parts. We compared three different models used to explain how inspiration works (Dictation, Communal and Plenary) and saw that only the Plenary view satisfies a balanced Catholic definition of inspiration. Along these lines, we defined "Fundamentalism" and explained some of the fallacies that often accompany such approaches to Scripture.

Following this, we addressed questions that pertain to the "truth" of Scripture. We discussed inerrancy and the Church's firm and unwavering conviction that God's Word is indeed "free from error." We discussed two approaches to inerrancy — the "restricted" and "unrestricted" view.

We suggested that after one weighs all the evidence, examines all the Scripture documents, etc., that the "unrestricted" view is the preferential approach.

Along these lines, we explained that robust Catholic view of unrestricted (or absolute) inerrancy does <u>not</u> depend upon or embrace the insufficient or knee-jerk reasons offered by others (e.g., Fundamentalist Christians) who happen to hold this view.

Here, we pointed out that adhering to unrestricted inerrancy: 1) does <u>not</u> mean that later biblical manuscripts (copies) are preserved from scribal errors; 2) <u>does</u> presuppose a correct interpretation of biblical texts, and in particular, a clear understanding of *literary genres*; 3) <u>does</u> apply to matters of history, while emphasizing that apparent historical errors <u>can</u> often be resolved, once one understands ancient customs and other literary expressions (e.g., mustard seed). Finally, 4) absolute inerrancy <u>does</u> <u>not</u> ignore or pretend that there are *apparent* errors, contradictions, or other serious difficulties found in the Scriptures — there are. When we encounter them, we should acknowledge such natural tensions, seeking to resolve them if possible through the above means and/or deeper study — and in the meantime, pray for God's wisdom.

Lastly, we discussed the reliability of the biblical manuscripts.

In short, we saw that everything our Church teaches on the inspiration, truth, and reliability of Scripture is based upon the firm belief that the Holy Spirit guided human authors in the writing of the sacred books, and that we can place all of our confidence, indeed our very lives, in them.

FOR REFLECTION	*Who have been the "guardians of the Word" that have personally influenced my life and faith? What quality or qualities were most compelling or attractive? What quality, characteristic or virtue would I like to cultivate? Ask God to place this desire on your heart and for the willingness to work on this, with the help of the Holy Spirit.*

Questions for Reflection

1. Which of the questions in this chapter were of most interest to me? Why?

2. What have I understood about the "truth" (inerrancy) of God's Word? What in particular is challenging for me about this doctrine of the Faith?

3. Which of the models of inerrancy (restricted, unrestricted) is most sensible to me? Why?

4. What have I believed about the "reliability" of the Scriptures in the past? How do I hope this chapter will help me grow in my knowledge of Scripture? Confidence in Scripture?

For Further Study

Achtemeier, Paul J. *Inspiration and Authority: Nature and Function of Christian Scripture.* Peabody, MA: Hendrickson, 1999. Adequate discussion of various models of biblical inspiration, along with their strengths and weaknesses.

Barbeau, J. W. "Newman and the Interpretation of Inspired Scripture," *Theological Studies,* 63 no 1 (2002), 53–67.

Béchard, Dean, ed. and trans. *The Scripture Documents: An Anthology of Official Catholic Teachings.* Collegeville, MN: Liturgical Press, 2002.

Benoit, Pierre. *Aspects of Biblical Inspiration.* Chicago: Priory Press, 1965. Benoit focuses first on St. Thomas' articulation of biblical inspiration and juxtaposes it with an analysis of more "minimalistic" responses in contemporary models.

Bouyer, Louis. *The Meaning of Sacred Scripture.* Notre Dame, IN: University of Notre Dame Press, 1958.

Burtchaell, J. T. *Catholic Theories of Biblical Inspiration Since 1810: A Review and Critique.* Cambridge: Cambridge University Press, 1969.

Dulles, Avery. *Models of Revelation.* Dublin: Knopf Doubleday, 1983.

Evans, Craig. *Fabricating Jesus: How Modern Scholars Distort the Gospels.* Downers Grove, IL: InterVarsity Press, 2006.

Grillmeier, A. "Dogmatic Constitution on Divine Revelation, Chapter III," *Commentary on the Documents of Vatican II,* ed. H. Vorgrimler, 199–215. New York: Crossroads, 1969.

Hagerty, C. *The Authenticity of Sacred Scripture.* Houston, TX: Lumen Christi Press, 1969.

Hahn, S. W. "Inspiration," *Catholic Bible Dictionary,* ed. Scott W. Hahn, 384. New York: Doubleday, 2009. A brief but helpful overview of the topic.

McGowan, A.T.B. "The Divine Spiration of Scripture," *Scottish Bulletin of Evangelical Theology* 21 no 2 (2003), 199–217.

Murphy, Dennis, ed. *The Church and the Bible: Official Documents of the Catholic Church* (Rev. second ed. Saint Paul: Alba House, 2007).

Newman, John Henry. *On the Inspiration of Scripture,* ed. J. D. Holmes, J.D. and R. Murray. London: Chapman, 1967. A classic text by Newman exploring biblical inspiration and its implications.

Nichols, Aidan. "The Authority of Scripture: Inspiration," *The Shape of Catholic Theology: An Introduction to its Sources, Principles and History,* 110–130. San Francisco: Ignatius Press, 1991. Both this chapter and the following one are substantial, historically grounded discussions into the complexities of biblical inspiration and inerrancy. As typical, Nichols captures the most essential elements of a theological question, and offers lucid and reliable analysis.

———. Authority of Scripture: Inerrancy," *The Shape of Catholic Theology: An Introduction to its Sources, Principles and History,* 131–140. San Francisco: Ignatius Press, 1991. (See above note.)

Trembath, Kern Robert. *Evangelical Theories of Biblical Inspiration: A Review and Proposal.* Oxford: Oxford University Press, 1987. A fairly recent evangelical Protestant perspective.

Vawter, Bruce. *Biblical Inspiration: Theological Resources.* London: Westminster, 1972.

Notes

37 Ibid.

38 Cf. CCC 120.

39 The additions to other books are found in Esther, additions to Daniel (parts of Ch. 3, 13 and 14) and the Letter of Jeremiah (i.e., Ch. 6 of the biblical book of Baruch). Ch. 13 of Daniel appeared as a separate book in the Greek Old Testament (LXX), known as *Susanna.* Likewise, Ch. 14 occurs as a separate book known as *Bel and the Dragon.*

40 *DV* §11 (emphasis added).

41 Cf. S. W. Hahn, "Inspiration," *Catholic Bible Dictionary.* Scott W. Hahn, Ed. (New York: Doubleday, 2009), 384.

42 Cf. Paul Achtemeier, The Inspiration of Scripture: Problems and Proposals (Philadelphia: Westminster, 1980); A.T.B. McGowan, "The Divine Spiration of Scripture," Scottish Bulletin of Evangelical Theology, 21 no 2 (2003), 199-217; J. W. Barbeau, "Newman and the interpretation of inspired Scripture," *Theological Studies, 63 no 1 (2002), 53-67;* P. Benoit, Aspects of Inspiration (Chicago: Priory, 1965); Raymond Brown, The Critical Meaning of the Bible (Ramsey, NJ: Paulist Press, 1981); James T. Burtchaell, Catholic Theories of Biblical Inspiration Since 1810 (New York: Cambridge, 1969); C. Hagerty, The Authenticity of Sacred Scripture (Houston, TX: Lumen Christi Press, 1969); A. Grillmeier, "The Divine Inspiration and Interpretation of Sacred Scripture," Commentary on the Documents of Vatican II, vol. 3. Herbert Vorgrimler, ed. (New York, NY: Herder and Herder, 1969); J. B. Webster, "Biblical Reasoning," *Anglican Theological Review, 90 no 4 (2008), 733-751.*

43 This masterpiece of Michelangelo Merisi da Caravaggio (1602) hangs in Contarelli chapel altar in the church of the French congregation San Luigi dei Francesi in Rome.

44 Melchior Cano, *De locis theologicis,* II, 17 (emphasis added).

45 Cf. K. Rahner, *Inspiration in the Bible.* Quaestiones Disputatae, 1 (New York: Herder & Herder, 1966).

46   E.g., "Inspiration has been too closely identified with the individual author and with the written word ... The vehicle of inspiration ... is the community of the people of God, Israel and the Church." J.L. McKenzie, "The Social Character of Inspiration," *Catholic Biblical Quarterly*, 24 (1962) 115-125.

47   Note: The symbols used in the above table (+,-) are only intended as a "snapshot" of the process, i.e., how integrated the Divine and human authors were (or not). Thus, in Table 1, the Plenary model is represented by two plus signs, indicating the full involvement of the Divine and human counterparts; whereas, in the Dictation and Communal models, one or the other is diminished.

48   CCC 126. *"With an eye to the churches ..."* Recall what was said above about the "Communal Inspiration" model. Here the *Catechism* affirms what was earlier in the chapter; namely, that there is a real dynamic and interplay that exists between the "authors" of the Gospels and the "communities" to whom they were connected. As such, the Apostles took into consideration "the situation of the churches" in formulating their Gospel. *"But always in such a fashion that they have told us the honest truth about Jesus ..."* Here, note that the Catechism affirms the vital role of the eyewitnesses themselves, without which there would be no written gospel.

49   *DV* § 12 (emphasis added).

50   John Paul II, Encyclical Letter *Fides et Ratio*, §100. Available online at: http://www.vatican.va/holy_father/john_paul_ii/encyclicals/documents/hf_jp-ii_enc_15101998_fides-et-ratio_en.html.

51   *PD* §18.

52   Nichols, *The Shape of Catholic Theology*, 138.

53   *DV* §11.

54   *PD* §40.

55   *DV* §11.

56   Bart Ehrman, *Misquoting Jesus: The Story behind Who Changed the Bible and Why* (San Francisco: HarperSanFrancisco, 2005), 5, 11, 12.

57   Source: K. Aland, *The Text of the New Testament* (Grand Rapids: Eerdmans, 1987), 29. This is just a sampling of the pertinent data; cf. Aland for the complete set of data and accompanying discussion.

58   Ibid.

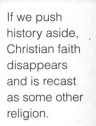

Principle 2
God's Word Is Revealed in History

Principle #2: Catholic Biblical Interpretation is profoundly concerned with history because of the nature of biblical revelation and the Living Word who revealed himself to humanity in history (John 1:14). Yet, Scripture can never be reduced to the natural order but fully affirms the supernatural and God's intervention in history.

Interpretation of a biblical text must be consistent with the meaning expressed by the human authors. Thus, Catholic exegetes must place biblical texts in their ancient contexts, helping to clarify the meaning of the biblical authors' message for their original audience and for the contemporary reader.

In the previous chapters, we discussed biblical inspiration — the "foundational" principle of all exegesis and proclamation of Scripture that is truly Catholic. We now turn to our next principle: "God's Word is Revealed in History."

As we will see, there is a logical connection between these two principles: if the Scriptures are indeed inspired, then the God who "breathed into" them and revealed to us His will did so using *human language* in and through *human history*.

The Word Enfleshed

"The Word became flesh and dwelt among us" (John 1:14). With these words, St. John confronts all of humanity with a hopeful yet surprisingly disturbing fact: *God has entered history*. This is indeed joyful news for the world. As Christians, we believe divine love has indeed been revealed to us in Jesus Christ. God has "spoken to us" in Jesus, the Word become flesh; through whom God also created the world (Heb. 1:2). He who is Love calls us into a loving relationship with the Father through the ultimate act of love: "Greater love has no man than this, that he lay down his life for his friends" (John 15:13). As St. Augustine wrote, "We would have despaired of ourselves had he not become flesh and dwelt among us."[59]

"The uniqueness of Christianity is manifested in the event that is Jesus Christ, the culmination of revelation, the fulfillment of God's promises and the mediator of the encounter between man and God. He who 'has made God known' (John 1:18) is the one, definitive word given to mankind."

— Pope Benedict XVI, *Verbum Domini* § 14

For St. Augustine, the hinge of his reality turned on the Incarnation of Jesus Christ. For example, Paul seems to be thinking incarnationally when he writes, "The life I now live *in the flesh* I live by faith in the Son of God, who loved who me *and gave Himself for me*" (Gal 2:20). Paul grasped that the flesh of His beloved Lord was not "given" but also "taken" in His death and crucifixion. But for Paul, this was no mere intellectual exercise; rather, this core belief in the Son of God, who "tabernacles among us," radically changed his life. The "enfleshment" of Jesus enabled Paul to conceive of his own life in entirely new terms, as one who was saved "in Christ" (2 Tim. 1:9) alive "in Christ" (Rom 6:11; Col 1:24), and joined to all the members of the Church, Christ's own body (Rom 12:5).

For Augustine, Paul and for all Christians, the Incarnation is *very good news*: God has not only "entered history," He has intervened in history, "changing its story," as it were, from something that would be otherwise meaningless to something overflowing with meaning and infinite joy. Even death, Paul writes, *"is swallowed up in victory"* (cf. 1 Cor 15:54–55). *O death, where is thy victory? O death, where is thy sting?* God's entered history in the Incarnation with this intention: that none would perish (John 3:16–17), but that all might inherit eternal life *and live in the light of the Resurrection*:

> Indeed I count everything as loss because of the surpassing worth of knowing Christ Jesus my Lord. *For his sake I have suffered the loss*

of all things, and count them as refuse, in order that I may gain Christ and be found in him, not having a righteousness of my own, based on law, but that which is through faith in Christ, the righteousness from God that depends on faith; *that I may know him and the power of his resurrection,* and may share his sufferings, becoming like him in his death, that if possible I may attain the resurrection from the dead. (Phil 3:8–11)

FOR REFLECTION

Growing up, to what extent was my experience of the Christian life "joyful?" What attitudes, events or persons enhanced or diminished the experience of joy? Today, how has this changed? Spend time in the presence of the Lord, asking for a greater measure of joy, despite the past, despite any present anxieties.

Hence, the Incarnation and the Resurrection of Christ are inextricably bound together. We cannot understand the one without contemplating the other. And it goes deeper still: for if we are not seeking to live now "in the hope of the resurrection," then we are not fully living the Christian life:

"The point of the resurrection ... is that the present bodily life is not valueless just because it will die ... What you do with your body in the present matters because God has a great future in store for it ... What you do in the present — by painting, preaching, singing, sewing, praying, teaching, building hospitals, digging wells, campaigning for justice, writing poems, caring for the needy, loving your neighbor as yourself — will last into God's future. These activities are not simply ways of making the present life a little less beastly, a little more bearable, until the day when we leave it behind ... They are part of what we may call building God's kingdom."[60]

Pope Benedict described this experience of all who belong to the Risen Christ as "a plunging ever anew into the vastness of being, in which we are simply overwhelmed with joy."[61] St. Paul admonishes us, "May the God of hope fill you with all joy and peace in believing, so that by the power of the Holy Spirit you may abound in hope" (Rom 15:13). And where there is genuine hope, there is genuine freedom:

Now the Lord is the Spirit, and where the Spirit of the Lord is, there is freedom. And we all, with unveiled face, beholding the glory of the Lord, are being changed into his likeness from one degree of glory to another; for this comes from the Lord who is the Spirit. (2 Cor 3:17–18)

The Incarnation, when viewed with the Resurrection, is indeed cause for immeasurable joy — and cause for the greatest gratitude and devotion to the Lord that we can muster today. God has entered our history: the Word has dwelt among us and continues to dwell among all people, in the Eucharist:

> In the mystery of the Incarnation, the Lord Jesus, born of woman and fully human, entered directly into a relationship not only with the expectations present within the Old Testament, but also with those of all peoples.[62]

What began with the Incarnation continues throughout all ages, as Christ "tabernacles" among us. And in the Incarnational-eucharistic presence of Jesus, we are changed, as Pope Benedict recently reminded us:

> Here we can see the full human import of the radical newness brought by Christ in the Eucharist: the worship of God in our lives cannot be relegated to something private and individual, but tends by its nature to permeate every aspect of our existence … Today there is a need to rediscover that Jesus Christ is not just a private conviction or an abstract idea, but a real person, whose becoming part of human history is capable of renewing the life of every man and woman. Hence the Eucharist, as the source and summit of the Church's life and mission, must be translated into spirituality, into a life lived "according to the Spirit."[63]

Yet this Incarnational proclamation of St. John remains in the past, as a claim of historic Christianity. In a sense, this perplexity on the part of many concerning the Incarnation is understandable. *How could this be?* As human persons, there is a struggle to comprehend (and actualize) such a great mystery, the reality of God taking on human flesh and really "dwelling among us."

Et Incarnatus Est

Particularly for the modern rationalist, the good news proclaimed by the Evangelist is confounding and even disturbing. Since the age of the Enlightenment, the field of biblical scholarship has been approached largely through a rationalistic lens, and not through an Incarnational lens. That is to say, a good deal of modern biblical scholarship has, by the very nature of the methods of study adhered to, set aside the supernatural and examined Scripture purely from a natural dimension.

Beginning in the eighteenth century and reaching its full-flowering in the nineteenth century, the "historical-critical" (HC) method has been the principle approach of most biblical scholars. Thus, it is important that we clearly understand what impact the HC method has had upon Incarnational faith, i.e., what opportunities and what challenges it presents.

Et incarnatus est — when we say these words, we acknowledge God's actual entry into real history.

— Pope Benedict XVI, *Jesus of Nazareth*

For our purposes, the historical-critical method may be defined as the "specific procedures" employed by historical biblical criticism. As such, it seeks to understand:

> The ancient text in light of its historical origins, the time and place in which it was written, its sources, if any, the events, dates, persons, places, things, customs, etc., mentioned or implied in the text. Its primary goal is to ascertain the text's primitive or original meaning in its original historical context.[64]

We should add to the above definition the following clarification. Namely, there is not, properly speaking, simply "one" HC method; rather, the term represents numerous approaches and foci. For example, some types of critical study are concerned primarily with trying to uncover the written sources "behind" a biblical text, i.e., "source criticism"; whereas other types of study involve the origin and development of the biblical text as a manuscript, i.e., "textual criticism."

As an historic approach to biblical studies, this method plays, at least in theory, a vital supporting role to our first principle: it seeks to discover the meaning of *the human author(s)* of Scripture. For this reason, Pope Benedict rightly referred to the historical-critical method as "an indispensable dimension of exegetical work."[65] As an Incarnational faith, Christianity is about real events that occurred *in real time* and *in real space*, and not merely "stories symbolizing supra-historical truths."[66] As the pope adds,

> The *factum historicum* (historical fact) is not an interchangeable symbolic cipher for biblical faith, but the foundation on which it stands: *Et incarnatus est* — when we say these words, we acknowledge God's actual entry into real history.[67]

In a manner of speaking, when it comes to biblical studies, "the Incarnation changes everything." "Christianity," writes Pope Benedict XVI in *Verbum Domini*, "perceives in the words the Word itself, the Logos who displays his mystery through this complexity and the reality of human history."[68] There is on the one hand a "Christological analogy"[69] between the Incarnation of Jesus Christ, the Living Word who entered history in the flesh and on the other hand, the "incarnational nature" of the Word of God, revealed in and through history:

> For as the substantial Word of God became like to men in all things, "except sin," so the words of God, expressed in human language, are made like to human speech in every respect, except error.[70]

As we conclude our look at the first part of our principle, several points should be clear. First, our faith is an Incarnational one: the Word has indeed taken on flesh and dwelt among us (John 1:14) — and dwells among us even now, in the whole life of the Church, and especially in the Eucharistic liturgy. Our entire approach to the Word of God is thus informed by this "Christological analogy." As a result, *history is not optional* for Catholic believers: we apprehend Scripture in and through history just as Jesus, the Logos entered human history, for the sake of our salvation:

> The word of God is thus expressed in human words thanks to the working of the Holy Spirit. The missions of the Son and the Holy Spirit are inseparable and constitute a single economy of salvation. The same Spirit who acts in the incarnation of the Word in the womb of the Virgin Mary is the Spirit who guides Jesus throughout his mission and is promised to the disciples.[71]

FOR REFLECTION | *Which methods of biblical interpretation are most life giving ... most challenging or troublesome for me? Why?*

A second point flows from the previous one. We must seek out the best historical methodologies that allow us to bring us as close as possible to understanding the motives of the original authors of Scripture. Given this Incarnational reality of Scripture, the importance of sound historical-critical methods becomes all the more clear: it ought to assist us in our inquiry as to the ancient context of the biblical authors, as we seek to identify "what meaning the sacred writer intended to express and actually expressed in [his] particular circumstances."[72] More specifically, the various tools employed by the method (e.g., the careful study of the original languages used by the biblical authors) help us to arrive at the meaning intended by the author:

> For it is the duty of the exegete to lay hold, so to speak, with the greatest care and reverence of the very least expressions which, under the inspiration of the Divine Spirit, have flowed from the pen of the sacred writer, so as to arrive at a deeper and fuller knowledge of his meaning.[73]

The Historical-Critical Method and the Church's Response

Despite the "indispensable" role of the historical-critical method in uncovering meaning, there are significant limitations of the method that we should be aware of as well. The most crucial strength of the method is also its greatest weakness: the historical analysis of the *human* author(s) and the text *they* composed. That is, the historical-critical approach is, by definition, restricted to objective criteria concerning historical realities. It does not possess criteria for the supernatural, the divine. Rather, it can only discuss, for example, Jesus' multiplication of the seven loaves and three fish[74] in terms of the natural dimensions of the story (e.g., setting, dialogue, reaction, consequent meaning for those present). The method has no means of dealing with the miracle itself, in supernatural terms. It can attempt to demythologize it, deconstruct it, or simply describe it in terms of natural data, but cannot, strictly speaking, engage it on the level of supernatural phenomenon.

The historical fact is a constitutive dimension of the Christian faith. The history of salvation is not mythology, but a true history, and it should thus be studied with the methods of serious historical research.

— Pope Benedict XVI, *Verbum Domini* § 32

So, the overall contribution of the historical-critical method has been (and continues to be) hotly debated. As one pair of scholars put it,

> "If the historical-critical method by definition rules out God as an agent in history, *of what help can it be to church or synagogue in understanding the Bible*, since like the Bible itself, these institutions view God and history in that way?"[75]

This sort of question was precisely the focus of a number of official documents of the Catholic Church over the past century. To better understand how the Church has dealt with the problems of the historical-critical method, let us review some of these developments. There have been three stages of response to such problems over the hundred or so years, beginning with Pope Leo XIII's 1893 encyclical on the study of Sacred Scripture, *Providentissimus Deus*. These periods are as follows:

1. Initial Responses and Renewed Resolve (1893–1942)
2. Full Participation in "Biblical Science" (1943–1965)
3. Interpretation of the Bible in the Church (1966–1993)

1) "Initial Responses and Renewed Resolve" (1893–1942)

The first stage of the Church's response began in 1893 with Pope Leo XIII's encyclical, *Providentissimus Deus* ("On the Study of Sacred Scripture"). Leo XIII was a pioneer, in that his encyclical was the Church's first "Scripture document" — not merely in the modern era, but *ever*. And it was urgently needed, as the Church was confronting two urgent challenges: the seeming contradiction between science and Scripture; and the rise of rationalist biblical thought. The vision and contents of Leo's momentous encyclical cannot be discussed here.[76]

However, the second challenge, i.e., the so-called Modernist (or Rationalist) controversy requires explanation. Just before the turn of the twentieth century, the difficulties emerging from within historical-critical scholarship were quite evident: the rationalistic, "historical reductionism" of many had presented a great challenge to Christian belief. This is clear in the tone of the encyclical itself:

> Now, we have to meet the Rationalists, true children and inheritors of the older heretics, who, trusting in their turn to their own way of thinking, have rejected even the scraps and remnants of Christian belief which had been handed down to them. They deny that there is any such thing as revelation or inspiration, or Holy Scripture at

all; they see, instead, only the forgeries and the falsehoods of men; they set down the Scripture narratives as stupid fables and lying stories: the prophecies and the oracles of God are to them either predictions made up after the event or forecasts formed by the light of nature; the miracles and the wonders of God's power are not what they are said to be, but the startling effects of natural law, or else mere tricks and myths; and the Apostolic gospels and writings are not the work of the apostles at all. These detestable errors, whereby they think they destroy the truth of the divine Books, are obtruded on the world as the peremptory pronouncements of a certain newly-invented "free science;" a science, however, which is so far from final that they are perpetually modifying and supplementing it. And there are some of them who, notwithstanding their impious opinions and utterances about God, and Christ, the gospels and the rest of Holy Scripture, would be considered both theologians and Christians and men of the Gospel, and who attempt to disguise by such honorable names their rashness and their pride.[77]

In short, the encyclical roundly condemned all rationalistic proposals that made faith "the enemy of science,"[78] and those "inheritors of the older heretics" who dismissed the supernatural and, against the steadfast tradition of the Church, concluded that the Bible was essentially to be understood as myth, legend and fable.

Hermeneutics alone cannot illuminate their enshrouding mystery but only the Church, given by God as our teacher and guide.

— Pope Leo XIII

In the encyclical, Leo XIII identified two theaters of operation where key victories would need to be won in defense of the Church and of Sacred Scripture.

Leo's first theater was *the study of the biblical languages.* The pope urged all professors and theologians, as well as students of Sacred Scripture to "master those tongues in which the sacred Books were originally written."[79] Leo's second theater was what he referred to as mastering the art of "true criticism."[80] The pope recognized that there was a proliferation of higher criticism that did not adhere to sound principles of historical inquiry. Instead, it merely gave rise to "disagreement and dissension."[81]

Another major development of this first phase began in 1902. Just nine years after *Providentissimus Deus*, Leo XIII established the Pontifical Biblical Commission (PBC), which was charged with "explaining and safeguarding the Sacred Books."[82] Later in this same period, Pope Benedict XV urged critical study of Scripture, but again re-affirmed the Church as the authentic interpreter of Scripture and emphasized the approach of the Fathers in reading Scripture from the heart of the Church.

2) "Full Participation in 'Biblical Science'" (1943–1992)

A new era in the Church's response began in 1943 — that of full participation in biblical studies, or as Pope Pius XII intentionally referred to it, full participation in "biblical science."[83]

Unlike preceding documents, *Divino Afflante Spiritu* truly opened up the doors of historical-critical methods for Catholic exegetes to make use of (cf. Table 4, below). Pius XII acknowledged that the situation had changed quite dramatically and allowed the Church definitively (but cautiously) to integrate modern methods of inquiry into study of Sacred Scripture:

Pius XII's confidence in announcing this new opening in biblical studies was in no small measure now possible for the following reason. By the 1940s there were numerous Catholic exegetes, mostly graduates of the newly founded Pontifical Biblical Institute (1909) and other Pontifical schools with a greater proficiency in the biblical languages and in "theological and biblical sciences"[84] who were able to properly train a new generation of seminarians and other students of Scripture. Building on the work of his predecessor, Pius XII was much more specific and directive in insisting on the return to the biblical languages. In fact, he issued the study of biblical Hebrew and Greek as a sort of "mandate" for all biblical students to strive towards.

Divino Afflante Spiritu is a seismic shift in the direction of "scientific" study of Scripture; the very thing that represented a threat was now brought under proper scrutiny so that "method" was properly separated from "abuses" within such methods. In light of this, historically-grounded approaches to Scripture — provided they were at the service of arriving at a "deeper and fuller knowledge" of the sacred and inspired texts were not only allowed but now were fully recognized as the "duty" of the biblical scholar.

In addition, the encyclical also promoted the inquiry into careful textual criticism:

> In the present day ... this art [of] textual criticism ... used with great and praiseworthy results in the editions of profane writings, is quite rightly employed in ... the Sacred Books, because of that very reverence ... due to the Divine Oracles. For its very purpose is to insure that the sacred text be restored, as perfectly as possible, be purified from the corruptions due to ... carelessness of the copyists and be freed, as far as may be done, from glosses and omissions, from ... repetition of words and ... other kinds of mistakes, which ... make their way gradually into writings handed down through many centuries.[85]

That *Divino Afflante Spiritu* encyclical officially opened up this endeavor to Catholic exegetes is a very important point. It should also be recognized that Pius XII acknowledged that in the transmission process of the biblical texts themselves, there were "corruptions" and "mistakes" that had developed.

Such a topic could not have been as easily addressed fifty years prior to *Divino Afflante Spiritu*; now, the pope confidently called on biblical exegetes to acquire such skills, all in service to the Church, as a means of the restoration of such impurities due the "Divine Oracles."

Unquestionably, the most significant contribution of *Divino Afflante Spiritu* was the full opening of H-C methods to Catholic biblical exegetes:

> Let the interpreter then, with all care and without neglecting any light derived from recent research, endeavor to determine the peculiar character and circumstances of the sacred writer, the age in which he lived, the sources written or oral to which he had recourse and the forms of expression he employed.[86]

From this time, Catholic exegetes were officially given the green light to engage in the various approaches of the H-C method — approaches previously utilized only by Protestant biblical scholars. The specific approaches in question included such H-C methods as textual criticism as well as form and source criticism.[87] The importance of this instruction in *Divino Afflante Spiritu* cannot be emphasized enough, as it had (and continues to have) a very profound effect on all Catholic biblical exegesis until today. Scholars such as Raymond Brown, Joseph

Table 4: Three Periods of Response of the Church to the Historical-Critical Method		
Period of Response	**Major Teaching Documents**	**Major Contributions**
1) Initial Responses and Renewed Resolve (1893–1942)	• *Providentissimus Deus* (Encyclical Letter of Pope Leo XIII: "On the Study of Sacred Scripture," 1893). • *Vigilantiae studiique* (Apostolic Letter of Pope Leo XIII: "Instituting a Commission for Biblical Studies," 1902). • *Responses of the PBC* (1905–1921). • *Pascendi dominici gregis* (Encyclical Letter of Pope Pius X: "On the Doctrine of the Modernists," 1907).	The Church confronts critical problems of Modernist interpretations of Scripture in *Providentissimus Deus* and other documents. Approaches that diminished or denied God's divine intervention or the supernatural dimension were roundly denounced. Positively, the study of ancient languages is heralded and a Commission is established to aid in proper biblical interpretation.
2) Full Participation in "Biblical Science" (1943–1992)	• *Divino Afflante Spiritu* (Encyclical Letter of Pope Pius XII: "Promoting Biblical Studies," 1943). • *Sancta Mater Ecclesia* (Pontifical Biblical Commission: "Instruction on the Historical Truth of the Gospels," 1964). • *Dei Verbum* (Second Vatican Council: Dogmatic Constitution on Divine Revelation, 1965). • *Catechism of the Catholic Church* (1992).	In *Divino Afflante Spiritu*, Pius XII formally approves the use of H-C methods, provided they are governed by sound "biblical science." The historicity of the gospels is defended. At Vatican II, the Church's overall understanding of "divine revelation" is delineated; its approach to and confidence in the Apostolic origins of Scripture are promulgated at Vatican II.
3) Interpretation of the Bible in the Church (1993–)	• *Interpretation of the Bible in the Church* (Pontifical Biblical Commission, 1993). • *Verbum Domini* (Apostolic Exhortation of Pope Benedict XVI, "The Word of the Lord," 2010).	The re-allocated PBC completes a major document on the study of Scripture and its role in the Church; greater emphasis is placed on the (proper use of the) H-C method. At the same time, the place of patristic exegesis and Scripture's crucial role in liturgy, pastoral ministry, and ecumenism are highlighted.

Fitzmyer, Roland Murphy and many others would soon change the way Catholic biblical scholarship in general was conducted.[88] Following on the heels of *SME* was of course the Second Vatican Council and, in particular, *Dei Verbum*, which, in some ways, consolidated all of the concerns discussed previously, into one Conciliar document.[89] In addition to its all-important proclamations concerning: 1) The nature of divine revelation itself;[90] 2) Sacred Scripture and Sacred Tradition as the "one deposit of faith;"[91] 3) The Apostolic origins, inspiration and inerrancy of Scripture;[92] and 4) The Old Testament[93] and New Testament;[94] the Constitution deals with various aspects of "human authorship" of the Scriptures. In the process, *Dei Verbum* mentions the need for linguistic semantic analysis of Scripture,[95] Source Criticism,[96] Form Criticism,[97] and even Redaction Criticism.[98] However, the Council documents would not be the most appropriate forum for a longer discussion of these H-C methods; this would come three decades after *Dei Verbum*, in the PBC document *The Interpretation of the Bible in the Church* (cf. below).

As a final development of this period, we should note the publication of the *Catechism of the Catholic Church* in 1994. The new *Catechism* — the first in over four hundred years — is saturated with Scriptural quotes.[99] But it is more than its numerous citations of biblical texts; rather, it is that the Scriptures are integrated into the catechesis. For example, Galatians 4:4–5[100] *is the very foundation of the catechesis* for Paragraph 422.[101] This kind of thing is found across the *Catechism* and leads John Cavadini (Chair of Theology at Notre Dame University) to refer to the larger project as a "scriptural catechesis."[102] In a fine article, Cavadini points out how superbly the *Catechism* integrates and balances historical-critical scholarship on the one hand, and scriptural catechesis on the other.[103] Additionally, Cavadini notes that the "rule of faith" and "canonical context" (cf. below) of biblical interpretation are woven together in "scriptural tapestries" throughout the *Catechism*, as is the *resourcement* ("return to the sources"), with respect to the Church fathers and what he calls their "scriptural rhetoric."[104]

FOR REFLECTION

"Scripture is like a river, broad and deep, shallow enough here for the lamb to go wading, but deep enough there for the elephant to swim."
— *St. Gregory the Great,* Moralia in Iob, *Book I.*

We now turn to the last of three periods of official Church teaching on Sacred Scripture, which takes us from the early 1990s to the present day.

3) "Interpretation of the Bible in the Church" (1993–)

Since this most recent stage was and is marked by more specific attention to various issues and methods of biblical "interpretation," we are referring to it as "Interpretation of the Bible in the Church." This is a fitting title on a second level, as the Pontifical Biblical Commission released a document addressing such topics, known as *The Interpretation of the Bible in the Church* (*IBC*).[105] The *IBC* document was published by the PBC on April 15, 1993. To date, the most thorough analysis of *IBC* was done in 2000 by Peter Williamson. [106]

As Prefect of the Congregation of the Doctrine of the Faith, Cardinal Ratzinger situated the importance of the PBC's task in his remarks, which can be found in the Preface to the document:

> In the history of interpretation, the rise of the H-C method opened a new era. With it, new possibilities for understanding the biblical word in its originality opened up. Just as with all human endeavor, though, so also this method contained hidden dangers along with its positive possibilities. The search for the original can lead to putting the word back into the past completely so that it is no longer taken in its actuality. It can result that only the human dimension of the word appears as real, while the genuine author, God, is removed from the reach of a method which was established for understanding human reality.[107]

The *IBC* laid out a detailed explanation of how historical-critical methods (and others) play a very important role in the study of the Scriptures:

> The historical-critical method is the indispensable method for the scientific study of the meaning of ancient texts. Holy Scripture, inasmuch as it is the "word of God in human language," has been composed by human authors in all its various parts and in all the sources that lie behind them. Because of this, its proper understanding not only admits the use of this method but actually requires it.[108]

The liturgy, and especially the sacramental liturgy, the high point of which is the Eucharistic celebration, brings about the most perfect actualization of the biblical texts.

— Pontifical Biblical Commission

In the following sections of the document, *IBC* delves into the history and development of the historical-critical method[109] and its principles;[110] and describes the specific means in which study was to be accomplished, i.e., in light of Form Criticism, Source Criticism, etc.[111] In its evaluation, *IBC* offers this evaluation of the method:

> To be sure, the classic use of the historical-critical method reveals its limitations. It restricts itself to a search for the meaning of the biblical text within the historical circumstances that gave rise to it and is not concerned with other possibilities of meaning which have been revealed at later stages of the biblical revelation and history of the church. Nonetheless, this method has contributed to the production of works of exegesis and of biblical theology which are of great value.[112]

IBC argues that Catholic exegesis should be carried out in a manner that is as objective as possible. It requires a "scientific orientation" in that it is based on the Catholic beliefs of objectivity, discoverability and the unity of truth. It recognizes that Catholic exegesis is to actively contribute to the development of new methods and to the progress of research, and suggests that Catholic scholars seek areas in which to collaborate with other scholars.[113] Finally, the document calls for integrating its principles into the life of the Church, through actualization, inculturation, in pastoral ministry and ecumenism and, most of all, in the liturgy:

> In principle, the liturgy, and especially the sacramental liturgy, the high point of which is the Eucharistic celebration, brings about the most perfect actualization of the biblical texts, for the liturgy places the proclamation in the midst of the community of believers, gathered around Christ so as to draw near to God. Christ is then "present in his word, because it is he himself who speaks when Sacred Scripture is read in the church." Written text thus becomes living word.[114]

Verbum Domini (2010)

In September 2010, Pope Benedict XVI released his Post-Synodal Apostolic Exhortation[115] on the Word of God, *Verbum Domini* ("The Word of the Lord"). You may have observed numerous citations from Verbum Domini throughout this book.

Given its length, a comprehensive review of *Verbum Domini* is not possible here. Nevertheless, seven salient points are offered below.

First, *Verbum Domini* is as encompassing a document as one would expect from this world-class biblical scholar. The pope leaves no stone unturned with respect to the Word of God and its role in the life and ministry of the Church today. Essentially all of the fifty-plus propositions from the 2008 Synod are dealt with in a positive and pastoral fashion. And much more. In short, Verbum Domini is a major teaching document that must be taken seriously — and is perhaps the most significant Scripture document since Vatican II's *Dei Verbum*.[116]

Second, the very shape of the document, and this is the third point, reveals the pope's interest in presenting principles of sound Catholic biblical exegesis in a decidedly Johannine fashion. In particular, Pope Benedict seizes upon John's Prologue (and specifically 1:14) as sort of a navigational star for raising essential principles of biblical interpretation. In this way, *Verbum Domini* can be read as an extended discussion of Catholic biblical exegesis that is "built upon" the foundation of St. John's Gospel.

Third, *Verbum Domini* hones in on biblical inspiration. In the Exhortation, the pope identifies inspiration as the fundamental principle for all true and proper interpretation of God's Word today. As he explains, the Word of God cannot be properly understood or proclaimed *apart from its being firmly and unequivocally rooted in God himself.*

From the perspective of Pope Benedict in *Verbum Domini*, we cannot embrace the divine without embracing the human element. Neither can we reject the one without rejecting the other, risking the whole interpretative enterprise.

Fourth, in *Verbum Domini*, the pope emphasizes that Scripture is not only in *believing* but also of *receiving* and *being transformed by* God's inspired Word. Here, he encourages the Church to re-discover the ancient spiritual art of *lectio divina*, as another means of meeting the Lord in Scripture, and being changed by Him:

Listening together to the word of God, engaging in biblical *lectio divina*, letting ourselves be struck by the inexhaustible freshness of God's word which never grows old, overcoming our deafness to those words that do not fit our own opinions or prejudices, listening and studying within the communion of the believers of every age: all these things represent a way of coming to unity in faith as a response to hearing the word of God.[117]

Therefore, he urges us to more attentive listening to the Word, in silence and in prayer.

Fifth and very importantly, in *Verbum Domini*, the pope calls the Church to forge a stronger bond between the Scriptures on the one hand and the Holy Eucharist on the other:

Word and Eucharist are so deeply bound together that we cannot understand one without the other: the word of God sacramentally takes flesh in the event of the Eucharist. The Eucharist opens us to an understanding of Scripture, just as Scripture for its part illumines and explains the mystery of the Eucharist. Unless we acknowledge the Lord's real presence in the Eucharist, our understanding of Scripture remains imperfect.[118]

Sixth, the pope emphasizes the need for Scripture to play a much more central role in *homilies*. Admittedly, too many Catholics have experienced homilies that treat the Scriptures only in a cursory way. The pope urges all preachers to re-double their efforts to make sure that the homily is a place where the radiance of the Scriptures is evident to all. Homilies must rest upon the Scriptures and explain the Scriptures, in a way that helps the faithful understand the meaning of the biblical author — and the meaning of the Scriptures in their own lives today.

Seventh and finally, in *Verbum Domini*, the pope speaks of the power of the Word of God, to touch hearts, to uplift the weary and to convert souls to Jesus Christ. He emphasizes the role of Sacred Scripture in the New Evangelization and, in so doing, reminds *all Christians* that it is the duty of all to "proclaim the Gospel":

We cannot keep to ourselves the words of eternal life given to us in our encounter with Jesus Christ: they are meant for everyone, for every man and woman. Everyone today, whether he or she knows it or not, needs this message. *May the Lord himself, as in the time of the prophet Amos, raise up in our midst a new hunger and thirst for the word of God* (cf. *Am* 8:11). It is our responsibility to pass on what, by God's grace, we ourselves have received.[119]

A final remark about the third period of the Church's active engagement and reflection on the role of Scripture in the Church is this: *it is ongoing.* It remains to be seen what topics and issues the Church will deal with next.

Conclusion

What has Chapter 2 contributed to our understanding of Scripture? A close examination of the second principle of Catholic biblical interpretation yielded a number of important discoveries.

In the first part of our discussion, we stressed the Incarnational (and Eucharistic) dimension of our faith. For Catholic students of Scripture, *history is not an optional thing.* Just as we encounter the Living Word in history, so must we approach Scripture in and through history, and with the best historical tools to help us apprehend the message of the human authors of Scripture, as they gave us God's words in human manner and in real history.

Following this, we turned to the remaining portion of Principle #2. Here we discussed one of the primary means today by which biblical scholars seek to uncover the intended meaning of the human authors of Scripture, i.e., the Historical-Critical method. We indicated the benefits of this approach — but also its shortcomings, abuses and biases of those that misuse it.

Finally, we reviewed three major stages of direct Church response to the needs and challenges of biblical interpretation in the modern period. As we examined numerous Scripture documents, we saw that our Church is indeed *a teaching Church* when it comes to understanding the Word of God. In various ways, the Church reiterated her deeply held conviction that the Scriptures are indeed the inspired Word, of the God who speaks and teaches us His truth, in a truly human way (*Dei Verbum*). Likewise, the Church reaffirmed the historicity and integrity of the Four Gospels and their apostolic origins. In the more recent documents, such as the *IBC* document the Church explained the usefulness of the historical-critical method, but also its limitations. In *Verbum Domini*, the Church reaffirmed all of these things, and underscored the need today for a deeper and more personal encounter with the Word of God, in praying and listening to the Scriptures (*lectio divina*), in the Word's integral link to the Holy Eucharist, in more biblical homilies, in ecumenical and interreligious dialogue and in the New Evangelization.

FOR REFLECTION

> *"Contemplation is the highest expression of man's intellectual and spiritual life. It is that life itself, fully awake, fully active, fully aware that it is alive. It is spiritual wonder. It is spontaneous awe at the sacredness of life, of being. It is gratitude for life ... It is a vivid realization of the fact that life and being in us proceed from an invisible, transcendent and infinitely abundant Source. Contemplation is, above all, awareness of the reality of that Source."*
>
> — *Thomas Merton,* New Seeds of Contemplation

Questions for Reflection

1. To what degree has my Christian faith been lived incarnationally? To what degree has the "enfleshment" of Jesus affected: My prayer life? My participation in the Eucharistic liturgy and Eucharistic adoration? My reading and study of Scripture?

2. What part of this principle ("God's Word is Revealed in History") was particularly challenging? Why?

3. How conversant am I with the Church's teaching documents on Scripture? Have I read them carefully? Which texts do I need to go back and re-read for further insight?

For Further Study

Athanasius, Saint. *On the Incarnation.* Crestwood, NY: St. Vladimir's Seminary Press, 1996. Features a nice introduction by C. S. Lewis.

Bartholomew, Craig. *"Behind" the Text: History and Biblical Interpretation.* Scripture and Hermeneutics Series. Grand Rapids: Eerdmans, 2003.

Cavadini, John C. "The Use of Scripture in the *Catechism of the Catholic Church,*" *Letter & Spirit* 2 (2006), 43–54. Excellent article exploring the number of ways (some obvious, some less obvious) in which Scripture is utilized in the *Catechism*.

Healy, Mary. "Inspiration and Incarnation: The Christological Analogy and the Hermeneutics of Faith," *Letter & Spirit* 2 (2006), 27–41.

Mariano, Magrassi. *Praying the Bible: An Introduction to Lectio Divina,* trans. Edward Hagman. Collegeville, MN: Liturgical press, 1988. More recently, see: Tim

Gray, *Praying Scripture for a Change: An Introduction to Lectio Divina*. West Chester, PA: Ascension Press, 2009.

Nichols, Aidan. *The Splendour of Doctrine: The Catechism of the Catholic Church on Christian Believing*. Edinburgh: T & T Clark, 1995.

Ratzinger, Joseph Cardinal. *Gospel, Catechesis, Catechism. Sidelights on the Catechism of the Catholic Church*. San Francisco: Ignatius Press, 1997.

Schönborn, Christoph. *Living the Catechism of the Catholic Church (Volume I: The Creed)*, trans. David Kipp. San Francisco: Ignatius Press, 1995.

Wojtyla, Karol. *Sources of Renewal: The Implementation of Vatican II*, trans. P. S. Falla. San Francisco: Harper & Row, 1972.

Internet Resources

Magnificat Publications. www.magnificat.net.

Notes

59 St. Augustine, *Confessions*, X 43, 69.

60 N. T. Wright, *Surprised by Hope: Rethinking Heaven, the Resurrection and the Mission of the Church*. (New York: Harper Collins, 2008), 193.

61 Benedict XVI, *Spe Salvi* §29.

62 Benedict XVI, *Sacramentum Caritatis* §54. Post-Synodal Exhortation "On the Eucharist as the Source and Summit if the Church's Life and Mission" (2007). Available online at: www.vatican.va/holy_father/benedict_xvi/apost_exhortations/index_en.htm.

63 Benedict XVI, *Sacramentum Caritatis* §71, 77 (emphases added).

64 R. N. Soulen and R. K. Soulen, *Handbook of Biblical Criticism*, 3rd ed. (London: Westminster John Knox Press, 2001), 79.

65 Benedict XVI, *Jesus of Nazareth*, xv.

66 Ibid.

67 Ibid.

68 Pope Benedict XVI, *Verbum Domini* §44.

69 Cf. Mary Healy, "Inspiration and Incarnation: The Christological Analogy and the Hermeneutics of Faith," *Letter & Spirit* 2 (2006), 27-41.

70 *DAS* §37; cf. Heb 4:15). Peter Williamson points out that like all analogies, this "Christological analogy" is not perfect: "The christological analogy between the two natures of the Incarnate Word and the divine and human dimensions of Scripture is useful, but ambiguous … The problem of the analogy of Scripture to the Incarnate Word is to define in what respects Scripture reflects the perfections of its divine Author and in what respects it reflects the limitations of its human authors." For a fuller discussion, cf. Williamson, *Catholic Principles for Interpreting Scripture*, 38.

71 Pope Benedict XVI, *VD* §17.

72 *DV* §10.

73 *DAS* §15.

74 The multiplication of loaves and fish is among Jesus' best attested miracles, and is found in all Four Gospels: Matt 14:15-21; 15:32-39; Mark 8:1-9; Luke 9:10-17; John 6:1-14.

75 Soulen and Soulen, *Handbook of Biblical Criticism*, 78.

76 In short, the Church's position, as laid out in *PD*, is that "nothing can be proved either by physical science or archaeology which can really contradict the Scriptures … "Truth cannot contradict truth." Cf. *PD* §23.

77 *PD* §10.

78 *PD* §22.

79 *PD* §17.

80 Ibid.

81 Ibid.

82 Leo XIII, *Vigilantiae studiique* §3. Apostolic Letter, "Instituting a Commission for Biblical Studies" (1902), *The Scripture Documents: An Anthology of Official Catholic Teachings*. Dean P. Béchard, ed. and trans. (Collegeville, MN: Liturgical Press, 2001), 63.

83 *DAS* §5.

84 Cf. *DAS* §10.

85 *DAS* §17.

86 *DAS* §33; cf. §40.

87 Redaction criticism (*Redaktionsgeschichte*) was only being pioneered in the mid-1940s and was not addressed by the encyclical. It would be discussed in the *IBC* document (below).

88 Raymond Brown, Joseph Fitzmyer, and Roland Murphy gained respect among Protestant and Catholic scholars alike. All three served as presidents of the traditionally Protestant Society of Biblical Literature. Each authored numerous works on the Bible, and together they wrote the *New Jerome Biblical Commentary*.

89 We have cited *DV* extensively in the previous chapter, and our discussion of it here will be brief.

90 Cf. *DV* §2-6.

91 *DV* §10.

92 Cf. *DV* §7-11.

93 Cf. *DV* §14-16.

94 Cf. *DV* §17-20.

95 *DV* §12: "For the correct understanding of what the sacred author wanted to assert, due attention must be paid to customary and characteristic styles of feeling, speaking and narrating which prevailed at the time of the sacred writer, *and to the patterns men normally employed at that period in their everyday dealings with one another*."

96 *DV* §19: "The sacred authors, in writing the four Gospels, selected certain of the many elements *which had been handed on, either orally or in written form* …"

97 DV §12: "To search out the intention of the sacred writers, attention should be given, among other things, to 'literary forms.' For truth is set forth and expressed differently in texts which are variously historical, prophetic, poetic, or of other forms of discourse. The interpreter must investigate what meaning the sacred writer intended to express and actually expressed in particular circumstances by using contemporary literary forms in accordance with the situation of his own time and culture."

98   For example, *DV* §19 refers to the Evangelists' treatment of their sources and states that "others synthesized or explained with an eye to *the situation of the churches.*"

99   Previous catechisms quoted Scripture, but not to the magnitude that the *Catechism of the Catholic Church* does.

100   Gal 4:4-5 "But when the time had fully come, God sent forth his Son, born of woman, born under the law, to redeem those who were under the law, so that we might receive adoption as sons."

101   CCC 422. *422 'But when the time had fully come, God sent forth his Son, born of a woman, born under the law, to redeem those who were under the law, so that we might receive adoption as sons.'* This is 'the gospel of Jesus Christ, the Son of God': God has visited his people. He has fulfilled the promise he made to Abraham and his descendants. He acted far beyond all expectation - he has sent his own 'beloved Son.'

102   John C. Cavadini, "The Use of Scripture in the *Catechism of the Catholic Church,*" 44; *Letter & Spirit* 2 (2006), 43-54. Another excellent treatment of the topic is found in Cardinal Joseph Ratzinger, "The Catechism's Use of Scripture," *On the Way to Jesus Christ*, Michael J. Miller, trans. (San Francisco, 2005) 146-53.

103   Cavadini, "The Use of Scripture in the *Catechism of the Catholic Church,*" 49-52.

104   Cavadini, "The Use of Scripture in the *Catechism of the Catholic Church,*" 48-49 and 52-54.

105   *The Interpretation of the Bible in the Church.* Pontifical Biblical Commission (Toronto, ON: Pauline Books and Media, 1996).

106   Peter Williamson, vol. 22, *Catholic Principles for Interpreting Scripture: A Study of the Pontifical Biblical Commission's The Interpretation of the Bible in the Church*, Pontificia Università Gregoriana, 2000, Subsidia Biblica (Roma: Pontificio Istituto biblico, 2001). The present book acknowledges Williamson's pioneering work and commends it to readers interested in further study of "principles of interpretation." There are similarities and differences between *The Word of the Lord* and Williamson's work. What they share in common is a discussion of principles vital to Catholic biblical interpretation. Whereas he discusses *twenty* principles for interpreting Scripture (and focuses solely on the *IBC* document), we present seven principles and examine a number of the Catholic Scripture documents, not only *IBC*.

107   Cardinal Joseph Ratzinger, Preface, *IBC*.

108   *IBC*, I.A.1.

109   Ibid.

110   Cf. *IBC*, §I.A.2.

111   Ibid. Other methods of biblical interpretation, such as Rhetorical Criticism, Narrative Criticism, canonical approaches, as well as other approaches (e.g., those of liberation and feminist theologies) are presented in Part I of the document. More on form, source and redaction criticism below.

112   *IBC*, I.A.4 (emphases added).

113   Cf. *IBC*, III.C.a.

114   *IBC*, IV.C.1. Cf. *Sacrosanctum Concilium* §7. More on these topics will be addressed below.

115   In the realm of papal writings, the weightiest documents are known as an Apostolic Constitution. These are followed by the Encyclical Letters, Apostolic Exhortations, Apostolic Letters, and finally, Letters and Messages. When Apostolic Constitutions contain dogma, they are referred to as Dogmatic Constitution (e.g., *Dei Verbum*). Thus, while Apostolic Exhortations are not as weighty as a Constitution or Encyclical (in that the latter concern the development of doctrine), they are certainly weightier than other official papal writings, as well as unofficial writing projects.

116   The new Exhortation makes no small number of references to *Dei Verbum* — perhaps more than all of the other of the Church's official "Scripture documents" combined. Additionally, however coincidental it may be, the very proximity of the names of the two documents, i.e., *Dei Verbum/ Verbum Domini* was not lost on this observer.

117   Pope Benedict XVI, *VD* §46.

118   Pope Benedict XVI, *VD* §55.

119   Pope Benedict XVI, *VD* §91.

120   Cf. Aidan Nichols, *The Shape of Catholic Theology*, 111.

CHAPTER 4

Principle 3
God's Word: Sacred Tradition and Sacred Scripture

> Tradition is the heritage of Christ's Church. This is a living memory of the Risen One met and witnessed to by the Apostles who passed on his living memory to their successors in an uninterrupted line, guaranteed by the apostolic succession through the laying on of hands, down to the bishops of today ... It is not an unchanging repetition of formulas, but a heritage which preserves its original, living kerygmatic core. It is Tradition that preserves the Church from the danger of gathering only changing opinions, and guarantees her certitude and continuity.
>
> *John Paul II, Apostolic Letter*
> *Orientale Lumen, 8*

Principle #3: Catholic Biblical Interpretation is grounded in the firm belief that there is one source of Divine revelation: Sacred Scripture and Sacred Tradition. The living presence of God's Word in the Church's life through time "flow from the same one divine wellspring" (DV, 9) and "form one sacred deposit of the word of God" (DV, 10). It was by the apostolic Tradition that the Church discerned which writings are to be included in the biblical canon (DV, 8) and it is above all Sacred Tradition that helps us to truly and properly understand the Word of God.

"Do you understand what you are reading?"

Principle #3: "God's Word: Sacred Tradition and Sacred Scripture" flows directly out of the previous principles of inspiration and history. Since Scripture is simultaneously the work of God and human authors and, since this collaboration occurred in human history, it is a thoughtful process in which there is *genuine human reflection involved.*

This notion of "human reflection" upon Scripture, unfolding in history as an active process can help us to understand what Sacred Tradition is, and how it is related to Sacred Scripture. Therefore, let us stay with this idea a bit further.

The divine Presence is no longer to be localized in a single place, the material tabernacle: henceforth, God will be in Jesus Christ, everywhere.

— Pope Benedict

First, if we look back at ancient Israel, we can see that quite early on, she understood her own identity in relation to unwritten things. It is true that later, she became a "people of the book," and in fact, remains so to this day. Yet, its authoritative sources did not at first originate in books, but in often-unwritten sources. In particular, four things could be mentioned here: 1) oral traditions; 2) customary laws; 3) priestly instruction at the Temple (and later, in the synagogues, too); and 4) in the proclamations of the prophets.[120] At the time of the Davidic monarchy and following, such sources were the "traditions" that guided Israel. It was not until after the Babylonian Captivity (587–539 B.C.) that the canon of the Hebrew Scriptures began to take on something of its recognizable shape. Even with the written Torah and other Scriptures available to them, the above sources, were all part of the "living process" by which God's people reflected upon the Lord and lived accordingly.

This notion of "human reflection," unfolding in history as an active or "living process" can help us to understand what Sacred Tradition is, and how it is related to Sacred Scripture.

This historically Jewish understanding of tradition was just as operable in Jesus' day. Thus, even as the New Testament Scriptures were being composed, the Apostles themselves indicated that they were not *self-interpreting* but required such *reflection* and *guidance* in order to truly understand the meaning intended by the biblical author:

So Philip ran to him, and heard him reading Isaiah the prophet, and asked, *"Do you understand what you are reading?"* And he said, *"How can I, unless someone guides me?"* And he invited Philip to come up and sit with him. (Acts 8:30–31)

Just as the Ethiopian man needed the Apostle Philip to guide him in reading the book of Isaiah, so do the entire people of God rely upon the guidance of the apostolic Church. Pope Benedict XVI refers to this dynamic in *Jesus of Nazareth*, where he writes:

> The Scripture emerged from within the heart of a living subject — the pilgrim People of God — and lives within this same subject. One could say that the books of Scripture involve *three interacting subjects.*[121]

First, the pope tells us that there is the *individual author* (or authors) who actually composed the biblical books.[122] Yet, as he observes, these individuals were not independent composers, as in the modern sense of authorship. Rather, they are part of a "collective subject, the 'People of God,' *from within whose heart* and *to whom* they speak."[123] So, as the pope explains, this "collective People of God," to which the biblical authors belong, is in fact a *second subject.* This second subject of the Church itself, the pope writes, is actually "the deeper author"[124] of the biblical books.

Yet, going beyond these two subjects, the pope explains that there is in fact a third entity that goes beyond both a) the true human authors and b) the Church: "This people does not exist alone; rather, it knows that it is led and spoken to, by God himself, who — through men and their humanity — is at the deepest level the one speaking ... The People of God — the Church — is the living subject of Scripture; *it is in the Church that the words of the Bible are always in the present.* This also means, of course, that the People has to receive its very self from God, ultimately from the incarnate Christ; it has to let itself be ordered, guided and led by him."[125]

FOR REFLECTION

Spend some time reflecting on Acts 8:26–36, then meditate on the following:

Who have been the "St. Philips" in my life; those individuals who directly or indirectly touched my life in a powerful way through their explanation and teaching of the Scriptures? In what ways do they continue to influence me today as I approach Scripture? Who is God perhaps asking me to be a "Philip" to at present? (e.g., sibling, friend, brother seminarian, parishioner, etc.) Will I make time to "sit" with the person and share my love for Scripture?

Written Text Becomes Living Word

Grasping this threefold dynamic — of the apostles and prophets, the Church to which they belong, and God Himself — will help us to better understand "the Word of God." Yet, there is more to the Word of God than that which was written on in the sacred page alone. As Paul himself writes, "So then, brethren, stand firm and hold to the traditions which you were taught by us, either by word of mouth or by letter" (2 Thess. 2:15):

> "In order that the full and living Gospel might always be preserved in the Church, the apostles left bishops as their successors. They gave them their own position of teaching authority." Indeed, "the apostolic preaching, which is expressed in a special way in the inspired books, was to be preserved in a continuous line of succession until the end of time."[126]

As the above quote from the *Catechism* states, the purpose of the written Word was to "preserve" the Gospel for all Christians at all times; not merely those that were alive in the age of the apostles. More specifically, this preservation of truth occurred in the context of the living relationship between the Apostles who wrote the books and the Church that received them: as the Apostles appointed bishops as their successors with "teaching authority." Notice then, that what we refer to as Scripture the *Catechism* rightly calls "*apostolic preaching*"; yet, while this *kerygma* resides in the "inspired books" in a unique way, for all people at all times, it is not limited to the written form alone. Rather, the "living voice of the Gospel *rings out in the Church*,"[127] which is, the pope reminded us, "the deeper subject" of Scripture.[128] This living embodiment of truth, which is the work of the Holy Spirit, is what we call Sacred Tradition. From Sacred Tradition, the Church "perpetuates and transmits to every generation all that she herself is, all that she believes."[129]

Though distinct from Sacred Scripture, Sacred Tradition is "closely connected to it,"[130] since both "flow from the same divine wellspring."[131] In a sense, the two "merge into a unity"[132] and are in a sort of dialogue or communication with one another.[133] In a special way, we should think of the works of the Church fathers as a key element of Sacred Tradition.[134] We would do well to read them, along with our devout reading of Scripture, as a witness to the living Tradition of the Church and all of its riches.

Yet, more broadly, Sacred Tradition is primarily the *unwritten* expression of the Word of God, entrusted to the Church.[135] Near the end of *IBC*, we read, "It is above all *through the liturgy* that Christians come into contact with Scripture, particularly during the Sunday celebration of the Eucharist."[136] Sacred Tradition, then, is embodied in the Church's sacred liturgy, and particularly, in the Eucharistic celebration of the Mass:

> In principle, the liturgy, and especially the sacramental liturgy, the high point of which is the Eucharistic celebration, brings about the most perfect actualization of the biblical texts, for the liturgy places the proclamation in the midst of the community of believers, gathered around Christ so as to draw near to God. Christ is then "present in his word, because it is he himself who speaks when Sacred Scripture is read in the church." *Written text thus becomes living word.*[137]

Pope Benedict refers to Sacred Tradition as a "living river ... the great river that leads us to the gates of eternity."[138] Sacred Tradition is not the stuff of history, but a "bringing forward" that which is ever new and ever alive. As the pope adds, this living river of Tradition puts us in touch not just with our "roots," but with the Church itself, which draws all of her life from the Holy Trinity, as the Church is "the holy Temple of God the Father, built on the cornerstone, Christ, through the life-giving action of the Spirit."

In Chapter 1, we talked about Scripture as a "mirror" through which we see God (and ourselves) reflected back to us. Now, with this fuller understanding of divine revelation as both Sacred Scripture and Sacred Tradition, we can re-visit and complete the image, with the help of *Dei Verbum*,

> In order to keep the Gospel forever whole and alive within the Church, the Apostles left bishops as their successors, "handing over" to them the authority to teach in their own place. This sacred tradition, therefore, and Sacred Scripture of both the Old and New Testaments are like a mirror in which the pilgrim Church on earth looks at God, from whom she has received everything, until she is brought finally to see Him as He is, face to face.[139]

FOR REFLECTION

"Lord, you are the companion of my pilgrimage. Wherever I go, your eyes are always upon me. Your seeing is also your moving. Therefore, you move with me and never cease moving as long as I move. If I am at rest, you are with me; if I ascend or descend, so do You; wherever I go, You are there (Ps 138:8)."
— *Nicholas of Cusa, "On the Vision of God."* B. McGinn., trans. In Nicolai de Cusa Opera Omnia, Vol. VI. *Hamburg: Felix Meiner Verlag, 1998, Ch. 5.*

Thus, the mirror by which we look at God (and ourselves) is even more encompassing than we may have thought; it is the dual "reflective power" of both Sacred Scripture and Sacred Tradition. Together, they are divine revelation, and these sources of Truth continually and authoritatively "show us God" (and ourselves) until we see Him "face to face" (cf. 1 John 3:2).

In short, Sacred Tradition is a crucial part of the Christian's journey toward God and absolutely essential for us to truly and properly understand Scripture. In fact, the primary role of Sacred Tradition is to provide us with a *pre-understanding* of "what it is that Scripture is talking about."[140] Therefore, Catholic exegetes must deliberately place themselves within this stream of the living Tradition of the Church[141] and seek to be faithful to the revelation handed on by this great living Tradition, of which the Bible is itself a witness.[142]

The Last Word on the Word: The Vital Role of the Magisterium

If Sacred Tradition provides us with a *pre-understanding* in the science of biblical interpretation, then, in a manner of speaking, the Church's Magisterium provides us with a *post-understanding* of all biblical interpretation. That is, because of the unique role the Church had in receiving from God both the Living Word (Jesus Christ) — and the written Word (Sacred Scripture), she is in a most privileged position to "give us the last word" on the correct and proper interpretation of Scripture. Moreover, this right and responsibility applies to the right interpretation of Sacred Tradition, and not only Sacred Scripture. As *Dei Verbum* summarizes:

The task of authentically interpreting the word of God, whether in its written form or in the form of tradition, has been entrusted to the Teaching Office of the Church which is not above the word of God but serves it by teaching only what has been handed on.[143]

In a sense, we could say that any given individual or community certainly has a "right" to interpret Scripture as he/they see fit. Yet, as the Council clearly indicates, it is the Church that has both the *authority* and the *privileged responsibility* of providing an "authentic interpretation" of Scripture. This does not pit the Church against the Word of God as its master; to the contrary, the Church is its "servant."[144] Moreover, this responsibility is not self-appointed, but is divinely appointed and "exercised in the name of Jesus Christ."[145] It is this unique role of the Magisterium — and all the bishops in communion with the pope[146] — which distinguishes it from all other individuals or bodies with an interpretative voice.

Similar echoes are heard in *The Interpretation of the Bible in the Church*, with respect to the final and authoritative role of the Church in the interpretation of divine revelation:

It is the believing community that provides a truly adequate context for interpreting canonical texts. In this context faith and the Holy Spirit enrich exegesis; *church authority, exercised as a service of the community, must see to it that this interpretation remains faithful to the great tradition which has produced the texts.*[147]

We should not think of this authority to interpret Scripture as an innovation of the Church. Rather, it is a continuation of the responsibility that the believing community of God's people has always bore, since the time of ancient Israel:

The communities of the Old Covenant ... received these texts as a patrimony to be preserved and handed on.[148]

In the same way, the apostolic Church continued the responsibility to preserve, rightly interpret and hand on the books of Scripture:

[The text of the Old and New Testament] were recognized by the communities of the Former Covenant and by those of the apostolic age as the genuine expression of the common faith. It is in accordance with the interpretative work of these communities and together with it that the texts were accepted as Sacred Scripture.[149]

The "problem" with most Scripture passages is not that they are obscure, but rather, that there is an embarrassment of riches and an abundance of meaning.

The Church's Role as Authoritative Interpreter

In short, for all of the above reasons, we look to the Magisterium of the Church for a "definitive word" on the interpretation of the Word. With that being said, a clarification is necessary, and with it, I offer some pastoral advice. While the Church clearly has this particular and authoritative role, we must understand that like a good Mother, the Church certainly is not interested in shackling her children or exercising her authority in any sort of excessive way. In fact, one can probably count on one hand the number of biblical passages for which a sort of "definitive hermeneutic" has been ascribed to it by the Church. Yet, even when the Church does involve itself in an interpretation of a specific biblical text, the role of the Church as the "authoritative interpreter" should not be perceived as somehow *exhausting* the meaning of the text, but rather, of *illuminating* it in a particular way — typically towards the understanding of various doctrines. This is not a problem, but it does require that we are aware of this, and seek to identify the "meanings" of a text as we study God's Word.[150]

FOR REFLECTION

To what extent does my study of Scripture rely upon or at least consider what the Catechism has to say on topics relevant to a given passage? What evangelical impulses arise in me as I think about particular people in my life and their beliefs about the Scriptures and the Church?

Some additional advice is offered with respect to Sacred Scripture, and the role of the Church in conversations with other Christians. In personal encounters with numerous non-Catholic Christians (and a good number of Catholics, I might add!), the role of the Church as the authoritative interpreter of Scripture is not well understood. Some even mistakenly believe that "somewhere" the Church has a definitive commentary on all or most of the texts in the Old and New Testaments, and thus "makes us read it a certain way." Yet, this is hardly the case. In fact, there are really very few passages of Scripture which the Church has sort of "definitively interpreted."

In many instances, such misunderstandings may be resolved with some good conversation — and we should begin by listening and by acknowledging that it can be difficult to understand. For my part, I have found the *Catechism* — which even non-Catholics will accept as "authoritative," at least with respect to Catholic questions — extremely helpful. Additionally, I have found it helpful to indicate just how rare it is that the Church actually offers any interpretation of specific biblical passages

I recall such a conversation with an Evangelical friend, who had been reading the *New Jerome Biblical Commentary* "for the official Catholic position" on a biblical text. Hearing this, I soon realized that my friend unknowingly and incorrectly assumed that this biblical commentary represented the Church's magisterium — it doesn't. I explained that while the scholars who oversaw the project were Catholic scholars (Raymond Brown, Joseph Fitzmyer, etc.) the commentary itself was only the work of individual biblical scholars and not the whole Church. Catholics, I explained, could agree or disagree with a particular conclusion in the *New Jerome Biblical Commentary* (or any other) — provided our agreement (or disagreement) was in no way an expression of opposition to the Church's tradition or a denial of her teachings.

Begin With the Church's Teachings in Our Sights

The above story illustrates the need for greater care when approaching commentaries. We should ask, who wrote the commentary — and why? What is their background? Are they Catholic — and if so, are they faithful to the teachings of the Church? Simply because someone professes to be a Catholic, we shouldn't assume they represent "the Catholic position" on a passage.

It's important to know as much about a biblical commentator, and we should do what we can to ascertain something about them. Neither should we be quick to judge. Similarly, in the event that the commentator is a non-Catholic biblical scholar, be prudent. We may learn a good deal from their work, and should not automatically fear that the book will be of no use.

Whatever we pick up and read, it is hoped that the seven principles in this book can provide a more sound basis for assessing the "catholicity" and "hermeneutic" (biblical point of view) of the author. Perhaps the best advice is to have your Bible and commentary in one hand, and the *Catechism* in the other. Every Catholic should possess a *Catechism* — and be well acquainted with it — particularly the sections dealing with Scripture. As you read Scripture and learn from various commentaries, allow the teachings of the Church to guide you forward.

Every Catholic should possess a *Catechism* — and be well acquainted with it — particularly the section dealing with Scripture.

Additionally, it's important to begin with faith — as well as *charity*; give the person the benefit of the doubt. Charity opens us up to an encounter of another so we can hear their voice. When we first encounter any author or listen to a teacher on Scripture, we ought to be especially attentive with regard to the "faithfulness" of their message. As we become more acquainted with them and their work, we should continue to be attentive and vigilant, but "let them do their thing." And, if it turns out that we still come across something that seems questionable, we should seek an opportunity to gain clarity about the issue. In the process, we should continue to exhibit kindness, compassion, patience and most of all Christian love towards the person, through our actions, our words, and certainly our prayers (cf. Col 3:12–13).

FOR REFLECTION	*"Our own curiosity often hinders us in reading the Scriptures, because we wish to understand and argue when we should simply read on with humility, simplicity, and faith."*
	— *Thomas À Kempis,* Imitation of Christ *(London: Paternoster House, 1903), 11.*

Pope Benedict is an excellent example in this regard. As former Prefect of the Congregation of Doctrine of the Faith and newly elected Pope, what kind of tone would he take in his volume concerning the life and ministry of Jesus Christ? In his first book as pontiff, *Jesus of Nazareth* (Volume I), he displays just the kind of charity and invitation that we are speaking of. Although he could have approached it as an "official" sort of text, he clearly indicates very early in the book that it is "in no way an exercise of the Magisterium" and that "everyone is free to disagree with me."[151] Given his position as the Chief Shepherd of the Church, this is a remarkable gesture of humility and charity. Along the same lines, he then invites the reader for "that initial goodwill without which there can be no understanding."[152]

Conclusion

Having completed our discussion on the teaching authority of the Church's Magisterium (along with some clarification and pastoral advice on the matter), we move forward to our next principle. As we do so, I offer the following image as a way of making sense of the Magisterium's authoritative role in relation to our own role as students of Scripture.

In a way, we might liken the Church's relationship to the Catholic biblical exegete as a loving mother to a son or daughter. Imagine the mother allowing the child access to their enormously big backyard and encouraging him or her to fully explore it; climbing its trees, discovering its beauty, and running this way and that. At the same time, imagine just beyond the yard a very steep and very dangerous slope, covered in jagged rocks. A solid fence separates the yard from the slope of the cliff. Yet, the fence that separates the yard from the dangerous territory beyond is not an "imposition" that impinges on the freedom of the child.

FOR REFLECTION

"As the soul goes ever after God with love so true, imbued with the spirit of suffering for His sake, God's majesty often and regularly grants it joy, and visits it sweetly and delectably in the spirit; for the boundless love of Christ, the Word, cannot see the afflictions of His lover without comforting him or her."
— St. John of the Cross, "The Dark Night of the Soul" (From Classics of Western Spirituality, Mahwah, NH: Paulist Press, 1987), 124.

Rather, its presence represents the wise boundaries of a responsible and loving parent, always seeking the good of the child, so that they avoid harm, and enjoy the security and safety of the yard, in which their freedom can be explored with confidence, certainty and joy. But it is a fence and not a wall — it can be easily breached, if we choose to do so. If and when we do so, what we leave behind are not fetters which bind us, but the freedom and truth of the Church, who, as a loving Mother, is always desiring us to grow into the responsible expression of freedom, as we search for truth in joy. And it is always truth that sets us free (John 8:32).

Questions for Reflection

1. Who have been the Philips in my life, i.e., those key individuals who have helped/are helping me "to understand what I am reading" when it comes to Scripture? (You are invited to thank God for those individuals and pray on their behalf.)
2. What has been my view of …
   a. Sacred Tradition and its relationship to Scripture?
   b. The Magisterium and its relationship to Scripture?
3. To what extent should the work of individual Catholic biblical scholars be influenced by — and in service to — the Magisterium of the Church? Why?
4. To what extent have I approached Sacred Tradition as the Word of God (i.e., the mostly unwritten "Word")? How would I explain the relationship of Scripture and Tradition … to a parishioner? … to an Evangelical Christian?
5. Similarly, how would I explain the relationship of the Magisterium to Sacred Scripture and Sacred Tradition?

For Further Study

Balthasar, Hans Urs von. *The Office of Peter and the Structure of the Church*. San Francisco: Ignatius Press, 1986.

Butler, B. C. *The Church and Infallability*. London, Sheed and Ward, 1954.

Congar, Yves. *Tradition and Traditions*. London: Burn and Oates, 1966. A classic text on the nature of Sacred Tradition and its role in the Church. See also: Congar, Yves and Avery Dulles. *The Meaning of Tradition*. San Francisco: Ignatius Press, 2004.

Hahn, S. W. *Letter and Spirit: From Written Text to Living Word in the Liturgy*. New York: Doubleday, 2005.

———. *Scripture Matters: Essays on Reading the Bible from the Heart of the Church*. Steubenville, OH: Emmaus Road, 2003.

Nichols, Aidan. *Epiphany: A Theological Introduction to Catholicism*. Collegeville, MN: Michael Glazier Press, 1996. A readable synthesis of Catholicism. See especially: Ch. 2 ("Revelation and its Sources"); Ch. 3 ("The Historian's Jesus"); and Ch. 4 ("The Church's Jesus").

Sullivan, F. A. *Magisterium: Teaching authority in the Catholic Church*. New York: Paulist Press, 1985.

Notes

121 Benedict XVI, *Jesus of Nazareth*, xx.

122 Ibid.

123 Ibid, xxi (emphases added).

124 Ibid.

125 Ibid (emphasis added).

126 CCC 77. Cf. *DV* §7, 8.

127 CCC 79 (emphasis added).

128 Benedict XVI, *Jesus of Nazareth*, xxi.

129 CCC 78.

130 CCC 78.

131 *DV* §9.

132 Ibid.

133 Ibid.

134 CCC 78.

135 Cf. CCC 78.

136 *IBC* IV.C.1.a, b. (For the enclosed quotation, cf. *Sacrosanctum Concilium* §7.)

137 *IBC* IV.C.1.a, b. (For the enclosed quotation, cf. *Sacrosanctum Concilium* §7.)

138 Benedict XVI, *The Origins of the Church: The Apostles and Their Co-Workers*, Huntington, IN: OSV Publications, 30.

139 *DV* §7.

140 *IBC*, III.b

141 *IBC*, III.b

142 *IBC*, Conclusion, e.

143 *DV* §11.

144 CCC 86.

145 CCC 85.

146 Ibid. "This means that the task of interpretation has been entrusted to the bishops in communion with the successor of Peter, the Bishop of Rome."

147 Cf. *DV* §10.

148 *IBC*, III.B.1.b.

149 *IBC*, III.A.3.a.

150   Cf. Ch. 6: "God's Word has meanings" (below).

151   Benedict XVI, *Jesus of Nazareth,* xiii.

152   Ibid, xiv.

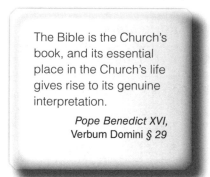

CHAPTER 5

The Bible is the Church's book, and its essential place in the Church's life gives rise to its genuine interpretation.

Pope Benedict XVI,
Verbum Domini § 29

The Canon of Sacred Scripture

The previous chapter, which discussed Principle #3 ("God's Word: Sacred Scripture and Sacred Tradition") helped us to better understand the role of the Church as the authentic interpreter of the Word of God. Yet, before the Church could exercise this authority to interpret the Word of God, it first had to *receive it and acknowledge it as such.* Before we examine our next principle, we need to discuss the idea and development of the biblical canon.

The Process of Canonization

The English term *canon* originates from the Greek and Latin, which in turn derives it from the older Hebrew term, *kaneh*, meaning "reed." As a reed was long, thin and straight, it provided the ancient peoples a sound tool by which one could measure something. Yet, there is dual sense in which we can think of our biblical canon as a reed. On the one hand, it is *the measure of genuine and authoritative books,* i.e., the Old and New Testaments we hold as sacred Scripture. In a deeper spiritual sense, the canon of Scripture is itself a kind of reed *that measures us* — with respect to our knowledge of Christ (1 Cor 6:22), love for the truth (John 8:32), and the obedience of faith (Rom 16:26).

The process by which books were accepted into the Scriptures is called *canonization.* Canonization occurs only after a book has been a part of the liturgy and the "believing community" and the book reflects the faith of the community. Naturally, as a human process, there was debate both among the Jews about which books should be allowed into the Hebrew canon and similarly among Christians regarding the list of books of the New Testament. While there is a good deal of distinction between Jews, Catholics and Protestants as to the canon of the Old Testament, there is unanimity between Catholics and other Christians as to the books of the New Testament and it reflects the faith of virtually all Christians.[153]

Table 5: The Canon of the Old Testament

Hebrew Canon	Catholic Canon	Protestant Canon
Torah/Books of Moses *Bereshith*/Genesis *Shemot*/Exodus *VaYikra*/Leviticus *BaMidbar*/Numbers *Devarim*/Deuteronomy	**Pentateuch (Law)** Genesis Exodus Leviticus Numbers Deuteronomy	**Pentateuch (Law)** Genesis Exodus Leviticus Numbers Deuteronomy
Nevi'im/Former Prophets Joshua Judges Samuel (1 and 2) Kings (1 and 2)	**Historical Books** Joshua Judges Ruth 1 Samuel 2 Samuel 1 Kings 2 Kings 1 Chronicles 2 Chronicles Ezra Nehemiah Tobit Judith Esther (longer version) 1 Maccabees 2 Maccabees	**Historical Books** Joshua Judges Ruth 1 Samuel 2 Samuel 1 Kings 2 Kings 1 Chronicles 2 Chronicles Ezra Nehemiah Esther (shorter version)

Nevi'im/Latter Prophets
Isaiah
Jeremiah
Ezekiel
The Book of the Twelve:
  Hosea, Joel,
  Amos, Obadiah,
  Jonah, Micah,
  Nahum, Habakkuk,
  Zephaniah, Haggai,
  Zechariah, Malachi
	Prophets
	Isaiah
	Jeremiah
	Lamentations
	Baruch
	Ezekiel
	Daniel (14 chapters)
	Hosea
	Joel
	Amos
	Obadiah
	Jonah
	Micah
	Nahum
	Habakkuk
	Zephaniah
	Haggai
	Zechariah
	Malachi
		Prophets
		Isaiah
		Jeremiah
		Lamentations
		Ezekiel
		Daniel (12 chapters)
		Hosea
		Joel
		Amos
		Obadiah
		Jonah
		Micah
		Nahum
		Habakkuk
		Zephaniah
		Haggai
		Zechariah
		Malachi

Hebrew Canon	Catholic Canon	Protestant Canon
***Kethuvim*/Writings**	**Wisdom Books**	**Wisdom Books**
Psalms	Job	Job
Proverbs	Psalms	Psalms
Job	Proverbs	Proverbs
Song of Songs	Ecclesiastes	Ecclesiastes
Ruth	Song of Songs	Song of Songs
Lamentations	Wisdom of Solomon	
Ecclesiastes	Sirach	
Esther (shorter version)		
Daniel (12 chapters)		
Ezra-Nehemiah		
The Book of Chronicles (1 and 2)		

Prior to the age of the Church, the people of ancient Israel recognized a threefold collection of sacred texts, as revealed by God: the *Tanak*.[154] The *Tanak* is comprised of *Torah* ("Law"), *Nebi'im* ("Prophets") and *Kethubim* ("Writings"). In terms of the development of the Hebrew canon, it is clear that the Torah was completed prior to the other two divisions in the canon (i.e., *Nebi'im* and *Kethubim*).

Exactly when the Hebrew Scriptures were actually composed is a question that continues to be debated, and such a discussion is beyond the scope of this book. Yet, many believe that the "Books of Moses," or the Torah, were composed somewhere between the eighth or perhaps ninth century B.C. at the earliest and the fourth century B.C. at the latest. The overall shape of the Hebrew canon likely occurred during or after the exile in Babylon (587–539 B.C.), a crucial period of ancient Jewish history.

Despite this consensus of the Hebrew canon around the time of the exile and return to Jerusalem, the full canonization process was by no means completed at this time. There was no real controversy among ancient Jews about the "inspired status" of the five books of Moses (i.e., the Torah). Yet, beyond their settled view of the Torah, there remained among the ancient rabbis *continual and robust debate* as to which other books were also considered as sacred.

Although the question of the canon was not settled at the time of Jesus, rabbinic scribes were not without criteria in voicing their views as to which books were "worthy of faith" and which were not. Meanwhile, the lack of a fixed Hebrew canon certainly did not dissuade Jesus, the Apostles, or the early Fathers from quoting the Hebrew Scriptures, as is evidenced by the *vast number of quotations and allusions* from them, both in the New Testament and in patristic literature.

Given such argumentation, various "canons" emerged. In rabbinic circles, there was no single authoritative body which could or did issue some sort of definitive canon and thus settle the matter. So, even after the crucifixion of Jesus, in the latter half of the first century, there is evidence of the continued ambiguity with respect to the Hebrew canon.

Q: "So, when was the canon closed, from the Jewish perspective?"

It is difficult to say with true precision when the Hebrew canon was actu-ally closed. A working hypothesis in the twentieth century suggested that after the destruction of the Jerusalem Temple in A.D. 70, the epicenter of rabbinic Judaism moved to Jamnia in the 80s or 90s. According to this proposal, the so-called Council of Jamnia definitively established (or "fixed") the Hebrew canon at this time.[155] A German scholar, Heinrich Graetz, introduced this possibility in 1871. Based largely upon *later* Jew-ish tradition, Graetz thus "worked backward" to the first-century and concluded that there must have been a Council of Jamnia which decided the canon near the end of the first century. This view became the schol-arly consensus for much of the twentieth century.[156]

Yet it is hardly an open and shut case. In fact, beginning in the 1960s, various scholars began to challenge this proposal, on grounds that there was not substantial evidence to support Graetz's theory. [157] More recently, respected Jewish biblical scholar Jacob Neusner has argued the case well that when all the evidence is laid on the table, Jewish canon was still open at least though the fourth century A.D. and perhaps as late as the sixth century A.D.[158]

Continuity and Discontinuity: The Development of the New Testament Canon

Christianity was a movement that exploded into Jerusalem, Judea and the wider Roman Empire. It followed and really grew out of the mantle of its "older brother," ancient Judaism. After all, Jesus was a Jewish rabbi and the first Christian converts were from Judaism. Like the process of canonization of the Hebrew Scriptures, the development of the New Testament canon was a process that unfolded over centuries and with ongoing debate and dialogue.

First, it should be noted that although we do not have a definitive New Testament canon in the apostolic age, it should be emphasized that the "Fourfold Gospel" (Matthew, Mark, Luke and John) was proclaimed in all of the apostolic churches and their liturgies. As early as A.D. 115, St. Ignatius, bishop of Antioch, refers to "The Gospel" as a singular apostolic work.[159] By the time of Irenaeus, in the 180s, the acceptance of "The Gospel" and the idea of a fourfold Gospel had become so axiomatic in the Church that he refers to it as an established fact as obvious as the four points of the compass or the four winds.[160]

From the earliest period then, the gospels were accepted as the definitive record of the apostles about the life, teachings and Passion of the Lord Jesus Christ. They were universally accepted as authoritative and sacred texts, and instrumental in the liturgy and catechesis of the early Christians. Most of the remaining texts of the New Testament, especially the Epistles, were precipitated by specific situations (e.g., Paul's letter to the Romans, in advance of his visit to them). These were also admitted to the liturgies and used for teaching, on the basis of their apostolic status, along with the Four Gospels. It is very likely that the particular churches held in highest regard letters received from an apostle(s), along with the more universal gospels, which were ultimately intended "for all Christians,"[161] and not strictly isolated communities.

By the time of Irenaeus the idea of a fourfold Gospel had become so axiomatic in the Church that he refers to it as an established fact as obvious as the four points of the compass or the four winds.

Second, it is likely that the particular churches (e.g., Thessalonica, Rome, Corinth, as well as those at Alexandria and elsewhere) added to their particular collection of apostolic texts (i.e., The Fourfold Gospel, apostolic letters received) by exchanging and sharing copies of the authoritative books with other churches in order to have them read publicly and proclaimed in the liturgy.

For these reasons (and others), the written collections of authoritative/apostolic collections of the early Christians were amassed rather expeditiously and disseminated widely throughout the Mediterranean world. Despite this, a considerable number of years passed before all of the individual churches possessed "the apostolic books in full" (Gospels and Acts, Epistles, The Book of Revelation). Consequently, this led to an absence of a fixed "list" of approved books and left room for variations and questions which lasted several centuries.

The earliest extant list of New Testament books was drawn up at Rome by the bishop Marcion of Sinope in A.D. 140. His canon included ten Pauline epistles and just one gospel, i.e., "The Gospel of Marcion." His "canon" was nothing more than a wholesale rejection of the entire Hebrew Bible. He excluded the other New Testament writings and instead, advanced a form of Christianity that ripped it apart from what he saw as corrupt and evil Jewish doctrines. What is important, for our purpose, is that the Marcionite canon was condemned by the Church. But in the process, he stimulated the Church to address the question of what books were canonical, a process that would unfold over the next several centuries.

Another early list, also from Rome, originated at the end of the second century A.D. known as the *Muratorian Fragment*. Unfortunately the beginning of the text is corrupt and unreadable, but it appears to mention the Gospels of Matthew and Mark, since it does refer to Luke as the third gospel. It also refers to John's Gospel, Acts of the Apostles, Paul's nine letters to various churches (Romans, 1 and 2 Corinthians, Galatians, Ephesians, Philippians, Colossians and 1 and 2 Thessalonians), as well as four others to specific individuals (Philemon, Titus, 1 and 2 Timothy). It also mentions Jude, two Epistles of John, Revelation, and Peter's letters. In addition, *Shepherd of Hermas* is mentioned as "worthy to be read" in the liturgy but was not included in the number of prophetic or apostolic writings.

Later, in A.D. 363, the local Synod of Laodicea listed all of the books of the New Testament save one, The Book of Revelation.[162] Yet, it attributed to St. Athanasius the first list of <u>all</u> twenty-seven books of what would become the canon of the New Testament. By the end of the third century, two North African ecclesiastical councils would classify all of the books of the New Testament named by Athanasius as "canonical," first at Hippo (A.D. 393) and then at Carthage (A.D. 397).

FOR REFLECTION	*"Even when carrying out needful tasks, keep meditating inwardly and praying. Thus you can grasp the depths of divine Scripture and the power hidden it, and 'pray without ceasing.'"*
	— *Abba Philimon,* Philokalia, Volume II

Given the developments that took place in the first three centuries of Christianity, we might conclude that the matter of the canon was now closed. Yet, it is important to realize that despite this rather "rapid" developmental process of the canon (at least in comparison with that of the Hebrew canon), a formal dogmatic declaration by the Church was still a long way in the future. The absolute ratification of the canons of both the Old Testament and the New Testament would not take place until the Council of Trent in the 1500s. On April 8, 1546, a decree was issued in which, for the first time in the history of the Catholic Church, the contents of the Bible — all forty-six books of the Old Testament and the twenty-seven books of the New — was ratified as an *absolute article of faith*.[163]

In conclusion, we can see that the canonization process of the New Testament began with the early liturgical proclamation of the Gospel in the apostolic era. Yet, it was also the desire for copies of "authoritative books" by the churches (and individuals) that accelerated the proliferation of "apostolic collections." Yet, it is crucial to underscore that the New Testament books did not become authoritative for the Church because they were formally included in any canonical list; rather, the Church included them in her canon *because she already venerated them in and out of the liturgy.*

Moreover, the excommunication of Marcion ended a controversy — and opened the era of dialogue and debate that would continue until the 300s, with the appearance of Athanasius' Festal Letter in A.D. 367, naming all twenty-seven books, and two ecclesial councils at the end of the 300s (i.e., Hippo and Carthage). Yet, the final ratification as an article of faith came well over a thousand years later, much later at the Council of Trent.

The Magisterium, i.e., the pope and the bishops in union with him, *definitively* settled the question of the canon. Only an infallible Church could produce an infallible canon of Scripture. Thus, we can and should embrace all of the Scriptures given to the Church by God, and deeply appreciate the incredible process by which the Spirit of God gave us, a permanent *kaneh*, i.e., a "measuring rod" of genuine and authoritative inspired books. For in the settled canon of Scripture we affirm, along with the entire Church, the divinely inspired books given to the Church by God. Most importantly, we embrace all of the books of Sacred Scripture — Old and New Testament — as *our measuring rod*, by which we can, and indeed must, continually measure our own Christian lives in light of the Living Word, who is our salvation and our hope.

Questions for Reflection

1. What has been my previous understanding of the development of the biblical canon? How has this chapter deepened my appreciation for the Church's role in the development of the canon of Scripture?
2. How familiar/comfortable am I with the various parts of the biblical canon (Law, Prophets, Writings, etc.)?
3. How would I respond to a non-Christian person who asked why I revere the "holy books" of my religion?
4. How would I respond to a non-Catholic Christian, regarding the status of the deutero-canonical books of the Old Testament?

For Further Study

Childs, Brevard. *Introduction to the Old Testament as Scripture.* Philadelphia: Fortress Press, 1979.

———. *The New Testament as Canon: An Introduction.* Philadelphia: Fortress Press, 1984.

Farmer, William R. and D. Farkasfalvy. *The Formation of the New Testament Canon.* New York: Paulist, 1983. Written from both Protestant (Farmer) and Catholic (Farkasfalvy) points of view.

Lienhard, Joseph T. *The Bible, the Church, and Authority: The Canon of the Christian Bible in History and Theology.* Collegeville, MN: Liturgical Press, 1995.

McDonald, L. M and J. A. Sanders. *The Canon Debate.* Peabody, MA: Hendrickson, 2002.

Metzger, Bruce. *The Canon of the New Testament: Its Origin, Development, and Significance*. Oxford: Oxford University Press, 1997.

———. *New Testament: Its Background, Growth and Content*. Nashville: Abingdon Press, 2003.

Nichols, Aidan. "The Authority of Scripture: Canonicity," *The Shape of Catholic Theology: An Introduction to its Sources, Principles and History, 99–109*. San Francisco: Ignatius Press, 1991.

Sundberg, A.C. "The Old Testament: A Christian Canon," *Catholic Biblical Quarterly* 30 (1968), 143–55.

Tov, Emmanuel. *Exploring the Origins of the Bible: Canon Formation in Historical, Literary, and Theological Perspective*. Grand Rapids: Baker Academic, 2008.

Turo, J.C. and R. E. Brown. "Canonicity," *The New Jerome Biblical* Commentary, ed. R. E. Brown, J. A. Fitzmyer and R. E. Murphy, 515–34. Prentice Hall, NJ: Prentice Hall, 1969.

Internet Resources

www.bible-researcher.com/canon.html. This website contains many helpful charts and tables concerning the development of the biblical canon.

Notes

153   Cf. Table 6, ("The Canon of the Old Testament") for the specific divisions and books included in the Hebrew canon, in contrast to the Catholic canon of the Old Testament (below). Likewise, the Catholic and Protestant canons are further distinguished in that the Protestant canon does not include the Deuterocanoical books (Sir, Wisd, 1 and 2 Macc, Baruch, Jdt and Tob; as well as additions to certain books in Hebrew canon).

154   Cf. Table 6 (above).

155   It is questioned today whether a "council" ever formally convened at Jamnia during the A.D. 80s-90s. It is more likely that this was a scribal school and not an authoritative body that fixed the canon.

156   Cf. L.M. McDonald, J. A. Sanders, *The Canon Debate* (Peabody, MA: Hendrickson, 2002).

157   Ibid.

158   Jacob Neusner, *Judaism and Christianity in the Age of Constantine: History, Messiah, Israel, and the Initial Confrontation*. Chicago Studies in the History of Judaism (Chicago: University of Chicago Press, 1987). Especially helpful is his treatment of the Christian canon and Jewish canon (pp. 128-139).

159   "Indeed, I heard some men saying, 'if I do not find it in the official records of *the gospel*, I do not believe. And when I made the answer, 'It is written,' they replied, 'that is the point at issue.' But to me, the official record is Jesus Christ; the inviolable record of his cross, his death, and his resurrection, and the faith which he brings about. " Cf. *Didache*, 11.3 (A.D. 80-120); *Epistle of Barnabas*, 5.5 (A.D. 70-79); Justin Martyr, *First Apology*, 65 (A.D. 148-55).

160   "It is not possible that the Gospels can be either more or fewer in number than they are. For, since there are four zones of the world in which we live, and four principal winds, while the Church is scattered throughout all the world, and the pillar and ground of the Church is the Gospel and the spirit of life; it is fitting that she should have four pillars, breathing out immortality on every side, and vivifying men afresh. From which fact, it is evident that the Word, the Artificer of all, He that sits upon the cherubim, and contains all things, He who was manifested to men, has given us the Gospel under four aspects, but bound together by one Spirit" (*Against Heresies*, 3:11:8).

161   One of the suppositions underneath much modern biblical criticism is that each of the gospels was written for a specific community. This tenant is not questioned here. A preponderance of data from the gospels indeed reveals this to be a valid supposition. Yet, some scholars over emphasize *the role and influence of these early communities,* to such an extent that *the community — and not the individual eyewitnesses,* emerge as the "controlling voice" under the gospels. This extreme notion, though accepted by many scholars, is questioned. In response, it is argued that the impetus for proclaiming and writing the Gospel of John, for example, was not *primarily* the "sitz im Leben" (life setting) of a "Johannine community." Rather, it was written that "*all who have ears to hear*" would come to believe that Jesus of Nazareth is "the Christ, the Son of the living God" — and by believing, "have life in His name" (John 20:31). For an excellent critique of deficient theories of "gospel audiences" — and fascinating insights on how (when all the evidence is sifted) the gospels appear to be intended for a very wide audience, see: Richard Bauckham, *The Gospels for All Christians: Rethinking the Gospel Audiences* (Grand Rapids: Eerdmans, 1997).

162   "Let no private psalms nor any uncanonical books be read in the church, but only the canonical ones of the New and Old Testament ... [After listing the books of the Old Testament, it continues as follows.] And these are the books of the New Testament: Four Gospels, according to Matthew, Mark, Luke, and John; the Acts of the Apostles, seven Catholic epistles, namely, one of James, two of Peter, three of John, one of Jude, fourteen epistles of Paul, one to the Romans, two to the Corinthians, one to the Galatians, one to the Ephesians, one to the Philippians, one to the Colossians, two to the Thessalonians, one to the Hebrews, two to Timothy, one to Titus, and one to Philemon" (Synod of Laodicea, A.D. 363, Canon 56, 60).

163   "The holy ecumenical and general Council of Trent ... following the example of the orthodox Fathers receives and venerates all the books of the Old and New Testament ... and also the traditions pertaining to faith and conduct ... with an equal sense of devotion and reverence ... If, however, anyone does not receive these books in their entirety, with all their parts, as they are accustomed to be read in the Catholic Church and are contained in the ancient Latin Vulgate edition as sacred and canonical, and knowingly and deliberately rejects the aforesaid traditions, let him be Anathema."

> "Remember not the former things, nor consider the things of old. Behold, I am doing a new thing; now it springs forth, do you not perceive it?"
>
> *Isaiah 43:18–19*

Principle 4
God's Word: Revealed in the Unity of the Old and New Testaments

Principle 4: Catholic biblical interpretation insists upon the unity and coherence of the whole canon of Scripture, both Old and New Testaments. This unitive dimension of the Word of God is evident in many ways; Catholic exegetes should be particularly aware of three:

- *The Theme of Covenant*
- *Biblical Typology*
- *Recapitulation in Christ*

In these and other ways, we affirm Augustine's conclusion: "The New Testament lies hidden in the Old and the Old Testament is unveiled in the New."

The forest and the trees

Principle #4 follows logically and sequentially from the previous three principles of Catholic biblical interpretation:

Principle #1: God is the ultimate author of Scripture, and He simultaneously guides the human authors in expressing His message in human language ...

Principle #2: He does so in and through actual history, and we must learn to uncover the original meaning, as best as we can, using sound historical and theological inquiry ...

Principle #3: this "divine word in history" was first apprehended by Christ's apostles, and preserved for all people in both written and unwritten forms (Scripture and Tradition). And it was the Church that recognized this revelation as "from God" and so developed the canon of Scripture.

As Catholic students of Scripture, we are called to interpret individual texts of Scripture in light of the whole canon of Scripture.[164] Any conclusions we reach about a specific passage of Scripture must be viewed in terms of the unity and coherence of both the Old and New Testament. As *Dei Verbum* instructs,

> Since Holy Scripture must be read and interpreted in the sacred spirit in which it was written, no less serious attention must be given to the content and unity of the whole of Scripture if the meaning of the sacred texts is to be correctly worked out. (*DV* §12)

Let us consider various aspects of this principle, beginning with the idea that there indeed are clear and recognizable "patterns" — patterns in biblical interpretation, and patterns within the Scripture itself.

The Dynamic Pattern of Biblical Interpretation and the Unitive Pattern of Scripture

The Pontifical Biblical Commission has referred to the interpretation of Scripture in the Church as a "dynamic pattern" of interaction between God's Word and the Church that receives it.[165] The PBC rightly suggests that both the writing of Scripture and its interpretation by the Church are best understood as a *response of the believing community*. Here, "community" refers to (a) the apostolic authors who, in the act of composing new Scriptures, are responding to previously composed biblical texts and, more broadly; (b) the response of the Church to the Word, through Sacred Tradition and the Magisterium. This is what is meant by the "dynamic pattern of biblical interpretation" and this pattern is already evident in the early apostolic Church and its reception of the Hebrew Scriptures.

For example, when St. Paul describes Jesus as the New Adam (cf. 1 Cor 15:45) or when St. John describes Jesus as the New Moses (cf. John 6:49–58), these apostles are *responding* to the previous biblical texts of Genesis and Exodus, where we encounter the original Adam and Moses. Thus, as the Apostles build upon these previous texts, taking them in new directions, their writings become part of the dynamic. In so doing, the apostles respond to Scripture in an interpretative way, and in the process, new Scriptures emerge. Continuing in this process, the Church today, through her living Tradition, thoughtfully and prayerfully deepens her understanding of God's revelation in Scripture:

Thus, we can rightly speak of a "dynamic pattern" between the written Scriptures on the one hand and the Church who receives and interprets them on the other.[166] Yet, to speak of this interplay — of the Church interacting with the Word — does not go far enough. Underneath this dynamism lies a still deeper pattern and the very reason for such lively interchange in the first place. *Specifically, there exists a unitive pattern between the Scriptures of Ancient Israel and the life of Jesus as experienced by the first Christians. This deeper pattern reflects the mystery of the one Source behind all of the Scriptures and His continual presence with His people.*

"According to the Scriptures"

As we read the Gospels, it is reasonable to conclude that many of Jesus' followers, even His closest disciples, often misunderstood who Jesus really was (e.g., Luke 8:18–19; John 10:1–7). Even Jesus' own disciples were not capable of truly deciphering what He was saying much of the time:

> On the next day, when they had come down from the mountain, a great crowd met him. And behold, a man from the crowd cried, "Teacher, I beg you to look upon my son, for he is my only child; and behold, a spirit seizes him, and he suddenly cries out; it convulses him till he foams, and shatters him, and will hardly leave him. And I begged your disciples to cast it out, but they could not." Jesus answered, "O faithless and perverse generation, how long am I to be with you and bear with you? Bring your son here." While he was coming, the demon tore him and convulsed him. But Jesus rebuked the unclean spirit, and healed the boy, and gave him back to his father. And all were astonished at the majesty of God. But while they were all marveling at everything he did, he said to his disciples, "Let these words sink into your ears; for the Son of man is to be delivered into the hands of men." *But they did not understand this saying, and it was concealed from them, that they should not perceive it; and they were afraid to ask him about this saying.* (Luke 9:37–45)

Not even Jesus' death on the Cross was able to lift the veil of mystery surrounding Jesus' identity. In the following passage from the Gospel of John, the Evangelist offers a comment that helps us comprehend exactly when the disciples began to make better sense of Jesus and His "hidden" identity:

The next day a great crowd who had come to the feast heard that Jesus was coming to Jerusalem. So they took branches of palm trees and went out to meet him, crying, "Hosanna! Blessed is he who comes in the name of the Lord, even the King of Israel!" And Jesus found a young ass and sat upon it; as it is written, "Fear not, daughter of Zion; behold, your king is coming, sitting on an ass's colt!" *His disciples did not understand this at first; but when Jesus was glorified, then they remembered that this had been written of him and had been done to him.* (John 12:12–16)

FOR REFLECTION

Learn how to let go of God through God, the hidden God through the naked God ... Get out of the water, so that you can make wine. My child, be patient and release yourself, because no one can dig out from the ground of your heart. O deep treasure, how will You be dug up? O high perfection, who may attain You? O flowing fountain, who can exhaust You?
— St. Francis de Sales, Letters of Spiritual Direction (Letter XXXIII). Library of St. Francis de Sales, 7 vol. Volume IV. Letters to Persons in Religion, 158–60. Trans. by H. Mackey (London: Burns & Oates, 1873–1910).

Notice that this event takes place at the beginning of Jesus' entrance into Jerusalem, Palm Sunday. Also note again, that "*His disciples did not understand this at first*" (v. 16). All of the symbolic actions that Jesus undertook intentionally built upon prophecies in Zechariah. They left a lasting impression on the disciples, yet with natural human capacities, it was not clear to them *what* Jesus was doing, or *how* He was about to fulfill them. But note as well the Evangelist's explanatory comment in the same verse: "*When Jesus was glorified, then they remembered that this had been written of him and had been done to him.*"

"This Jesus, whom I proclaim to you, is the Christ." This is the message of the Apostles; and it is how we as Catholic exegetes are called to read, teach and proclaim the Scriptures today.

What was obscure to the disciples prior to Jesus' hour of "glory," i.e., the Resurrection, became crystal clear to them afterwards, and the Holy Spirit guided them "into all truth" (John 16:13). Moreover, recall that Jesus Himself spent the forty days between His Resurrection and His Ascension explaining His miraculous words and deeds and His prophetic and sacramental actions to His disciples. He explained everything they witnessed and things beyond their human ability to see; the myriad of "things concerning Himself *in all the Scriptures*" (Luke 24:27). It was this Spirit-inspired revelation, along with Jesus' own catechesis that unlocked the mystery of Jesus' true identity as the Son of God and Savior of the world. As Pope Benedict explains:

> In the paschal mystery "the words of Scripture" are fulfilled; in other words, this death which took place "in accordance with the Scriptures" is an event containing a *logos*, an inner logic: the death of Christ testifies that the word of God became thoroughly human "flesh," human "history." Similarly, the resurrection of Jesus takes place "on the third day in accordance with the Scriptures": since Jewish belief held that decay set in after the third day, the word of Scripture is fulfilled in Jesus who rises incorrupt.[167]

This Christ-awakening transformed the disciples' lives. Now, in the light of Easter, the disciples were able to *interpret* what they had witnessed. Not only could they understand it; they were able to communicate this Good News with power and clarity. Not only were they "knowers" of Jesus' true identity — but also "proclaimers" of this Good News, of the love of God poured out in Jesus Christ and the life-giving power of His Resurrection and His return to the Father in glory, and what they perceived to be His imminent return. And, they did all of this "in accordance with the Scriptures" (1 Cor 15:3).

Thus, afforded this divine catechesis by Christ Himself, and guided by the Holy Spirit, we see, beginning in the post-Resurrection appearances and throughout the book of Acts, a passionate urgency and a fearlessness as the Apostles "proclaim Christ" with fervor from the Hebrew Scriptures:

> Now when they had passed through Amphipolis and Apollonia, they came to Thessalonica, where there was a synagogue of the Jews. And Paul went in, as was his custom, and for three weeks he argued with them from the Scriptures, explaining and proving that it was necessary for the Christ to suffer and to rise from the dead, and saying, "This Jesus, whom I proclaim to you, is the Christ." (Acts 17:1–13)

This Jesus, whom I proclaim to you, is the Christ. This is the message of the Apostles; and it is how we as Catholic students of the Bible are called to read, teach and proclaim the Scriptures today. We are called to study Scripture with a keen awareness and of this deeper pattern of unity in mind, just as Jesus' first disciples were instructed to do so by our Lord. As we become increasingly aware of this coherence that connects the Old with the New and the New with the Old, our comprehension and proclamation of Jesus according to the Scriptures will become richly satisfying as well.

This unitive pattern in Scripture is perhaps no more evident than on the very day the Church was born, at Pentecost, when the inhabitants of Jerusalem witnessed …

> The Parthians, Medes and Elamites, residents of Mesopotamia, Judea and Cappadocia, Pontus and Asia, Phrygia and Pamphylia, Egypt and parts of Libya belonging to Cyrene, visitors from Rome … Cretans and Arabians … all speaking in their native tongues, they were astounded. (Acts 2:9–11)

The disbelieving crowd assumed that such men were drunk (Acts 2:13). Yet, notice how the Apostles respond; for those who mocked those Spirit-filled Jews needed to know the truth of the matter, as did those who were "amazed and perplexed," and who wondered what it all meant (cf. Acts 2:12). Thus, rather than offering some explanation of their own choosing, again and again we see the Apostles explaining who Jesus is *according to the Scriptures*. Peter stood with the other eleven[168] and preached Christ to them from the Old Testament Scriptures:

> Men of Judea and all who dwell in Jerusalem, let this be known to you, and give ear to my words. For these men are not drunk, as you suppose, since it is only the third hour of the day; but this is what was spoken by the prophet Joel: "And in the last days it shall be, God declares, that I will pour out my Spirit upon all flesh, and your sons and your daughters shall prophesy, and your young men shall see visions, and your old men shall dream dreams; yea, and on my menservants and my maidservants in those days I will pour out my Spirit; and they shall prophesy. And I will show wonders in the heaven above and signs on the earth beneath, blood, and fire, and vapor of smoke; the sun shall be turned into darkness and the moon into blood, before the day of the Lord comes, the great and manifest day. And it shall be that whoever calls on the name of the Lord shall be saved." (Acts 2:14b–21; cf. Joel 2:28–32)

In beginning to draw on the Scriptures in his Pentecost homily, St. Peter is, in a manner of speaking, reminiscent of Al Pacino's character in the great film *Scent of a Woman* ... he's "just getting warmed up."

Here, St. Peter reminds his Jerusalem audience of the vivid image of "the glorious disclosure,"[169] the coming day of the Lord, anticipated by Joel, the ancient Jewish prophet. Given the events that had just taken place, its use in Peter's sermon is clear: God's promises are now fulfilled through the outpouring of the Holy Spirit at Pentecost.

St. Luke makes reference to the passage elsewhere in the book, yet interestingly, in both instances, it is not associated with the outpouring of the Spirit, but with "calling on the name of the Lord."[170] Moreover, Luke is not the only New Testament writer to draw on this passage; St. Paul uses Joel's imagery in his letter to the Romans, also in reference to "calling on the name of the Lord" (Rom 10:13). Yet, in his epistle to Titus, Paul uses the imagery from Joel, but connects the outpouring of the Spirit to the coming of Christ:

> For we ourselves were once foolish, disobedient, led astray, slaves to various passions and pleasures, passing our days in malice and envy, hated by men and hating one another; but when the goodness and loving kindness of God our Savior appeared, he saved us, not because of deeds done by us in righteousness, but in virtue of his own mercy, by the washing of regeneration and renewal in the Holy Spirit, which he poured out upon us richly through Jesus Christ our Savior, so that we might be justified by his grace and become heirs in hope of eternal life. (Titus 3:3–7)

Notice too, that Paul's use of the prophet Joel in Titus 3 is closely connected with the sacrament of baptism: this sending of the Spirit, which was now "poured out" through Christ (v. 6), brings salvation through the "washing of regeneration and renewal" (v. 5). Elsewhere, St. Matthew draws on this same text from the prophet Joel, placing it in his eschatological discourse in chapter 24,[171] as does St. Mark in his "little apocalypse" in chapter 13 of his Gospel.[172] In both instances, the Evangelists use Joel's imagery to discuss the coming of the Son of Man, <u>not</u> the outpouring of the Spirit.

At least two observations can be made from the above examples of the apostolic authors and their use of the Old Testament:

1) From the very beginnings of the Church at Pentecost, the Apostles continually drew upon many Hebrew Scriptures to proclaim that Jesus is the Christ, God's anointed messiah.

This is clear enough from the above examples related to Peter's Pentecost homily. Immediately after the reference to Joel 2 and the outpouring of the Spirit, Luke records that St. Peter spoke about the "signs which God performed" through Jesus (cf. Acts 2:22), and his crucifixion and resurrection (vv. 23–24). In so doing, Peter's sermon brings in Psalm 16:8–11, 132:11, 2 Sam. 7:12, and Psalm 110:4 — all of which expand from Scripture just how Jesus is the Davidic messiah whom they have crucified (Acts 2:36). St. Peter does not limit himself to one reference to Scripture, but brings a multiplicity of biblical passages together in proclaiming Christ.

In drawing on Scripture in his Pentecost homily, St. Peter is, in a manner of speaking, reminiscent of Al Pacino's character in the great film *Scent of a Woman* … he's "just getting warmed up." Peter's preaching and his dynamic use of the Scriptures unfolds. In more ways than one is the true biblical account in Acts 2 rather cinematic in its scope. Peter's message has a dramatically powerful effect and as a result, the scales fall from many eyes, as three thousand believe, repent and are baptized (Acts 2:38, 41).

In similar fashion, the other apostles and writers of the New Testament go back to the Old Testament hundreds of times to explain Christ. This frequent usage of the Old Testament in the New, from the very origins of the Church, is a most important aspect of the unitive pattern in Scripture, and leads to a second observation closely related to the one just described:

2) For the early Christians, every book of the Hebrew Scriptures was saturated with meaning and explanatory power. As a consequence, the Scriptures were drawn upon deeply and often in numerous ways — yet, always for the larger purpose of showing the fulfillment of God's promises to His people, through Jesus Christ and the Holy Spirit.

Clearly, the above passage from Joel (while central to understanding the events of Pentecost) was for the Apostles pregnant with meaning and instrumental in explaining other things about the Spirit and about Jesus (the outpouring of the Spirit, Salvation in Jesus' name, Christian baptism, etc.) This "saturation of meaning" is not germane only to Joel 2, or a select few passages of the Old Testament; rather, it typifies what was so often the case in the apostolic use of the Old Testament: *the unity of the Scriptures runs deep*. That is, rather than merely seeing <u>one</u> primary connection between Old and New, the same Scripture passage often served a number of purposes.

Covenant, Typology, Recapitulation

In Christ, the Apostles recognized the fulfillment of the Old Covenant, in ways that could not have been fully anticipated or understood before He graced our horizon with His earthly presence. As the *Catechism* observes:

> The Law of the Gospel "fulfills," refines, surpasses, and leads the Old Law to its perfection. In the Beatitudes, the New Law fulfills the divine promises by elevating and orienting them toward the "kingdom of heaven." It is addressed to those open to accepting this new hope with faith — the poor, the humble, the afflicted, the pure of heart, those persecuted on account of Christ and so marks out the surprising ways of the Kingdom.[173]

Despite the fulfillment of the Old Covenant in Christ, the Hebrew Scriptures, what we call the Old Testament always remains an "indispensable part of Sacred Scripture"[174] since it "has never been revoked."[175] The Old Testament prepares us for the coming of Christ, "to announce this coming by prophecy, and to indicate its meaning through various types."[176] In addition to this primary role, that of preparing the way for Christ, the Old Testament is vital for numerous other reasons as well:

> "Even though they contain matters imperfect and provisional," the books of the Old Testament bear witness to the whole divine pedagogy of God's saving love: these writings "are a storehouse of sublime teaching on God and of sound wisdom on human life, as well as a wonderful treasury of prayers; in them, too, the mystery of our salvation is present in a hidden way."[177]

Nevertheless, let us now focus on the role of the Old Testament as preparing the way for Christ. In the above paragraph, we noted that *Dei Verbum* mentions various ways that the Old Testament prepares us to meet Christ in the New Testament. One of the fundamental ways that is specifically mentioned is "prophecy." Indeed, as we read Scripture, we witness numerous examples of biblical prophecies in many books of the Old Testament. Most readers will be familiar with at least the major prophecies of the Old Testament, such as the following examples:

> **Isa 7:14** *Behold, a young woman shall conceive and bear a son, and shall call his name Immanu-el.*
>
> **Matt 1:122–23** *All this took place to fulfill what the Lord had spoken by the prophet: "Behold, a virgin shall conceive and bear a son.*

> **Zech 9:9** *Rejoice greatly, O daughter of Zion! Shout aloud, O daughter of Jerusalem! Lo, your king comes to you; triumphant and victorious is he, humble and riding on an ass, on a colt the foal of an ass.*
>
> **John 12:14–16** *And Jesus found a young ass and sat upon it; as it is written, "Fear not, daughter of Zion; behold, your king is coming, sitting on an ass's colt!" His disciples did not understand this at first; but when Jesus was glorified, then they remembered that this had been written of him and had been done to him.*

> **Psa 22:18** *They divide my garments among them, and for my raiment they cast lots.*
>
> **John 19:24** *So they said to one another, "Let us not tear it, but cast lots for it to see whose it shall be." This was to fulfill the Scripture, "They parted my garments among them, and for my clothing they cast lots."*

Three points should be added about our attentiveness to such biblical prophecies. First, the above are just three examples of the dozens of biblical prophecies from the Old Testament that have their fulfillment in the New Testament in Jesus Christ. Many — but certainly not all of the Old Testament prophecies are located in the prophetic books (Isaiah, Jeremiah, Daniel, etc.) Many more appear in the Pentateuch, Psalms and Wisdom literature.

The entirety of the Old Testament can be summarized as the story of God calling and setting apart a "holy people" as His own righteous sons — not for their sake alone, but that they would be a light to the nations, and thereby beckon the whole world to live under the reign of God. Yet, when this "righteousness" is not brought about, neither on the part of Israel nor the other nations, at "the appointed time" (Gal 4:4), God sent "His only begotten son" (John 3:16), *His messiah*, to be the Faithful and Righteous Israelite, for her sake and that of the whole world. Perhaps, in some sense, this is what St. Peter has in mind when he writes, "*For Christ also died for sins once for all, the righteous for the unrighteous*" (1

Pet 3:18). In any event, Jesus is the fulfillment of all of salvation history, and we ought to examine the whole of the Old Testament with great care, keenly watchful for this "messianic hope" and the numerous prophecies connected with the biblical hope.

Second, most of the biblical prophecies in the Old Testament point directly to Christ. Yet, there are other prophecies that have their fulfillment in other institutions and persons, such as the Church, the Sacraments, the Blessed Virgin Mary, and so on. As but one example, you may recall that Gen 3:15, the so-called *Protoevangelium* ("first gospel"), points forward to the Gospel and Jesus Christ, the New Adam, when God says to the serpent,

> *He shall bruise your head,*
> *and you shall bruise his heel.*

We should also see in the preceding phrase a prophecy pertaining to the New Eve, the Virgin Mary:

> *I will put enmity between you and the woman,*
> *and between your seed and her seed ...*

Third and finally, when selecting a Bible for purchase, it can be helpful to consider some sort of "study edition," which cross-references such Scriptures. In this way, one can more readily know when there is an Old Testament text underneath the New, and when a New Testament text lies hidden in the Old.

At present, what's important is recognizing that there are numerous ways the Old and New Testaments are interconnected and unified. So many are the ways and so mysterious and profound are the many connections that when we step back and consider them, we can't help be left with a sense of wonder and awe. Such complexity, such unity, such mystery cannot be the product of "chance," of "history" or of human orchestration. Such is the work of the Holy Spirit.

Recently, the Assembly of Bishops reiterated the utter necessity of recognizing this "unitive pattern" in the canon of Scripture when it concluded, "*the totality and organic unity* of the Canon of Sacred Scripture constitutes the criterion for interpreting the Sacred Book."[178]

Without such concern, I would suggest that all of our firm convictions in the Principles 1–3 (i.e., Inspiration, History, Sacred Scripture and Sacred Tradition) would be in vain. This is not to diminish the great importance of those principles in interpreting Scripture — hardly. It is to suggest that unless we are aware of and pay attention to the unity of

Scripture, we may be captivated by any number of beautiful trees and yet entirely miss the forest that we are passing through!

Whenever we attempt to uncover the meaning of any passage or verse of Scripture, we must take into account *the whole of Scripture*, and not only the passage or even its immediate context. Catholic exegesis requires that we interpret any individual text of Scripture in the light of the fullness of the Old and New Testament. As *Dei Verbum* instructs,

> Since Holy Scripture must be read and interpreted in the sacred spirit in which it was written, no less serious attention must be given to the content and unity of the whole of Scripture if the meaning of the sacred texts is to be correctly worked out.[179]

FOR REFLECTION

To what degree does my study and prayer bring "the whole of Scripture" to bear upon my study and prayer of any portion of it? Are there passages in Scripture that I return to so often that, if I'm honest, I am a little "stuck there"? What passages in Scripture are like "beautiful trees" to me, that I gaze at over and over ... which in itself is good, but can nevertheless prevent me from seeing the "forest" (i.e., the whole of Scripture)? How might a renewed resolve to appreciate "the forest" positively affect my knowledge of and love for those favorite "trees"? What are some ways that I might challenge myself to see "the whole forest" better (e.g., read through the Bible in a year, etc.)?

As Pope Benedict XVI observed, this "unitive" approach (sometimes referred to as canonical exegesis today) is no novelty; it lies at the heart of the Church's approach to Scripture at Vatican II:

> I would very much like to see theologians learn to interpret and love Scripture as the Council desired, in accordance with *Dei Verbum*: may they experience the inner unity of Scripture — something that today is helped by "canonical exegesis."[180]

Note that the pope indicates that such care for the whole of God's Word plunges us into the depths of this "inner unity" of Scripture. Moreover, the pope adds that reading Scripture in the way *Dei Verbum* instructs leads to a *spiritual encounter* of the Word; so that our exegesis is not purely external, "but rather an inner immersion in the presence of the Word."[181] Lastly, the pope comments that such attention to the unitive dimension of Scripture is in no way at odds with historic and scientific study of Scripture, but complements it:

> It seems to me a very important task to do something in this regard, to contribute to providing an introduction to living Scripture as an up-to-date Word of God beside, with and in historical-critical exegesis.[182]

In short, it is imperative that we seek to interpret Scripture in light of its profound unity, revealing the great mystery of man's restoration to God through Christ. Without such awareness, we may end up with fractured interpretations of biblical passages, such as lifting "proof-texts" Scripture without regard for the context or unity of Scripture.

Questions for Reflection

1. Aside from Mass, how much of the Old Testament have I read?
2. What is my favorite character or passage from the Old Testament? Why?
3. What hopes or fears do I have about learning more about the Old Testament?
4. What have I been taught about the "unity" of the Old and New Testament in the past? How has this chapter affected my previous understanding?

For Further Study

Beale, Gregory and D. A. Carson, eds. *Commentary on the New Testament Use of the Old Testament.* Grand Rapids: Baker Academic, 2007. This resource is unique in that it provides commentary on each book of the New Testament, with a specific focus on its use of Old Testament. The commentary goes beyond mere citations and helps readers understand the *context and nature* of the Old and New testament connections.

Bruggemann, Walter. *The Prophetic Imagination.* 2nd ed. Philadelphia: Fortress Press, 2001.

De Vaux, Roland. *Ancient Israel: Its Life and Institutions.* NY: McGraw-Hill, 1961.

McConville, J, Gordon and Mark Boda, eds. *Dictionary of the Old Testament: Prophets.* The IVP Bible Dictionary Series. Downers Grove, IL: InterVarsity Press, 2012.

Wright, Christopher. *Knowing Jesus Through the Old Testament.* Downers Grove, IL: InterVarsity Press, 1995.

Notes

164   *IBC*, I.C.b; III.D.4.b.

165   Cf. *IBC*, III.c.

166   Cf. *IBC*, III.c: "This dynamic pattern corresponds to the requirement that there be a lived affinity between the interpreter and the object, an affinity which constitutes, in fact, one of the conditions that makes the entire exegetical enterprise possible."

167   Pope Benedict XVI, *VD* §13.

168   Acts 2:14a. The eleven include Matthias, who has replaced Judas (cf. Acts 1:15-26).

169   Aidan Nichols, *The Splendour of Doctrine: The Catechism of the Catholic Church* on Christian Believing (Edinburgh: T & T Clark, 1995), 23.

170   Cf. Acts 2:39 ("For the promise is to you and to your children and to all that are far off, *every one whom the Lord our God calls to him;*" Acts 22:16: "And now why do you [Paul] wait? Rise and be baptized, and wash away your sins, *calling on his name.*'"

171   Matt 24:29: "Immediately after the tribulation of those days the sun will be darkened, and the moon will not give its light, and the stars will fall from heaven, and the powers of the heavens will be shaken."

172   Mark 13: 24-25: "But in those days, after that tribulation, the sun will be darkened, and the moon will not give its light and the stars will be falling from heaven, and the powers in the heavens will be shaken."

173   CCC 1967.

174   CCC 121.

175   Ibid.

176   *DV* §15; cf. Luke 24:44; John 5:39; 1 Cor 10:12; 1 Pet 1:10.

177   CCC 122 (cf. *DV* 15).

178   *Instrumentum laboris* §15,d. ("The Word of God in the Life and Mission of the Church"). XII Ordinary General Assembly of Bishops, 2008

179   *DV* §12 (emphasis added).

180   Benedict XVI, "Address to the Bishops of Switzerland," Nov. 7, 2006 (in *L'Osservatore Romano: Weekly Edition in English*, Nov. 22, 2006, 5, 10; cf. *Jesus of Nazareth*, xi-xxiv).

181   Ibid.

182   Ibid. (emphasis added).

> "I am the LORD, I have called you in righteousness, I have taken you by the hand and kept you; I have given you as a covenant to the people, a light to the nations, to open the eyes that are blind, to bring out the prisoners from the dungeon, from the prison those who sit in darkness."
>
> *Isaiah 42:6–7*

Scripture's Unitive Pattern
The Theme of Covenant

In the last chapter, we introduced Principle #4, "God's Word is Revealed in the Unity of the Old and New Testament." We ended with a discussion of the importance of biblical prophecy as one very significant manner in which the "unitive pattern" of Scripture is seen.

Yet, it is by no means the only way. And, as important as biblical prophecy is, we must learn to recognize the plurality of ways in which the Holy Spirit has connected the Old and the New. If we only look to the promise/fulfillment dynamic involved in biblical prophecy, we will miss many of the other fascinating ways that God's Word is brought mysteriously together in the Old and New Testaments.

With this in mind, we now move beyond the topic of biblical prophecy and turn our attention to three other ways in which this supernatural and unitive pattern is seen in Scripture:

1. The Theme of Covenant
2. Biblical Typology
3. Recapitulation in Christ

In this chapter and the next, we'll focus exclusively on the all-important theme of "Covenant." Following this, in a later chapter, we'll complete this discussion and our work on Principle #4 by focusing on the latter two ways (Typology and Recapitulation). Let's begin with the all-important theme of covenant.

"The Lord Will Provide" — The Theme of Covenant

No theme is more central to our apprehension of the whole of Scripture than that of "covenant." The *Catholic Bible Dictionary* defines covenant as a "kinship bond between two parties, with conditions or obligations, established by an oath or its equivalent."[183] Such bonds were an integral part of the relationships between ancient peoples in biblical times.[184] Yet, more than a fact of human relationships alone, the relationship of God to His people is covenantal in nature: a familial bond with its own particular conditions and requirements. As in the covenantal relationships outside the Bible itself, the bond between God and His people is enacted by ritual, such as a sworn oath or a communal meal, as the parties enter into the covenant with one another.[185]

No theme is more central to our apprehension of the whole of Scripture than that of "covenant."

More specifically, a covenant can be understood as "a *familial bond* established by a *legally binding* oath sworn during a *liturgical ritual*."[186] In salvation history, God takes the initiative to establish this "familial bond" with humanity. And just like our own families, there is an ever-increasing dimension to the covenant relationship between God and humanity.

In the ancient world, there are many forms of legally binding covenants.[187] Nevertheless, distinctive to the ancient Israelites was their belief that such a familial bond was possible with God. For other peoples, such kinship was experienced only on a naturalistic level — but not a supernatural level. This was unheard of!

Yet, what was distinctive of "the children of Abraham" (John 8:39) was the firm belief that God Himself *entered into a covenant relationship with them.* With other peoples, the gods did not offer any sort of relationship, but only rewards and/or punishments. In contrast, God, while enacting the covenant as the "superior party," reveals His infinite love to Israel, in the form of an intimate familial bond. In short, *God reveals Himself as a Father:* "And you shall say to Pharaoh, 'Thus says the LORD, Israel is my first-born son" (Exod 4:22).

FOR REFLECTION

To what degree is my relationship with Christ shaped by this "familial" understanding of the (New) Covenant? In what ways is God's 'fatherhood' presently felt in my life? In what ways do I need God to become 'more of a father' to me — and why? What role will the Scriptures play as I increase the awareness of being a 'son' of the Father and of Christ?

The God of Israel is a personal God, who walks and talks with His people; and He initiates a covenant with His people in a personal and familial way. More specifically, throughout salvation history, God reaches out as a Father to His children, seeking to establish them in His love, govern them in grace, and preserve them for His purposes, and for their true happiness and freedom.

All of this God does in a "human" way. Although God could bring about these conditions in various ways, in Scripture, we clearly see God working through various "mediators" in offering His covenantal love to His children.

Specifically, in the Old Testament, God inaugurates these actions with **Adam** along with his wife Eve, with all of humanity and all of creation: "*And God blessed them, and God said to them, "Be fruitful and multiply, and fill the earth and subdue it; and have dominion over the fish of the sea and over the birds of the air and over every living thing that moves upon the earth*" (Gen 1:28).

Through the willful disobedience and rejection of the Father's initiative of love (Gen 3:1–24) Adam brought sin and death to all of humanity. Nevertheless, the Father chooses to "create His family" anew with a righteous man, the mediator **Noah** (and his sons). Yet, the effects of this "original sin" persist and in fact intensify. Consequently, like their first parents, humanity continues to reject the Father's initiative of love — and chooses to "make a name for themselves" (Gen 11:4), rather than calling on the Father. Thus, God calls a new mediator, **Abraham**, through whom universal blessings will flow to all of humanity: This is indeed a new day, an entirely new beginning, and from this relationship with one man, God will reach out to a people, and establish them as *His people*:

Now the LORD said to Abram, "Go from your country and your kindred and your father's house to the land that I will show you.

And I will make of you a great nation, and I will bless you, and
make your name great, so that you will be a blessing. I will bless
those who bless you, and him who curses you I will curse; and
by you all the families of the earth shall bless themselves." (Gen
12:1–3)

This is the exciting beginning of all that God will do in salvation
history in calling a people to Himself, to live as His children, loved by the
Father! This covenant with Abraham brought numerous specific blessings: a new identity, a new home, a new destiny. And the Father would
bring about all of these blessings in a truly human way — *through the gift
of a son* — Isaac. Abraham's faithfulness "on the way" (Gen 12, 15, 17)
confirms the Father's choice of a righteous mediator.

As we know, there are other "mediators" that follow Abraham and
precede the coming of Christ. Isaac's son Jacob is the "father" of twelve
sons, and God's people now have a "family name" — Israel. In Exodus
we meet **Moses,** who shepherds God's people Israel out of Egypt and
towards the land He promised to Abraham, Isaac and Jacob. Now, God's
family has taken on the identity of a nation. Through His mediator Moses, the Father gives to His children the Torah (or "Law"). This Law is
another manifestation of God's fatherly love for His children. The commandments of God are a supreme grace that allow Israel to be "governed
by God" and not their own sinful hearts which would, were it not for
God and His Law, lead them into idolatry and death, instead of worship
and life. More than this, the Father calls Moses and Aaron to establish
a tabernacle according to His precise instructions (Exod 25–40) so that
His children may worship Him on the journey to the Promised Land.

Beyond Moses, we can think of a number of mediators that the
Father calls to guide His people into a deeper relationship with Himself:
Joshua, the Judges, the Prophets, and so on. But in the grand story of
the Father's covenant with His children, it is a king that represents the
culmination of this unfolding story: **David**. Now, Israel is made aware
of a deeper destiny that the Father has for His children — they are to
become a Kingdom:

When your days are fulfilled and you lie down with your fathers,
I will raise up your offspring after you, who shall come forth from
your body, and I will establish his kingdom. [13] He shall build a house
for my name, and I will establish the throne of his kingdom forever.
[14] I will be his father, and he shall be my son. (2 Sam 7:10–14)

Here, the Father tells David, "*I will make you a house*" (v. 11). David perceives this "house" to be a permanent tabernacle, a holy Temple. This is an important aspect of the covenant the Father makes with His mediator, David. (Even though it is his son, Solomon, who will establish the holy temple in Jerusalem). The Jerusalem Temple will become the center of life, worship, community for the people of Israel:

But the Father's desire is even greater than this earthly house, which is His home. Indeed, through David's offspring, the Father will build a dynasty — the House of David, and the throne of this kingdom will be "established forever" (v. 13). This promise looks forward not only to the Davidic kings of Judah, but to something greater than a "human lineage" of earthly kingship. No, it is *a kingdom* itself that God is building through His people.

The divine Presence is no longer to be localized in a single place, the material tabernacle: henceforth, God will be in Jesus Christ, everywhere.

— Henri de Lubac

The Father's covenant love, from the beginning with Abraham, *is never thwarted or derailed.* To the contrary, the promises were deeper than His people could comprehend with their minds. The promises would have to be apprehended by the heart.

All of the mediators, and all of the previous covenant developments anticipate their ultimate fulfillment in the fullness of these promises in Christ, who inaugurates a New Covenant with humanity:

Behold, the days are coming, says the LORD, when I will make a new covenant with the house of Israel and the house of Judah, not like the covenant which I made with their fathers when I took them by the hand to bring them out of the land of Egypt, my covenant which they broke, though I was their husband, says the LORD. But this is the covenant which I will make with the house of Israel after those days, says the LORD: *I will put my law within them, and I will write it upon their hearts; and I will be their God, and they shall be my people* (Jer 31:31–33; cf. Isa 55:1–3; Ezek 34:25).

As Henri de Lubac observes, we need to grasp the continuity between the Old Testament and the New Testament, in which the former was "a kind of sketch or model, a *prima* adumbration — a model of clay for vessels of gold."[188]

Yet at the same time, we must also recognize the discontinuity between the two, in the sense that the Old Testament is in sum, an "advance towards Christ; only when it attaints to Him does its real meaning which was gradually hinted at, become clear."[189] In this way, the New Covenant is not like the Old: "The divine Presence is no longer to be localized in a single place, the material tabernacle: henceforth, God will be in Jesus Christ, everywhere."[190] In Jesus, God does not only *inaugurate a covenant* with His people — he actually *becomes the covenant* for His people:

> Behold my servant, whom I uphold, my chosen, in whom my soul delights; I have put my Spirit upon him, he will bring forth justice to the nations. He will not cry or lift up his voice, or make it heard in the street; a bruised reed he will not break, and a dimly burning wick he will not quench; he will faithfully bring forth justice. He will not fail or be discouraged till he has established justice in the earth; and the coastlands wait for his law. Thus says God, the LORD, who created the heavens and stretched them out, who spread forth the earth and what comes from it, who gives breath to the people upon it and spirit to those who walked in it: "*I am the LORD, I have called you in righteousness, I have taken you by the hand and kept you; I have given you as a covenant to the people, a light to the nations, to open the eyes that are blind, to bring out the prisoners from the dungeon, from the prison those who sit in darkness.*" (Isa 42:1–7)

FOR REFLECTION | *To what degree do I view the Scriptures as "vessels of gold?" On a 1 to 10 scale, how important is reading, studying and praying the OT to me personally? What book of the OT would I desire to study in a more serious way? How do I feel such effort would affect ... my love for Christ? ... for others? ... my spiritual life as a whole? Why?*

God's people were called by God to be "a light to the nations" (v. 7) and draw many to her Living and True God. Yet, in reality Israel did not fulfill this prophetic mission. This does not mean that the children of Israel did not experience God's presence, His power, His covenant blessings — they did! It does mean that she did not live out in its entirety their call to be a "kingdom" that drew the nations to Zion, to the one true God. As such, Israel missed out on the blessings that accompanied this mission.

In the fullness of time (Gal 4:4), the redeemer of the world, Jesus Christ stepped into history as "the light of the world" (John 8:12). Only in a partial way was Israel this "light," only in a provisional way did she possess such holiness in herself as to attract the nations to Yahweh. In themselves, God's people are not capable of "being holy," of being His kingdom.

In this way, Israel was an "almost kingdom," unrealized not because she was not called, but because of her waywardness and her subjectivity and willful disobedience. Jesus steps into this near catastrophe, and changes the story dramatically and unexpectedly. His salvation brings not the anticipated end of this "almost kingdom," but what it had always pointed to: *Himself.* Jesus fulfills Israel's mission on behalf of her: "Jesus himself is the Kingdom; the Kingdom is not a thing, it is not a geographical dominion like worldly kingdoms. It is a person. It is He."[191]

And so He redeems her hopes of "everlasting joy" (Isa 61:7). Jesus becomes for Israel what she was called to be, but in her failings, did not fulfill: what man did not accomplish, the New Man can and does accomplish on man's behalf. Jesus is the righteous Israelite, fulfilling the stipulations of the Old Covenant in ways that God's people had not.

Questions for Reflection

1. Have I previously "seen" or "grasped" the importance of covenant in my previous reading of Scripture? Why or why not? How might the above discussion "unify" my reading of Scripture?

2. Recall the major "mediator" figures in the Old Testament (Adam, Noah, Abraham, Moses, David). In what I have learned about them, how do they "point forward" to Jesus? Can I think of ways in which Jesus is … the New Adam? The New Isaac? The New David?

3. How is it that a covenant can be called a "familial bond?" In the New Covenant, how is it that I too am part of this "familial bond" with Christ?

For Further Study

Gentry, Peter J. and Stephen J. Wellum. *Kingdom through Covenant: A Biblical-Theological Understanding of the Covenants.* Wheaton: Crossway, 2012.

Hahn, S. W. *Covenant and Communion: The Biblical Theology of Pope Benedict.* Ada, MI: Brazos Press, 2009.

———. *A Father Who Keeps His Promises: God's Covenant Love in Scripture.* Cincinnati: Servant Books, 1998. A straightforward and fairly simple approach to the theme of "covenant" in Scripture. For a more in-depth study, see *Kinship by Covenant* (below).

———. *Kinship by Covenant: A Canonical Approach to the Fulfillment of God's Saving Promises.* The Anchor Yale Bible Reference Library. New Haven, CT: Yale University Press, 2009. An in-depth evaluation of "covenant," and its development across the Old and New Testaments. For a less challenging approach to the topic, see *A Father Who Keeps His Promises* (above).

Ratzinger, Joseph. *Many Religions One Covenant: Israel, the Church and the World.* San Francisco, CA: Ignatius Press, 1999.

Wright, N. T. *Climax of the Covenant.* Philadelphia: Fortress, 1993. Wright focuses on what he sees as the misunderstanding on the part of many in reading Paul, particularly in Romans. This book challenges twentieth-century assumptions of biblical scholarship as to the "disconnect" between Paul and ancient Judaism.

Notes

183   "Covenant," in *Catholic Bible Dictionary*, 168.

184   E.g., Gen 21:22-23 (Abraham and Abimelech); David and Jonathon (1 Sam 18:1-40).

185   "Covenant," in *Catholic Bible Dictionary*, 168-170. For a more detailed examination of "covenant," cf. Scott W. Hahn, *Kinship by Covenant: A Canonical Approach to the Fulfillment of God's Saving Promises.* The Anchor Yale Bible Reference Library (New Haven, CT: Yale University Press), 2009.

186   "Covenant," in *Catholic Bible Dictionary*, 170 (emphasis added).

187   Two primary types of covenants are: 1) Kinship covenants, in which both parties swear an oath; and 2) Grant covenants, in which one party (i.e., the superior one) swears the oath. Both types are apparent in Scripture.

188   Henri de Lubac, *The Sources of Revelation* (New York: Herder & Herder, 1968), 101. "The New Testament is the fruit of the supernatural tree whose root, trunk and leaves are the Old Testament" (Ibid.).

> In this great mystery, Jesus is revealed as *the Word of the new and everlasting covenant:* divine freedom and human freedom have definitively met in his crucified flesh, *in an indissoluble and eternally valid compact.* Jesus himself, at the Last Supper, in instituting the Eucharist, had spoken of a "new and everlasting covenant" in the outpouring of his blood and shows himself to be the true sacrificial Lamb who brings about our definitive liberation from slavery.
>
> Pope Benedict, Verbum Domini §12

The Threefold Pattern of the Covenant

God's chosen mediators of the **Old Covenant** anticipate the fulfillment of the outpouring of grace in the **New Covenant**. And so we must look at these mediators and covenant actions. When we do so, we are beginning to contemplate Christ in the Old Covenant that prepares us to understand the unfolding of the Father's love in the New Covenant and the establishment of the **Church** and the Kingdom of God. In the following passage, three things are evident about the covenants in Scripture:

> *For you are a people holy to the* LORD *your God;* the LORD your God has chosen you to be a people for his own possession, out of all the peoples that are on the face of the earth. *It was not because you were more in number than any other people that the* LORD *set his love upon you and chose you, for you were the fewest of all peoples;* but it is because the LORD loves you, and is keeping the oath which he swore to your fathers, *that the* LORD *has brought you out with a mighty hand, and redeemed you from the house of bondage, from the hand of Pharaoh king of Egypt.*
>
> *Know therefore that the* LORD *your God is God,* the faithful God who keeps covenant and steadfast love with those who love him and keep his commandments, *to a thousand generations, and requites to their face those who hate him, by destroying them; he will not be slack with him who hates him, he will requite him to his face. You shall therefore be careful to do the commandment, and the statutes, and the ordinances, which I command you this day.*

And because you hearken to these ordinances, and keep and do them, the LORD your God will keep with you the covenant and the steadfast love which he swore to your fathers to keep; he will love you, bless you, and multiply you; he will also bless the fruit of your body and the fruit of your ground, your grain and your wine and your oil, the increase of your cattle and the young of your flock, in the land which he swore to your fathers to give you. (Deut 7:6–13)

Here, in Deuteronomy, a threefold pattern of the biblical covenant is evident:

1. **Covenental Election**. God initiated this covenant with His people. Abraham and his descendants.
2. **Covenental Faithfulness**. God faithfully pours His love upon His unfaithful people.
3. **Covenental Blessedness**. God promises to bless His people — and through them, all the peoples of the earth.

From the Old Covenant to the New, this threefold pattern of God's initial covenant with Abraham is transformed and taken up to a new level in Christ. In each element of the pattern, the form changes from the Old to the New, but the deeper quality characteristic to each remains intact.

Now, let us examine each of these three elements.

1. Covenental Election. The first feature of the threefold pattern of covenant is "election," or "chosen-ness." God chooses to bring Abraham and his kin into a familial relationship with himself:

Now the LORD said to Abram, "Go from your country and your kindred and your father's house to the land that I will show you. And I will make of you a great nation, and I will bless you, and make your name great, so that you will be a blessing. I will bless those who bless you, and him who curses you I will curse; and by you all the families of the earth shall bless themselves." (Gen 12:1–3)

In the Old Covenant, Abraham and his descendants are elected by God, as "His own possession" (Deut 7:6). The basic response to this great gift, repeated many times and in numerous ways is obedience to God. This response, of "choosing the God who has chosen us" is known in Scripture as holiness and righteousness: "And [Abraham] believed the

LORD; and he reckoned it to him as *righteousness*" (Gen 15:6). Throughout the remainder of the Old Testament, and in many ways, God reminds His people that He has chosen them:

Deut 7:6 "For you are a people holy to the LORD your God; *the LORD your God has chosen you to be a people for his own possession*, out of all the peoples that are on the face of the earth.

Psa 105:6–8 O offspring of Abraham his servant, sons of Jacob, *his chosen ones*! He is the LORD our God; his judgments are in all the earth. *He is mindful of his covenant forever, of the word that he commanded, for a thousand generations.*

Isa 45: 4–6 *For the sake of my servant Jacob, and Israel my chosen, I call you by your name, I surname you, though you do not know me.* I am the LORD, and there is no other, besides me there is no God; I gird you, though you do not know me, that men may know, from the rising of the sun and from the west, that there is none besides me; I am the LORD, and there is no other.

Sir 47:22 But the Lord will never give up his mercy, nor cause any of his works to perish; *he will never blot out the descendants of his chosen one*, nor destroy the posterity of him who loved him; so he gave a remnant to Jacob, and to David a root of his stock.

In the New Covenant, we see this same pattern of "election." However, in Jesus, election is expanded to accommodate a truly universal people, the Church, reaching all the peoples of the earth:

Matt 28:18–20 *Go therefore and make disciples of all nations*, baptizing them in the name of the Father and of the Son and of the Holy Spirit, *teaching them to observe all that I have commanded you;* and lo, I am with you always, to the close of the age.

Matt 28:26–28 Now as they were eating, Jesus took bread, and blessed, and broke it, and gave it to the disciples and said, "Take, eat; this is my body." And he took a cup, and when he had given thanks he gave it to them, saying, "Drink of it, all of you; for *this is my blood of the covenant, which is poured out for many for the forgiveness of sins.*"

John 3:16–17 For God so loved the world that he gave his only Son, that whoever believes in him should not perish but have eternal life. For God sent the Son into the world, not to condemn the world, but that the world might be saved through him.

Eph 3:3–5 Blessed be the God and Father of our Lord Jesus Christ, who has blessed us in Christ with every spiritual blessing in the heavenly places, *even as he chose us in him before the foundation of the world, that we should be holy and blameless before him.* He destined us in love to be his sons through Jesus Christ, according to the purpose of his will, to the praise of his glorious grace which he freely bestowed on us in the Beloved.

Thus, in the New Covenant, this first feature of the covenant, "election," has not been abolished or diminished in any way. To the contrary, in the New Covenant, *election is magnified!* In the Old Covenant, we see an ever-expanding dimension of "the elect," from the man Abraham to the nation and kingdom of Israel. Yet, this is but a shadow of the magnification and expansion of "election" in the New Covenant.

We could say that in the New Covenant, this first feature of the Old Covenant is "alive and well," as **election reaches its climax in Christ**: "*But to all who received him, who believed in his name, he gave power to become children of God; who were born, not of blood nor of the will of the flesh nor of the will of man, but of God*" (John 1:12–13).

2. Covenant Faithfulness. The second element of the threefold pattern of covenant "faithfulness" — God is loyal and faithful in remembering His people. There is a term in Hebrew that is frequently associated with God's faithfulness: *hesed*, which usually is translated as "faithfulness" or better still, "steadfast love." In light of God's *hesed* towards His people, He is ever loyal to the promises He made to Abraham, even when His people are disobedient. God continually shows *hesed* to His people:

Num 14:18–19 "The LORD is slow to anger, and *abounding in steadfast love*, forgiving iniquity and transgression, but he will by no means clear the guilty, visiting the iniquity of fathers upon children, upon the third and upon the fourth generation.' Pardon the iniquity of this people, I pray thee, *according to the greatness of thy steadfast love*, and according as thou hast forgiven this people, from Egypt even until now."

Deut 7:9 Know therefore that the L ORD your God is God, *the faithful God who keeps covenant and steadfast love* with those who love him and keep his commandments, to a thousand generations.

Psa 33:4–5 For the word of the L ORD is upright; and all his work is done in faithfulness. He loves righteousness and justice; *the earth is full of the steadfast love of the L ORD .*

Psa 63:3–4 *Because thy steadfast love is better than life*, my lips will praise thee. So I will bless thee as long as I live; I will lift up my hands and call on thy name.

In the New Covenant God expresses this "steadfast love" to His people, the Church, through Jesus Christ. Though the Hebrew term *hesed* is not there, the substance is — and is seen in a number of closely related Greek words, such as *agape* ("love"), *charis* ("grace") and *chrēstotēti* ("kindness, goodness"). A good example of this "transformation" of God's *hesed* in Jesus is seen in St. Paul's letter to the Ephesians. Paul uses not one, not two, but *three* words which together represent the *hesed* of Jesus Christ:

Eph 2:4–7 But God, who is rich in mercy, out of the great *love* (*agape*) with which he *loved us* (agape), even when we were dead through our trespasses, made us alive together with Christ — by grace (*charis*) you have been saved — and raised us up with him, and made us sit with him in the heavenly places in Christ Jesus, that in the coming ages he might show the immeasurable riches of his *grace* (*charis*) in kindness (*chrēstotēti*) toward us in Christ Jesus.

Likewise, what "faithfulness" looks like is altered in the New Covenant. Under the Old Covenant, the form this took was: a) sign of circumcision; and b) keeping the Law of Moses. Under the New Covenant, "faithfulness" is transformed through Christ (1 Cor 2:9). As such: a) "baptism" is the new *circumcision of the heart*; and b) the "Law of Christ" is *written on the heart*: "Bear one another's burdens, and so fulfill the Law of Christ" (Gal 6:2; cf. Jer 31:31–33).

In a similar way as with election, this second feature of the Old Covenant is "alive and well" in the New, and is not abolished or diminished in any way because **faithfulness reaches its climax in Christ.**

3. Covenant Blessedness. The third and final element of the three-fold pattern of covenant is "blessedness." In the Old Covenant, these blessings are very concrete: "*He will love you, bless you, and multiply you; he will bless the fruit of your body and the fruit of your ground, your grain, your wine and your oil, and increase your cattle and the young of your flock, in the land which he swore to your fathers to give you*" (Deut 7:13). The biblical roots of this "blessed state" of God towards His people is seen in the opening chapters of Genesis, where God blesses our first parents with every "good" thing (Gen 1:4, 10, 12, 18, 21, 25, 31).

Adam and Eve break God's covenant and introduce sin and death into human history. Nevertheless, God will initiate a covenant with Abraham, in which many blessings will be poured out upon the children of Adam:

> **Gen 12:2–3** Go from your country and your kindred and your father's house to the land that I will show you. And I will make of you a great nation, and I will bless you, and make your name great, so that you will be a blessing. I will bless those who bless you, and him who curses you I will curse; and by you all the families of the earth shall bless themselves.

The three great blessings God promises to Abraham can be summarized here as follows: **land, dynasty** and **family**. The first blessing that God promises is that his descendants will inherit *land,* "the land that I will show you" (v. 1). Later in the Old Testament, we learn this "promised land" is given a name, Jerusalem. It will become the place where God's people will dwell, and where God will dwell among them, in His holy Temple. Spiritually, this points forward to heaven, which is our promised land, the New Jerusalem :

> **Rev 21:2** *And I saw the holy city, new Jerusalem, coming down out of heaven from God,* prepared as a bride adorned for her husband; and I heard a loud voice from the throne saying, "*Behold, the dwelling of God is with men. He will dwell with them, and they shall be his people, and God himself will be with them*; he will wipe away every tear from their eyes, and death shall be no more, neither shall there be mourning nor crying nor pain any more, for the former things have passed away."

The second blessing God promises Abraham is *dynasty*: "I will make of you a great nation, and I will bless you, and make your name great, so that you will be a blessing" (v. 2). Later, we learn that this will involve an heir, a "son," through whom this promise will grow. Make no mistake, though — the promise here is not just of a "son," but of a *dynasty*. The descendants of Abraham will be a "great nation" (v. 2), a "kingdom of priests and a holy nation" (Exod 19:6).

As the book of Genesis ends, the blessing unfolds even further, as the promise of "kingship" comes specifically to the descendants of one of Jacob's twelve sons (i.e., one of Abraham's great grandsons), Judah:

> **Gen 49:10–12** *The scepter shall not depart from Judah, nor the ruler's staff from between his feet, until he comes to whom it belongs*; and to him shall be the obedience of the peoples. Binding his foal to the vine and his ass's colt to the choice vine, he washes his garments in wine and his vesture in the blood of grapes; his eyes shall be red with wine, and his teeth white with milk.

Much could be said about this prophetic and messianic text! Let us limit our remarks to three crucial ones. First, these royal promises to Judah *point back to Abraham*, and clearly echo the promises of "dynasty" God gave to Abraham (Gen 12:3). But not just a dynasty, a "kingdom." And if you have a kingdom, you have a king ("the scepter shall not depart," "the ruler's staff"). Second, these royal promises *point forward to David*, who is born of the tribe of Judah, and is the king that is foreshadowed here in Genesis. Third and finally, these royal promises point forward ever further — to God's anointed Messiah. On a second level, this is what the phrase *"until it comes to whom it belongs"* signifies, the coming messianic King. This is confirmed by the presence of messianic imagery, such as the "foal" and "ass's colt" (Gen 49:11), which are later depicted by the prophet Zechariah as the humble animal that will carry the victorious messiah to his people (see Zech 9:9; compare with Matt 21:5). On a spiritual and sacramental level, the images of "vine/choice vine" and "blood/grapes/wine" are profound foreshadowings of Jesus Christ and the Holy Eucharist.

The third promise God makes to Abraham is family: "And by you *all the families of the earth shall bless themselves*" (Gen 12:3). For the above promises of land and dynasty are promised to Abraham and *his descendants*. Yes, he will go to a land that God will show him; and yes, God will bring forth kings from him. But these blessings are bound up in the gift of a son.

Thus, God gave Abraham a son, Isaac, through whom the blessings will flow. Yet later, as we know, the faith of Abraham is severely tested, as God commands Abraham to sacrifice his "only son" as a burnt offering.

> **Gen 22:6–8** And Abraham took the wood of the burnt offering, and laid it on Isaac his son; and he took in his hand the fire and the knife. So they went both of them together. And Isaac said to his father Abraham, "My father!" And he said, "Here am I, my son." He said, "Behold, the fire and the wood; but where is the lamb for a burnt offering?" Abraham said, *"God will provide himself the lamb for a burnt offering, my son." So they went both of them together.*

Here, we understand why the *Catechism* says Abraham "fulfilled the definition of faith" (CCC 145). The Book of Hebrews interprets this scene as a prefigurement of Christ, and ascribes a divine insight to Abraham, in that in faith, Abraham foresaw the resurrected Christ in his own son:

> **Heb 11:17–19** By faith Abraham, when he was tested, offered up Isaac, and he who had received the promises was ready to offer up his only son, of whom it was said, "Through Isaac shall your descendants be named." *He considered that God was able to raise men even from the dead; hence he did receive him back and this was a symbol.*

But as fantastic as these blessings are, which God gave to Abraham, we should come back to the first Adam as we contemplate the New Adam. As was said above, the biblical roots of the "blessed state" of God towards His people is seen in the opening chapters of Genesis. The promises "tend towards" Abraham, but they originate in their primordial and purest form not in Mesopotamia or Ur, the land of Abraham, but in *Eden, the land of Adam.* After God's creative work has ceased, culminating in the creation of Man, God says "behold, it is very good" (Gen 1:31).

> **Gen 2:2–3** *And on the seventh day God finished his work which he had done, and he rested on the seventh day from all his work which he had done. So God blessed the seventh day and hallowed it, because on it God rested from all his work which he had done in creation.*

As Jacob Neusner writes, the Sabbath is more than a ritual of abstaining from work; rather, *"it is a way of imitating God."*[192] This is the essential blessing God offers to Adam, to Israel, and to all of His people:

a way of drawing us to Himself. This third feature of the Old Covenant is not abolished as we turn to the New Testament. Rather, like the previous two features we examined, "blessedness" is likewise transformed in the New Covenant. Just as the later blessings of *land, dynasty* and *family* are taken up and fulfilled in Christ, so too is this Edenic blessing:

As Pope Benedict XVI talks about, Jesus' statement in Matthew's Gospel, that "The Son of man is lord of the Sabbath" (Matt 12:8) is to be read in the context of the so-called *Jubelruf* ("joyful shout") of the Messiah, which is just several verses prior to it:[193]

> I thank thee, Father, Lord of heaven and earth, that thou hast hidden these things from the wise and understanding and revealed them to babes; yea, Father, for such was thy gracious will. All things have been delivered to me by my Father; and no one knows the Son except the Father, and no one knows the Father except the Son and any one to whom the Son chooses to reveal him. Come to me, all who labor and are heavy laden, and I will give you rest. Take my yoke upon you, and learn from me; for I am gentle and lowly in heart, and you will find rest for your souls. For my yoke is easy, and my burden is light. (Matt 11:25–30)

As Benedict XVI writes, Jesus is not advocating a "liberal understanding of the Law," for "following Christ is not comfortable."[194] No, a moral explanation alone will not suffice — a Christological one is necessary as well:

> "The rest that is intended here has to do with Jesus. Jesus' teaching about the Sabbath now appears in full harmony with his *Jubelruf* (messianic joy) and his words about the Son of Man being Lord of the Sabbath. Neusner sums up the overall content as follows: "My yoke is easy, I give you rest, the Son of Man is lord of the Sabbath indeed, because the Son of Man is now Israel's Sabbath: how we act like God."[195]

In conclusion, we could say that in the New Covenant, this final feature of the Old Covenant is "alive and well," as **blessedness reaches its climax in Christ**. Above all the "blessings" in the Old Testament, none is more primary than finding our Sabbath rest in Jesus Christ:

> **Heb 4:9–11, 16** So then, there remains *a sabbath rest for the people of God; for whoever enters God's rest also ceases from his labors as God*

did from his … Let us therefore strive to enter that rest, that no one fall by the same sort of disobedience. Let us then with confidence draw near to the throne of grace, that we may receive mercy and find grace to help in time of need.

For the Apostles and authors of the New Testament, "this Sabbath rest" in Christ brings new purpose and new meaning to our lives; His rest is our peace, His joy is our delight, His *Jubelreuf* our jubilation. In the Kingdom of God, Christians enter into this Sabbath rest at Baptism. We are able to experience daily life, no matter the "ups and downs" that attend it, and enter into all of it with the Lord of the Sabbath. Ultimately, for those born again in water and Spirit, this *Jubelreuf* leads far beyond daily consolations and the experience of God's presence in the here and now. For those who are in Christ, death is not our final rest, or a place of darkness — no. For those in Christ, death is merely a threshold that leads to new life, resurrection life, and the true *Jubelreuf* of the messiah, Here we arrive at our heavenly home and our true and eternal Sabbath rest: *"And night shall be no more; they need no light of lamp or sun, for the Lord God will be their light, and they shall reign for ever and ever"* (Rev 22:5). Let us desire more greatly to enter His Sabbath rest.

Table 6: The Threefold Pattern of the Covenant		
Threefold Pattern	**Old Covenant**	**New Covenant**
Covenantal Election	Feature: Chosenness Form: A Particular people (Children of Abraham)	Feature: Chosenness Form: A Universal People (The Church)
Covenantal Faithfulness	Feature: Obedience Form: Circumcision, Law of Moses	Feature: Obedience Form: Baptism, Law of Christ
Covenantal Blessedness	Feature: Sabbath Rest Form: Promised Land (Jerusalem)	Feature: Sabbath Rest Form: Promised Land (Eternal Life)

Conclusion: The Liturgical Enactment of the New Covenant

In the above discussion, we saw that no theme is more central to our apprehension of the whole of Scripture than that of covenant. Along with this, we focused our attention on the threefold pattern of the covenant: *covenantal election, covenantal faithfulness* and *covenantal blessedness.*

We looked at various ways in which these three patterns emerge in the Old Testament — and how they point forward to greater realities beyond the Old Covenant. Ultimately, we saw how each of these features is transformed and finds its climax of meaning on the pages of the New Testament, in the New and everlasting New Covenant of Jesus Christ.

Now, as we conclude this chapter, one final remark is necessary, to link all of these features together. And it is this:

At each progressive stage of the Old Covenant, God initiates the promises through various mediators. The covenant is ratified or *enacted* through *solemn words* (e.g., I will be your God and you will be My people) and *solemn deeds* (Circumcision, Passover, etc.) These solemn words and solemn rites are, in a manner of speaking, the **liturgical enactment of the Old Covenant**. In these liturgical enactments, *blood is shed:*

> **Heb 9:18–20** Hence even the first covenant was not ratified without blood. For when every commandment of the law had been declared by Moses to all the people, he took the blood of calves and goats, with water and scarlet wool and hyssop, and sprinkled both the book itself and all the people, saying, "This is the blood of the covenant which God commanded you."

Likewise, in the New Testament, God initiates His covenantal promises through his one Divine mediator, Jesus Christ (1 Tim 2:5), through *solemn words* and *solemn deeds*, the **liturgical enactment of the New Covenant:**

> And he took bread, and when he had given thanks he broke it and gave it to them, saying, "This is my body which is given for you. Do this in remembrance of me." And likewise the cup after supper, saying, "This cup which is poured out for you is the new covenant in my blood." (Luke 22:19–20)

As in the Old Covenant, blood is shed. Yet the blood of Christ, who Himself is "without blemish" secures our eternal redemption:

> **Heb 9:11–15** But when Christ appeared as a high priest of the good things that have come, then through the greater and more perfect tent (not made with hands, that is, not of this creation) he

entered once for all into the Holy Place, *taking not the blood of goats and calves but his own blood, thus securing an eternal redemption.*

For if the sprinkling of defiled persons with the blood of goats and bulls and with the ashes of a heifer sanctifies for the purification of the flesh, *how much more shall the blood of Christ, who through the eternal Spirit offered himself without blemish to God,* purify your conscience from dead works to serve the living God. Therefore *he is the mediator of a new covenant, so that those who are called may receive the promised eternal inheritance, since a death has occurred which redeems them from the transgressions under the first covenant.*

The institution of the Eucharist at the Last Supper *is the liturgical enactment of the New Covenant.* Through solemn words ("Behold the Lamb of God, behold Him who takes away the sins of the world") and solemn deeds (receiving the Body and Blood of the Lord) we participate in the covenant of grace, enacted in heaven on our behalf by the Risen Lord. "For as often as you eat this bread and drink the cup, you proclaim the Lord's death until he comes" (1 Cor 11:26).

In *Verbum Domini*, Pope Benedict offers a fitting reflection on Jesus, "the true sacrificial Lamb," who, in the heavenly Kingdom, continually re-enacts the New Covenant on our behalf:

> In this great mystery, Jesus is revealed as *the Word of the new and everlasting covenant*: divine freedom and human freedom have definitively met in his crucified flesh, *in an indissoluble and eternally valid compact.* Jesus himself, at the Last Supper, in instituting the Eucharist, had spoken of a "new and everlasting covenant" in the outpouring of his blood and shows himself to be the true sacrificial Lamb who brings about our definitive liberation from slavery.[196]

This completes our discussion of covenant, the master theme that unifies all of the Scripture, both Old and New Testaments. It is the theme that allows us — and requires us — to see Christ on every page of the Bible. Yet, as important as "covenant" is, it is not the only "unifying" element between the Old and New Testament. Now, we turn to a second such element, namely, biblical typology.

FOR REFLECTION | *What am I doing these days to enter more deeply into the experience of "resting" in God? What people, places, things or Scriptures are most profoundly influencing me towards a deeper awareness of the need for this rest?*

Questions for Reflection

1. Describe the following in your own words:
   • Covenantal election
   • Covenantal faithfulness
   • Covenantal blessedness
2. What are the "features" and "forms" in the Old Covenant? In the New Covenant?
3. How is it that Jesus does not abolish or diminish: these three aspects of the covenant, but is the "climax" of each one?
4. What is the role of the "solemn words" and "solemn deeds" of the Old Covenant? Why was the "shedding of blood" necessary?
5. What does it mean to say that Jesus is the "liturgical enactment" of the New Covenant? How might this affect our approach to receiving the Holy Eucharist?

For Further Study

Please see the resources listed in the previous chapter.

Notes

189   Ratzinger, *In the Beginning: A Catholic Understanding of the Story of Creation and the Fall*, 9.

190   De Lubac, *The Sources of Revelation*, 102.

191   Benedict XVI, *Jesus of Nazareth*, 49.

192   Jacob Neusner, *A Rabbi Talks with Jesus* (Montreal: McGill-Queen's University Press, 2000), 75.

193   Benedict XVI, *Jesus of Nazareth*, vol. 1, 109.

194   Ibid.

195   Ibid, 110; cf. Neusner, *A Rabbi Talks with Jesus*, 86.

196   Pope Benedict XVI, *VD* §12.

CHAPTER 9

> "As Moses lifted up the serpent in the wilderness, so must the Son of man be lifted up, that whoever believes in him may have eternal life."
>
> *John 3:14*

Biblical Typology and Recapitulation

Having completed our discussion of "Covenant," we turn in this chapter to a discussion of two other crucial ways in which the "unitive pattern" of the Old and New Testaments is evident: "Biblical Typology" and "Recapitulation in Christ."

Biblical Typology

Typology may be defined as the study of "persons, places, events, and institutions in the Bible that foreshadow later and greater realities made known by God in history."[197] The *Catechism* states that this method of reading Scripture has always been a part of the Church's study and veneration of Scripture:

> The Church, as early as apostolic times, and then constantly in her Tradition, has illuminated the unity of the divine plan in the two Testaments through typology, which discerns in God's works of the Old Covenant prefigurations of what he accomplished in the fullness of time in the person of his incarnate Son.[198]

Typology points to the advancement of salvation history as a "carefully orchestrated plan that God unfolds in stages of ever increasing fulfillment.[199] Accordingly, biblical typology is another lens alongside that of prophecy and covenant — which helps us "look" into the deeper pattern of unity in Scripture. For the Catholic student of Sacred Scripture, it's a vital avenue of biblical interpretation. As the above quote from the *Catechism* indicates, typology is anything but new.

Typology originates in ancient Jewish thought patterns, lying deep in the Old Testament itself. For instance, in the Book of Joshua we read the account of God miraculously parting the waters of the Jordan River and leading Joshua and the Israelites through unharmed (Josh 3:1–17).

The original Jewish readers of this book may have not called this "typology," but they recognized the pattern just the same: Joshua is the Moses-figure who delivers them; and God has again come to their rescue, parting the waters of the river just as He had done in the past, at the Red Sea (Exod 14).

Instrumental to biblical typology are what is known as "types" and "antitypes." In ancient Greek, the term *typos* referred to something that leaves an impression or a mark on another thing; such as a wax seal that leaves on a piece of parchment the impression of its original figure. In biblical typology then, the type is *the original feature* (person, place, event or institution) found in a Scriptural passage. The antitype is *the new feature* (person, place, event or institution) in a subsequent biblical text that is "pre-figured" in the previous one, i.e., the one in which the original is found. Not only are "type" and "antitype" analogous to one another, but in the antitype is seen a "greater than" fulfillment of the type which anticipated it is some real yet "lesser" way. So Moses is the 'type' who sets the pattern of redemption. This pattern is later echoed by Joshua, who is the antitype of Moses.

In a similar way, we often see patterns of typology that begin in the Old Testament and are completed only much later in the New Testament. For example, in the Old Testament, we recall that while Israel was in the harsh wilderness, Moses, through God's provision, provided the Israelites with manna, bread from heaven which was for them their daily sustenance:

> Then the LORD said to Moses, "Behold, I will rain *bread from heaven* for you; and the people shall go out and gather a day's portion every day, that I may prove them, whether they will walk in my law or not. (Exod 16:4)

Here in Exodus, we see that Moses is a type of Christ. When we turn to the Gospel of John, this image from Exodus is explicitly recalled, of God through Moses raining down this heavenly manna. In the process, Jesus is depicted as the antitype to Moses:

Jesus said to them, "*I am the bread of life*; he who comes to me shall not hunger, and he who believes in me shall never thirst" (John 6:35). Where Moses called down the Manna from heaven, Jesus *is* the Manna from heaven. Thus, Moses is a type of Jesus, and Jesus corresponds to — but surpasses the original figure of Moses. This correspondence between the two is bolstered in the remainder of the Bread of Life Discourse in

John 6: "*This is the bread which came down from heaven, not such as the fathers ate and died; he who eats this bread will live forever*" (John 6:58).

And this is not the only way this type/antitype is developed between Moses/New Moses. In the Old Testament Moses *parts the Sea* (Exod 14:21–24); in the New Testament Jesus *walks on the Sea* (John 6:16–21). In the Old Testament, *Moses' first sign* to Pharaoh is turning the water of the Nile to blood (Exod 7:17–20); in the New Testament, *Jesus' first sign* is turning the water at the Wedding feast at Cana to wine — which in turn *prefigures His blood.*

Let us consider another example of biblical typology, whose origins lie in the prophet Isaiah:

> Thus says the LORD, who makes a way in the sea, a path in the mighty waters, who brings forth chariot and horse, army and warrior; they lie down, they cannot rise, they are extinguished, quenched like a wick: "Remember not the former things, nor consider the things of old. Behold, I am doing a new thing; now it springs forth, do you not perceive it? I will make a way in the wilderness and rivers in the desert. The wild beasts will honor me, the jackals and the ostriches; for I give water in the wilderness, rivers in the desert, to give drink to my chosen people, the people whom I formed for myself that they might declare my praise. "Yet you did not call upon me, O Jacob; but you have been weary of me, O Israel!" (Isa 43:16–22)

In the above passage, the prophet Isaiah writes of the coming redemption of God's people, describing it terms that would be familiar to every Israelite. In preparing his audience for this future action of God, the prophet describes Yahweh as the God who:

> *Makes a way in the sea, a path in the mighty waters, who brings forth chariot and horse, army and warrior; they lie down, they cannot rise, they are extinguished, quenched like a wick* (vv. 16–17).

Here, in hymnic form, the image of Yahweh's deliverance of His people is put to use by the prophet in the uncertainty of Isaiah's times. Isaiah begins by helping his readers recollect God's deliverance through the Red Sea and their exodus from Egypt. But he does not stop there. Rather, he wants his readers to draw on this "saving image" to explain that now, God is doing something familiar, but in a fresh and new situation. Just as God in the past could be relied upon to save them through the water, now God is going to deliver His people in the wilderness. Isaiah's lesson now becomes clear: in meditating upon God's powerful acts in their past, His people draw strength and hope to trust Him with their present concerns. As Isaiah records:

> Remember not the former things, nor consider the things of old. Behold, I am doing a new thing; now it springs forth, do you not perceive it? I will make a way in the wilderness and rivers in the desert (vv. 18–19).

"Behold, I am doing a new thing" says the Lord to His people in Isaiah's setting. In recalling the great deeds of old, God asks his people to search their hearts for what He is yet to do among them in their present situation: *"Now it springs forth, do you not perceive it?"* Following this encouragement and hope comes a new challenge to God's people: "Yet you did not call upon me, O Jacob; but you have been weary of me, O Israel!" (v. 22). As a result, Israel is called to renounce her sins, and trust in the Lord's power, as later in the chapter, Isaiah records God's plea to His people:

> Put me in remembrance, let us argue together; set forth your case, that you may be proved right. Your first father sinned, and your mediators transgressed against me. Therefore I profaned the princes of the sanctuary, I delivered Jacob to utter destruction and Israel to reviling (vv. 26–28).

In short, what we see in the above passage in Isaiah is a typological approach: Israel's great struggle of the past is re-presented, in light of a New Exodus that God beckons His people to in the present.[200] Likewise, the whole story of Joshua is cast in the light of the story of Moses. For example, the crossing of the Jordan recalls the crossing of the Red Sea (Josh 3–5, Exod 14); Joshua parts the Jordan just as Moses parted the raging waters of the Red Sea (Josh 3:14–17, Exod 14:16–22).

Thus, the origins of typology are to be seen in this early stage of salvation history, and not something that "suddenly occurred" to those Jewish Christians who composed the books of the New Testament. Aidan Nichols rightly assesses those critics who dismiss typology as some sort of "imposition" onto the text of the Old Testament:

> The typological method cannot be called an extraneous imposition on the Old Testament, since on the contrary *it grows out of the Old*

Testament from within. Its connection with the Old Testament is organic and inherent.[201]

Clearly then, as we look at various passages in the Old Testament, we can see types of Christ (and Mary, Peter, the Sacraments, the Church). However, it is only when we arrive in the New Testament that we see the full flowering in the antitype to which the old figure was ultimately a symbol, a shadow, a hint of something greater yet to come. Aidan Nichols observes that his 1952 English missal has this inscription:

Oft in the olden types foreshadowed
In Isaac on the altar bowed
And in the ancient paschal food
And in the manna sent from heaven[202]

Early Christian catechesis made constant use of the Old Testament.

— *Catechism of the Catholic Church*

Jesus continually presented himself typologically, as the New Temple (John 2:21), the New Moses (John 6:33), one greater than Jonah, and Solomon (Matt 12:6), and in many other ways. Through these various types of Christ and others still, the authors of the New Testament re-interpreted the life and teachings of Jesus, His Passion and resurrection, as well as His final parousia through the signs and symbols within the Old Testament. A familiar example of this is seen in John 3, which records Jesus' speech to Nicodemus, in which the bronze serpent from the book of Numbers is a type of Christ, which anticipates Jesus' glorification as the Son of Man, who is "lifted up" on the Cross:

The LORD said to Moses, "Make a fiery serpent, and set it on a pole; and everyone who is bitten, when he sees it, shall live." So Moses made a bronze serpent, and set it on a pole; and if a serpent bit any man, *he would look at the bronze serpent and live.* (Num 21:8–10)

As Moses lifted up the serpent in the wilderness, *so must the Son of man be lifted up, that whoever believes in him may have eternal life.* (John 3:14)

St. Paul's thought patterns frequently run along typological lines, especially as he develops his Christology. In fact, Paul makes more use of typology than he makes explicit reference to the covenant! Additionally, in Paul's letters we see a sort of "eschatological typology," for example, passages in texts in which Adam is the prefigurement of the Christ, the New Adam, who "undoes" Adam's disobedience through His perfect obedience (Rom 5:12–21).

Elsewhere, we see a kind of ecclesial/sacramental typology in the Old and New Testaments. For example, the Old Testament image of the "foundation stone" of the Jerusalem Temple becomes for Paul a type of Christ, who is the "cornerstone" of the Church (Eph 2:20).

> **Isa 28:16** "Behold, I am laying in Zion *for a foundation a stone, a tested stone, a precious cornerstone, of a sure foundation*: 'He who believes will not be in haste.' (Isa 28:16)

> **Eph 2:19–22** So then you are no longer strangers and sojourners, but you are fellow citizens with the saints and members of the household of God, built upon the foundation of the apostles and prophets, *Christ Jesus himself being the cornerstone, in whom the whole structure is joined together and grows into a holy temple in the Lord; in whom you also are built into it for a dwelling place of God in the Spirit.*

Finally, in Peter's first epistle, we have one of the clearest examples of typology. In this instance, the image of the flood in Genesis is a type that prefigures Christian baptism:

> **1 Pet 3:18–21** For Christ also died for sins once for all, the righteous for the unrighteous, that he might bring us to God, being put to death in the flesh but made alive in the spirit; in which he went and preached to the spirits in prison, who formerly did not obey, *when God's patience waited in the days of Noah, during the building of the ark, in which a few, that is, eight persons, were saved through water. Baptism, which corresponds to this, now saves you, not as a removal of dirt from the body but as an appeal to God for a clear conscience,* through the resurrection of Jesus Christ, who has gone into heaven and is at the right hand of God, with angels, authorities, and powers subject to him.

In conclusion, biblical typology is an essential tool in the hand of the careful biblical exegete. Its roots lie deeply in the persons, places and things of the Old Covenant. The New Testament writers *plumbed the depths* of the Old Testament to "explain Christ" as the true fulfillment of these types of the Old Testament. As the *Catechism* summarizes:

> Christians therefore read the Old Testament in the light of Christ crucified and risen. Such typological reading discloses the inexhaustible content of the Old Testament; but it must not make us forget that the Old Testament retains its own intrinsic value as Revelation reaffirmed by our Lord himself. Besides, the New Testament has to be read in the light of the Old. Early Christian catechesis made constant use of the Old Testament. As an old saying put it, the New Testament lies hidden in the Old and the Old Testament is unveiled in the New.[203]

Finally, having looked earlier at biblical prophecy, and more extensively at the theme of covenant — and just now, biblical typology, we now turn to one more way in which the "unitive pattern" between the Old and New Testament is evident: "Recapitulation in Christ."

Recapitulation in Christ

While many readers of Scripture may be somewhat familiar with prophecy, and even covenant and typology, this final theme of recapitulation is one that is less familiar, or even unheard of by many. This is most unfortunate, as it is one of the most exciting "connectors" between the Old and New Testament that we are discussing in the book!

To understand what is meant by recapitulation, we turn to the wisdom and clarity of the *Catechism*. In Section One of the *Catechism*, the "mysteries of Christ's life" are prefaced with three short but highly useful paragraphs. In them, the *Catechism* discusses three key interrelated terms, all of which, it suggests, are characteristics common to the entire life of Christ. These qualities permeate and exemplify all of the mysteries. In other words, these three characteristics are seen again and again in the Gospels — not only in the Passion of Christ, but also throughout His entire life.

The *Catechism* describes three qualities that are common to all the mysteries of Christ as: *Revelation*, *Redemption*, and *Recapitulation*. For our purposes, we will only concern ourselves with the last of these characteristics, i.e., "recapitulation." But in order to understand recapitulation, let us look at the three paragraphs in the *Catechism* in which they are discussed (CCC 516–18). As we do so, I will make a few remarks in order to underscore their value and explain "how they work":

CCC 516 Christ's whole earthly life — his words and deeds, his silences and sufferings, indeed his manner of being and speaking — is *Revelation* of the Father. Jesus can say: "Whoever has seen me has seen the Father," and the Father can say: "This is my Son, my Chosen; listen to him!" Because our Lord became man in order to do his Father's will, even the least characteristics of his mysteries manifest "God's love … among us."

The first characteristic that is common to studying all the mysteries of Christ's life is "revelation." What does Jesus reveal? Above all, *He reveals God to us* (John 1:18). In gazing at Jesus, we are gazing at the Father ("Whoever has seen me has seen the Father"). As such, all the goodness that belongs to God is likewise exemplified perfectly and fully in Jesus. Thus, Jesus reveals the face of the Father; His divine mercy, His perfect justice and above all, His love for us. While all of these are important, in the context of this paragraph of the *Catechism*, I suggest that the particular concept that is being heralded is "truth." In other words, all of the mysteries of Christ — His Incarnation, His miracles, His parables, etc. — all of the mysteries reveal "truth" in some way. Whether Jesus speaks or not in a passage from the Gospels, in some way, the *Catechism* is saying, it is a "revelation of truth."

As but one example, in the mystery of Jesus in the desert, we can see that what is revealed is that Jesus did not condescend to the temptations of the Devil, but exemplifies that He is indeed the sinless Messiah, the spotless lamb. As such, we have a Savior who overcame the Devil at least twice: at the Cross and in advance of it, in the desert. Christ reveals the great love of the Father, who did not spare Jesus this encounter, but actually had the Spirit "drive Him to the desert," in order to show His filial obedience to the Father.

Did you notice how broadly the *Catechism* defined where we should be looking for this characteristic of Jesus in the Gospels? His "whole earthly life" and then it lists examples: "His words and deeds, his silences and sufferings, *indeed his manner of being and speaking*." Question: what would it look like if we were to study Scripture like this? What "truth" might we see, when listening to the "silence" of Jesus before His accusers? What might the "revelation" be in such passages? In Jesus' "hidden years," in his quiet labor at Nazareth? In the manger? In His parables? Spend some time looking at your favorite passages, and ask similar questions of the text.

The second characteristic common to all the mysteries of Christ is listed in the following paragraph of the *Catechism*:

CCC 517 Christ's whole life is a mystery of *redemption*. Redemption comes to us above all through the blood of his cross, but this mystery is at work throughout Christ's entire life:
   — already in his Incarnation through which by becoming poor he enriches us with his poverty;
   — in his hidden life which by his submission atones for our disobedience;
   — in his word which purifies its hearers;
   — in his healings and exorcisms by which "he took our infirmities and bore our diseases;"
   — and in his Resurrection by which he justifies us.

Here again, notice how inclusive the *Catechism* is in discussing the mystery of "redemption."

I suspect that for many of us, we have thought of "redemption" as something that pertains only to the Cross. Naturally, the *Catechism* affirms the centrality of the Cross ("Redemption comes to us above all through the blood of his cross").

It then lists a number of mysteries of Christ's life that we don't always associate with "redemption" — and then it suggests particular ways that redemption is seen in these less obvious scenes: "Already in his Incarnation through which by becoming poor he enriches us with his poverty." That sentence alone is a lot to ponder; that Christ's redemption is evidenced already in His Incarnation. It seems the *Catechism* is getting at the notion of our fallen human flesh, and how Christ's work of redemption — carried out on the Cross, is nonetheless begun in some mysterious way, by "dignifying" humanity by condescending to our human nature.

The next sentence offers just as much to meditate upon: "In his hidden life which by his submission atones for our disobedience." Have you ever thought of Jesus' hidden years at Nazareth as "redemptive?" The *Catechism* says we ought! Perhaps, Jesus' manual labor, His hard work at Nazareth, redeems the many ways we have made "work" something that is a curse rather than a blessing. Yet, lived in quiet humility and dignified human labor, human work, and the quietness of everyday life in these hidden years, thus brings redemption to this aspect of our lives.

We can look to "His word," "His healings and exorcisms," and "His Resurrection," all of which the *Catechism* lists as examples of His redemptive work. Again, I ask: What would it look like if we studied "redemption in Christ" such an all-encompassing part of our biblical study?

The third and final characteristic common to all the mysteries of Christ is listed in the following paragraph of the *Catechism*, i.e., "recapitulation."

Of these three characteristics common to Christ's life, it is the one that we will focus on, since, as we will see, of the three traits, it is the one that most represents yet another "unifying element" between the Old and New Testaments, and this is our chief interest in discussing "recapitulation" here.

> **CCC 518** Christ's whole life is a mystery of *recapitulation*. All Jesus did, said and suffered had for its aim restoring fallen man to his original vocation:
>
> > When Christ became incarnate and was made man, he recapitulated in himself the long history of mankind and procured for us a "short cut" to salvation, so that what we had lost in Adam, that is, being in the image and likeness of God, we might recover in Christ Jesus. For this reason Christ experienced all the stages of life, thereby giving communion with God to all men.

All that was lost in the first Adam is now restored, taken up, and "recapitulated" in Christ:

Like covenant and typology, reading Scripture with an eye to "recapitulation" provides us with yet another lens to see the unity of the Old and New Testament.

Yet, such careful reading requires us to *contend with the whole* of Scripture in order to understand *any of its many parts*, that is to say, any given text we are reading, studying or praying. But how does "recapitulation" work out in Scripture — how can we "see" recapitulation properly speaking?

To start with, when reading a gospel passage, we might try to think of *as many parallels* from the Old Testament that come to mind. Here then is an important clarification: Unlike typology, which works as a one-to-one correspondence, recapitulation is not restricted to such a manner. That is, we're not dealing with a set of types and antitypes. Rather, we begin by recognizing that Jesus is "recapping" *all of salvation history and healing/restoring it in Himself.* So, when hearing Jesus called "Son of David," for instance, by people seeking a miracle, we might think of various ways that David was unfaithful to God (his greed, his selfishness, his adulteress affair with Bathsheba, his murder of Uriah, her husband, etc.) Then, returning to the gospel passage, we are seeking to understand some of the ways that salvation history is taken up, fulfilled, restored, healed — recapitulated in Christ. So, not only is Jesus "Son of David" (prophecy/typology), but He is also the *true David* (recapitulation). To read, study and pray the Scripture in such a way is to be mindful of what the *Catechism* calls "recapitulation."

This "solo" is Jesus … The Son of Man recapitulates in himself earth and heaven, creation and the Creator, flesh and Spirit.

— Pope Benedict XVI, *Verbum Domini* §13

It cannot be stressed enough that when it comes to this idea of re-capitulation, the *Catechism* asks us to go back, back, back … all the way to the beginning of salvation history, to what was lost in Adam. It is with Adam first and foremost that Christ begins His work of "recapitulating" salvation history.

Let us explore the idea a bit further. Consider the term "recapitu-lation" itself. It is from a Latin root which has several meanings. With respect to biology, it refers to "repetition," as in the reappearance or re-iteration of previous stages of life. This can help us understand what the *Catechism* is getting at: recapitulation in Christ is a kind of "repetition" of our original state of humanity. Not as though we return to Eden, but in a sense, the experience of our parents, particularly their broken union with one other and their broken communion with God, is experienced as a "reversal" through Christ. "In Adam," Paul tells us, "all die, so also in Christ shall all be made alive" (1 Cor 15:22). As Pope Benedict writes in *Verbum Domini*,

> Calling to mind these essential elements of our faith, we can con-template the profound unity in Christ between creation, the new creation and all salvation history. To use an example, we can com-pare the cosmos to a "book" and consider it as "the work of an au-thor who expresses himself through the 'symphony' of creation. In this symphony one finds, at a certain point, what would be called in musical terms a 'solo,' a theme entrusted to a single instrument

or voice which is so important that the meaning of the entire work depends on it. This 'solo' is Jesus … *The Son of Man recapitulates in himself earth and heaven, creation and the Creator, flesh and Spirit.* He is the center of the cosmos and of history, for in him converge without confusion the author and his work."[204]

Thus, Pope Benedict XVI offers an important qualifier: recapitulation is *not simply repetition*, but *a grand reversal* of man's fortunes. The response of the man born blind to his accusers in John's Gospel, "I was blind, but now I see" (John 9:25) is more than an affirmation of physical sight. It is a declaration that the restoration of the original goodness and wholeness of humanity has begun in Christ. This is recapitulation.

"Behold, I will make all things new."

— Revelation 21:5

A second meaning of the term is of a literary sort; here, recapitulation denotes "putting under headings." Initially, this second definition may appear at first less relevant, but it is quite applicable to our discussion. Imagine your favorite book … without any breaks between chapters, paragraphs or even words. Without capital letters or grammatical marks. It would be nonsense:

> thatwhichwasfromthebeginningwhichwehaveheardwhichwehave
> seenwithoureyeswhichwehavelookeduponandtouchedwith
> ourhandsthatwhichwasfromthebeginningwhichwehaveheard
> whichwehaveseenwithoureyeswhichwehavelookeduponand
> touchedwithourhandsconcerningthewordoflifethelifewasmade
> manifestandwesawitandtestifytoit

Yet, when the author's natural order is restored ("put under proper headings") — when all of the breaks are re-inserted between words and paragraphs — it is again sensible:

> *"That which was from the beginning, which we have heard, which we have seen with our eyes, which we have looked upon and touched with our hands, concerning the word of life—the life was made manifest, and we saw it, and testify to it."* (1 John 1:1–2)

Without such order, a book, any book would make little or no sense. Like such a book without order, fallen man cannot make sense of himself. So it is that when Christ enters man's story, the book begins to makes sense again: humanity and all of life is recapitulated, re-ordered as the Author intended from the beginning.

With Christ, man becomes sensible. Man can "read his own story" and make sense of it from beginning to end. In fact, with Christ, it is as if man reads his story *afresh*, aware of meaning, order and beauty that was not previously seen when his story was jumbled. "Behold," Christ tells us, "I make all things new" (Rev 21:5).

FOR REFLECTION

> As I reflect on my life experiences and wounds, in what ways am I being renewed in Christ? Where has he transformed me the most profoundly? Where do I need to place my confidence in Him, and allow Him to bring an area of my life "under the headings" ... where do I need to read my own story "afresh" and give thanks for the things that He has made new in His mercy and grace?

Man's dignity as made in the image and likeness of God (Gen 1:26–27), which was obscured through sin and threatened by death, is reclaimed by Christ. Indeed, all that was "subjected to futility," including all of creation, is recapitulated and "made new" in Christ (2 Cor 5:17):

> For the creation waits with eager longing for the revealing of the sons of God; for the creation was subjected to futility, not of its own will but by the will of him who subjected it in hope; because *the creation itself will be set free from its bondage to decay and obtain the glorious liberty of the children of God* (Rom 8:19).

A final point to see is that the *Catechism* explains that recapitulation is not merely a lens by which to explore the deeper unity of the Scriptures — it really is a means of taking *us* deeper into the mysteries of Christ: "For this reason Christ experienced all the stages of life, thereby giving communion with God to all men."[205]

Conclusion

What are we to take away from these chapters, in which we explored three themes: Covenant, Biblical typology and Recapitulation?

Above all, we should appreciate that there is within Sacred Scripture *a clear and deep pattern of inner unity*. In response, we must take great care with the Word of God, and seek to read Scripture more prayerfully and more attentively. The more assiduously we read the Bible, the clearer this unity will become for us, for this "unitive pattern" encompasses *the entire Bible*.

So, for all of their distinctive qualities, the seventy-three books of Sacred Scripture present us with a deep unity, and what connects all of them together is the God-man, Jesus Christ. When we read, study and pray the Scriptures in such ways, we will perceive a multitude of connections that the ancient Israelites, the Apostles and the early Christians saw.

- When we look upon Scripture with "covenant" eyes, we see more clearly the unfolding story of God's election of His beloved people; of His covenant love for Israel and the Church, and for all people at all times. Finally, we see the many blessings that are part of the larger covenant plan of God — even our own place in this plan.

- When we read, study and pray Scripture typologically, vigorously but prudently recognizing types and antitypes, we are engaging in an interpretative method that as ancient as the Temple itself. For the Catholic student of God's holy Word, typology is a richly rewarding way to see and proclaim the fullness of Christ to the people of God.

- Lastly, when we comprehend what the *Catechism* means by "recapitulation in Christ," *we go beyond* the notion of the "revelation of Christ" and even "redemption in Christ" (as indispensable as they are), and arrive at a deeper understanding of how Christ makes all things new. When we are appropriately aware of covenant, typology, and recapitulation, we are not just reading the letter of Scripture, but also the spirit of the sacred page:

Reading the Scriptures in such ways leads to an awakening — a discovery of the profound unity within the Word of God. Such reading takes practice, patience, and grace. It requires hard work … and is deeply rewarding. After such ardent reading on our part, the Word of God shines with a surprising yet familiar splendor, more than compensating for our time and labor.

Questions for Reflection

1. What is "biblical typology?" What is "recapitulation in Christ?" How are they related — and how are they distinct ways of approaching Scripture?
2. What "types" of Jesus come to mind, from my own understanding of the Old Testament? Of Mary? Of the Sacraments? Of the Church?
3. Recall the initial explanation of "recapitulation," and how it is found in the Catechism, along with two other terms — what are they? How do they "operate" in Scripture? (See CCC 516–518.)
4. How might these three qualities invigorate your study of Scripture? Start right now — open your Bible to your favorite passage. If you cannot think of one, turn to "The Wedding Feast at Cana" (John 2:1–11).

    a) Where or how is "revelation" evident in this passage, i.e., "What" is revealed: what truth about the Father, Son and/or Holy Spirit? The Disciples? The Church? Mary? Etc. (You may want to look at CCC 516 for assistance.)

    b) Where is "redemption" evident in this passage? (You may want to look at CCC 517 for assistance.)

    c) Where is "recapitulation" evident in this passage? (You may want to look at CCC 518 for assistance — and this chapter, since it was just covered, and in more depth than the other two.

For Further Study

Beale, Gregory and D. A. Carson, eds. *Commentary on the New Testament Use of the Old Testament.* Grand Rapids: Baker Academic, 2007. This resource is unique in that it provides commentary on each book of the New Testament, with a specific focus on its use of Old Testament. The commentary goes beyond mere citation of Old Testament sources or allusions and helps readers understand the context and nature of the Old and New Testament connections. See also Michael Duggan, *The Consuming Fire: A Christian Guide to the Old Testament.*

Huntington, IN: Our Sunday Visitor, 2010, which shows the relationship of each Old Testament book to the New Testament.

Danielou, Jean. *From Shadows to Reality: Studies in the Biblical Typology of the Fathers.* London: Burns & Oates, 1960.

France, R. T. *Jesus and the Old Testament.* Vancouver: Regent College Publishing, 1992.

Nichols, Aidan. "Imagination and Revelation: The Face of Christ in the Old Testament," *The Way* 21 (1981) 270–77.

————. *Lovely Like Jerusalem: The Fulfillment of the Old Testament in Christ and the Church.* San Francisco: Ignatius Press, 2007. A brief but perspicacious reflection on the relationship between the Old and New Testament. Nichols handles the biblical texts masterfully and, in particular, explains "typology" better than many longer attempts to do so. Additionally, *Lovely Like Jerusalem* is a work of patristic *resourcement* and is highly recommended.

Notes

197 "Typology," in *Catholic Bible Dictionary*, 929.

198 CCC 128.

199 Ibid.

200 Later re-presentations of the exodus narrative can be seen in Psa 77 and Wisd 10-18. Cf. B. S. Childs, "Memory and Tradition in Israel," *Studies in Biblical Theology*, 37 (Naperville, IL: Allenson, 1962) 60–63.

201 Aidan Nichols, *Lovely Like Jerusalem: The Fulfillment of the Old Testament in Christ and the Church* (San Francisco: Ignatius Press, 2007), 172.

202 Nichols, *Lovely Like Jerusalem*, 176.

203 CCC 129; cf. *DV* §19. It is beyond the scope of this chapter to discuss typology in the patristic era. More on patristic interpretation of Scripture will be discussed below.

204 Pope Benedict XVI, *VD* §13.

205 CCC 518.

> He is a slave to a sign who uses or worships a significant thing without knowing what it signifies.
>
> — *St. Augustine, On Interpretation, 3.9*

> The sacred page is ... the soul of sacred theology.
>
> *Dei Verbum §24*

Principle 5
God's Word Has Meaning(s)

Put Out Into the Deep

Following on the heels of the previous chapters, in which we explored the close relationship of the Old and New Testaments, we now turn our attention to the richness of *meaning* that is found within this unified Word.

Principle #5: Catholic Biblical interpretation affirms that God's Word is rich in meaning and a multiplicity of approaches can assist the exegete in explaining texts. No one method of interpretation is adequate in itself to plumb the depths of Scripture. Catholic exegetes thus benefit from exploration of various methods, including ancient, medieval, and modern biblical scholarship. Such an array of approaches can cast valuable light on the Sacred Page, provided one "reads" them within the tradition of the Church and according to the hermeneutics of faith.

In this chapter, we are going to examine a number of such methods and possibilities. Before beginning our journey through history, in search of possible ways that Catholic exegetes can draw out meaning from God's Word, suggestions are offered — one from antiquity and one that is quite recent.

The first bit of advice comes from the Scripture itself; specifically, from the author of the Book of Sirach:

> *He who devotes himself to the study of the law of the Most High will seek out the wisdom of all the ancients, and will be concerned with prophecies; he will preserve the discourse of notable men and penetrate*

the subtleties of parables; he will seek out the hidden meanings of prov-
erbs and be at home with the obscurities of parables ... He will direct
his counsel and knowledge aright, and meditate on his secrets. He will
reveal instruction in his teaching, and will glory in the law of the Lord's
covenant. Many will praise his understanding, and it will never be
blotted out; his memory will not disappear, and his name will live
through all generations. Nations will declare his wisdom, and the con-
gregation will proclaim his praise; if he lives long, he will leave a name
greater than a thousand, and if he goes to rest, it is enough for him. (Sir
39:1–3, 7–11)

This passage offers salient tips for the biblical exegete. First, Sirach
notes that the art of biblical interpretation is indeed an ancient one (v. 1).
As we search for meaning in Scripture, we would be wise to remember
that the river of interpretation is deep and it is wide. Those "devoted to
the study of the law" may traverse over many seas, seeking wisdom from
the ancients (v. 1) — as well as from medieval, modern and even contemporary biblical thinkers.

Such navigation involves genuine effort and requires patience and
care. Yet, we are wise to make such efforts and not merely read and interpret Scripture on our own. So, along with Sirach, we could say that
the first thing necessary for the wise interpreter is to "put out into the
deep" (cf. Luke 5:4). Secondly, Sirach urges the biblical interpreter to be
thoughtful in what he learns: it is not enough to search for meaning; the
student of Scripture must also "*direct his counsel and knowledge aright*" —
carefully meditating on what he learned and assimilating this knowledge.

The other piece of advice is much more recent and comes to us
from the Pontifical Biblical Commission:

In devoting themselves to their task, Catholic exegetes have to pay
due account to the *historical character* of biblical revelation. For the
two testaments express in human words bearing the stamp of their
time the historical revelation communicated by God in various
ways concerning himself and his plan of salvation. Consequently,
exegetes have to make use of the historical-critical method. They
cannot, however, accord to it a sole validity. All methods pertaining
to the interpretation of texts are entitled to make their contribution to the exegesis of the Bible. In their work of interpretation

Catholic exegetes must never forget that what they are interpreting is the *Word of God*. Their common task is not finished when they have simply determined sources, defined forms or explained literary procedures. *They arrive at the true goal of their work only when they have explained the meaning of the biblical text as God's word for today.* To this end they must take into consideration the various hermeneutical perspectives which help toward grasping the contemporary meaning of the biblical message and which make it responsive to the needs of those who read Scripture today.[206]

While Catholic students must certainly pay attention to the "historical character of biblical revelation" (cf. Principle #2, above), the PBC insists here that the historical-critical (or frankly, any other) method cannot become the sole basis by which we interpret Scripture.

FOR REFLECTION	*In what ways am I prepared to put out into the deep? In what ways do I need to allow my academic study of Scripture to be informed and prepared for by prayer?*

"Open up the treasury door for us, Lord, at the prayers of our supplications; let our prayer serve as our ambassador, reconciling us with your divinity."
— Ephrem the Syrian, *Armenian Hymn No. 1*. (From *The Syriac Fathers on Prayer and the Spiritual Life*. Trans. by S. Brock. Kalamazoo, MI: Cistercian Publications, 1987, 36.)

As the PBC urges elsewhere in the document, "One of the characteristics of the Bible is precisely *the absence of a sense of systematization and the presence, on the contrary, of things held in dynamic tension.*"[207] Thus, we should *always* seek clarity, but at the same time, we should be wary of interpretations that are excessively "simplistic."[208]

If we heed the above pieces of advice, both ancient and modern, we will be better prepared to launch out into the deep and wide river in search of biblical meaning.

Before we put out into the deep, the last order of business is to be sure that we are clear about: (a) the four senses of Scripture; and (b) something known as *Sensus plenior*.

The Four Horses

First, the *Catechism* is very clear that, historically, we can trace one of two "planes of meaning" in all of Scripture. Broadly speaking, these two planes, or "senses of Scripture," are the ***literal*** and the ***spiritual***.[209]

Building on this primary division, the *Catechism* goes on to explain that the spiritual sense is further "subdivided into the ***allegorical***, ***moral***, and ***anagogical*** senses."[210] What makes Scripture so rich for all who read it and seek meaning from it are these four senses of Scripture. In the past, but not as much today, they were together known as the *Quadriga* (Latin: "Four Horses"). As the *Catechism* puts it, together, these four horses pull the cart of meaning, and guarantee "all its richness to the living reading of Scripture in the Church."[211] Following this, the *Catechism* provides a basic explanation as to each of the four senses of Scripture:

> **The literal sense** is the meaning conveyed by the words of Scripture and discovered by exegesis, following the rules of sound interpretation. "All other senses of Sacred Scripture are based on the literal."[212]
>
> **The spiritual sense**. Thanks to the unity of God's plan, not only the text of Scripture but the realities and events to which it speaks are signs.
>
> > 1. The *allegorical sense*. We can acquire a more profound understanding of events by recognizing their significance in Christ; thus the crossing of the Red Sea is a sign or type of Christ's victory and also of Christian Baptism.
> > 2. The *moral sense*. Events reported in Scripture ought to *lead us to act justly*. As St. Paul says, they were written "for our instruction."
> > 3. The *anagogical sense* (Greek: *anagoge*, "leading"). We can view realities and events in terms of their *eternal significance*, leading us toward our true homeland: thus the Church on earth is a sign of the heavenly Jerusalem.[213]

A medieval couplet from the thirteenth century helps us recall these four senses — and appreciate their instrumentality in drawing meaning from Scripture:

> *Littera gesta docet, quid credas allegoria, moralis quid agas, quid speras anagogia.*[214]

Translated, this means:

> *The Letter speaks of deeds; Allegory to faith;*
> *The Moral how to act; Anagogy our destiny.*

Unfortunately, in the modern era, some historical-critical scholars reacted negatively to this "multiplicity of meanings" in Scripture, suggesting that:

> A text cannot have at the same time more than one meaning. All the effort of historical-critical exegesis goes into defining "the" precise sense of this or that biblical text seen within the circumstances in which it was produced.[215]

However, such restriction of meaning to a single sense is unwarranted and has, as the PBC states, subsequently "run aground on the conclusions of theories of language and of philosophical hermeneutics, both of which affirm that written texts are open to a plurality of meaning."[216] Additionally, the following guidelines are offered regarding the four senses of Scripture:

1. The *literal* sense:
   a. Is not only legitimate, it is indispensable as the starting point from which all interpretation follows. It is "that which has been expressed directly by the inspired human authors. Since it is the fruit of inspiration, this sense is also intended by God, as principal author. One arrives at this sense by means of a careful analysis of the text, within its literary and historical context."[217]
   b. Is not to be confused with a "literalist" (or "literalistic") manner of reading Scripture, as is common among fundamentalist interpretations. "It is not sufficient to translate a text word for word in order to obtain its literal sense. One must understand the text according to the literary conventions of the time."
   c. Does not allow us to attribute whatever meaning we desire. To do so, the PBC suggests, is like "cutting off the biblical message from its root, which is the Word of God in its historical communication; it would also mean opening the door to interpretations of a wildly subjective nature."[218]

2. The *spiritual* sense(s):

    a. Can generally be understood as "the meaning expressed by the biblical texts when read under the influence of the Holy Spirit, in the context of the paschal mystery of Christ and of the new life which flows from it ... It is therefore quite acceptable to reread the Scriptures in the light of this new context, which is that of life in the Spirit."[219]

    b. "Is not to be confused with subjective interpretations stemming from the imagination or intellectual speculation."[220] Rather, all spiritual interpretation flows in one way or another from the paschal mystery, "in all its inexhaustible richness, which constitutes the summit of the divine intervention in the history of Israel, to the benefit of all mankind."[221]

    c. Is orientated towards the life of the Spirit. In fact, one can properly engage in spiritual interpretation to the extent that "one then holds together three levels of reality: the biblical text, the paschal mystery and the present circumstances of life in the Spirit."[222]

Sensus Plenior

Following its discussion of the spiritual sense of Scripture, the *IBC* document speaks of the *sensus plenior* ("fuller sense") of Scripture, which is:

> The deeper meaning of the text, intended by God but not clearly expressed by the human author. Its existence in the biblical text comes to be known when one studies the text in the light of other biblical texts which utilize it or in its relationship with the internal development of revelation.[223]

Sensus plenior has its roots in Principle #1 (Inspiration) and is based on the conviction that a Scriptural text might contain a meaning that even the author is not fully aware of. The *IBC* document gives the example of Matt 1:23 ("*Behold, a virgin shall conceive and bear a son, and his name shall be called Emmanuel*" which means, *God with us*"), which gives a fuller sense to the prophetic text in Isaiah (Isa 7:14). Thus, texts in which *sensus plenior* seems to be operative will illuminate even deeper truths and fresh possibilities in Scripture:

This deeper truth will be more fully revealed in the course of time—on the one hand, through further divine interventions which clarify the meaning of texts and, on the other, through the insertion of texts into the canon of Scripture. In these ways there is created a new context, which brings out fresh possibilities of meaning that had lain hidden in the original context.[224]

From the beginning, Jewish biblical exegesis employed a diversity of means to uncover meaning in Scripture.

With the above helps we now turn to some critical ways in which the Word of God has been interpreted over time.

Patristic and Medieval Biblical Interpretation

From the apostles and the apostolic Fathers onward, the landscape of Christian biblical interpretation of both Old and New Testament, is, to one degree or another, grounded in the person of Christ as the fulfillment of Scripture.

As the *IBC* document summarizes, the larger contribution of patristic exegesis in particular is inestimable:

> *The fathers of the church, who had a particular role in the process of the formation of the canon, likewise have a foundational role in relation to the living tradition which unceasingly accompanies and guides the church's reading and interpretation of Scripture. Within the broader current of the great tradition, the particular contribution of patristic exegesis consists in this: to have drawn out from the totality of Scripture the basic orientations which shaped the doctrinal tradition of the church and to have provided a rich theological teaching for the instruction and spiritual sustenance of the faithful.*[225]

It is beyond the scope of this chapter to treat every major development in the patristic and medieval eras. In our search for "meanings" in Scripture, let us mention some key figures and movements that exemplify the richness of early Christian and medieval interpretation, beginning with the early Church fathers.

St. Justin Martyr (A.D. 100–165)

Among the many key biblical insights from Justin, what is perhaps most crucial is his absolute confirmation of Christianity through the use of the Old Testament. Justin is one of the first to respond to the heretic Marcion, who rejected the Old Testament. Justin explained that major Christological features (e.g., Virgin birth, suffering, death, and resurrection) were all prefigured in the texts of Old Testament. Elsewhere, in *Dialogue with Trypho*, written as a dialogue between Justin and a Jewish rabbi over the course of several days, he discusses, for example, the Law and circumcision, with an eye to showing how the Old Covenant is fulfilled in the New Covenant.[226]

"This is the one who made the heavens and the earth, and who in the beginning created man, who was proclaimed through the law and prophets, who became human via the virgin, who was hanged upon a tree, who was buried in the earth, who was resurrected from the dead, and who ascended to the heights of heaven, who sits at the right hand of the Father, who has authority to judge and to save everything, through whom the Father created everything from the beginning of the world to the end of the age."

— St. Melito of Sardis, *Concerning the Passover*, 104

St. Irenaeus of Lyon (A.D. 130–200)

One of the greatest of the apostolic fathers, Irenaeus recognized that more advanced methods of interpretation were needed and he accomplished this. *Against Heresies* (c. 180), Irenaeus' masterwork, contains an extensive critique of many forms of Gnosticism and many other early heresies. Irenaeus defended the unity of the Old and New Testament. He carefully showed how they do not reveal two gods but one true God, who is the Lord of all history. He also showed how everything that has happened in history is part of God's divine plan for humanity:

> If anyone, therefore, reads the Scriptures with attention, he will find in them an account of Christ, and a foreshadowing of the new calling. For Christ is the treasure which was hid in the field, that is, in this world (for "the field is the world"); but the treasure hid in the Scriptures is Christ, since He was pointed out by means of types and parables … For every prophecy, before its fulfillment, is

to men [full of] enigmas and ambiguities. But when the time has arrived, and the prediction has come to pass, then the prophecies have a clear and certain exposition ... When at this present time the law is read to the Jews, it is like a fable; for they do not possess the explanation of all things pertaining to the advent of the Son of God, which took place in human nature; but when it is read by the Christians, it is a treasure, hid indeed in a field, but brought to light by the cross of Christ.[227]

Irenaeus held to two essential rules for the interpretation of Scripture: *Apostolic tradition* and *Clarity*. He considered the tradition of the apostles as the key to unlock the Old Testament.[228] In a related fashion, he suggested that the Valentinians (a Gnostic group) took what was obvious and clear from the apostles, and in fact made it unclear.[229]

The Church Fathers present a theology that still has great value today because at its heart is the study of sacred Scripture as a whole ... Their example can teach modern exegetes a truly religious approach to sacred Scripture, and likewise an interpretation that is constantly attuned to the criterion of communion with the experience of the Church.

— Pope Benedict XVI, *Verbum Domini* § 37

St. Jerome (A.D. 347–420)

Perhaps no figure from the patristic era is more associated with Scripture and its interpretation and translation than St. Jerome. Most notably of his many accomplishments, of course, was Jerome's translation of Scripture into Latin. The Vulgate, his translation, from the original languages into Latin, the common language of the day, did not gain wide approval initially. Yet, buy the ninth century it was utilized in practically the entire Church and was declared the "official text" of the Church at the Council of Trent on April 8, 1546.[230]

Jerome's great contributions are all the more impressive when one looks more closely at his personal devotion to Scripture, as the following quote attests:

Read assiduously and learn as much as you can. Let sleep find you holding your Bible and when your head nods let it be resting on the sacred page.[231]

So long as you are in your own country regard your cell as your orchard; there you can gather Scripture's various fruits and enjoy the pleasures it affords you. Always have a book in your hands and read it; learn the Psalter by heart; pray unceasingly; watch over your senses lest idle thoughts creep in.[232]

FOR REFLECTION

Which Church fathers have been the most fruitful in terms of my prayer and study of the Scriptures? Which have been the most challenging? Why?

St. Augustine (A.D. 354–430)

The great doctor of the Church, St. Augustine likewise made immense contributions to the study of Sacred Scripture: his disputation of various heretical interpretations,[233] his insistence on understanding the original biblical languages, the importance of the *rule of faith*, and the primacy of "love" in all Christian exegesis.

Like many of the Church fathers, much of Augustine's commentary on Scripture is homiletic in form. That is, it is designed to exhort as much as to instruct; to form in moral character and to strengthen Christian discipleship. Yet, aside from his many biblical commentaries, Augustine also gave us a masterwork on the work of biblical interpretation: *De Doctrina Christiana* ("On Christian Doctrine"). It consists of four books on how to philosophically approach Scripture, as well as how to interpret and teach it properly. In *De Doctrina*, he argues that the words of Scripture are absolutely true and any person of faith and goodwill could sufficiently interpret it; in contrast, any person who distorted the Scriptures, or simply did not understand them was not interpreting them in a spirit of charity. In Book I, he discussed the notion of things and "signs." Signs not only represent meaning; rather, they are themselves things and thus possess meaning in themselves. In his treatment of things and signs, and their proper use, Augustine concludes that the only thing truly to be enjoyed is God himself. In Book II, he continues this discussion of things and signs, and lists seven steps in the path of wisdom:

- Fear of God
- Obedience of faith
- Scientia (knowledge)

- Fortitude
- Good counsel
- Purity of heart
- And finally, Wisdom

In Book III Augustine concludes his examination of signs and things, believing that as his readers overcome ignorance of their particular qualities, they will better understand how to interpret and live by the Holy Scriptures. Here, he deals with "ambiguous" signs and lays out rules for determining if a sign is literal or figurative, with his essential rule being that no interpretation can be true which does not promote charity: love of God and love of man.

FOR REFLECTION

"'My soul is thirsty for the living God' (Psa 41:2) ... This is what I am thirsty for, to come and appear before Him. I am thirsty in my pilgrimage, in my running; I shall be filled upon my arrival."

— *St. Augustine,* Exposition on the Book of Psalms. *(Trans. by A. Cleveland Coxe,* A Select Library of the Nicene and Post-Nicene Fathers of the Christian Church, *ed. Phillip Schaff. First Series. Vol. III. New York: The Christian Literature Co., 1886–90), 132.*

Book IV constitutes the second half of *De Doctrina*, and a departure from the previous discussion of signs and things. Here, Augustine holds up the biblical authors as the most majestic of all orators and writers, far surpassing all others in both eloquence of rhetoric and in wisdom. Lastly, he urges all teachers of Scripture to be ever mindful of the great responsibility of their work, and the necessity of living in harmony with their teaching so that they may be an example to all. Augustine held that for some people, *the Christian teacher is "the only Scripture they will ever read," thus our character must exemplify Christ and His Apostles.*

The above comments, concerning Justin, Irenaeus, Jerome and Augustine, by no means exhaust what could be said about these great figures as regards to Scripture. Yet, our brief discussion alerts us to some of the primary characteristics of the patristic era with regard to Sacred Scripture. It also alerts us to the concerns that the fathers had with respect to the Bible, and that we too should be mindful of in our own study.

Two Rival Schools: Alexandria and Antioch

In the patristic era, there were two influential schools of thought with regard to the interpretation of Scripture. The first was the Catechetical School at Alexandria, which emphasized *allegorisis* (allegory). Origen (c. A.D. 185–253), whose biblical interpretation is typical of the Alexandrian approach, argued that not every text had a literal sense (though most did). However, he said that all texts had a spiritual sense, and the spiritual sense was the beginning point for all biblical inquiry. Beyond Origen, this emphasis on the spiritual and allegorical characterized all who ascribed to the Alexandrian approach, such as Clement of Alexandria, Cyril and Gregory of Nyssa, who wrote this in his commentary on the Song of Songs:

> In all these cases and others like them it is incumbent on us to search the Scriptures and to pay careful attention to the reading and to track it down in every way, *if we can somehow find a meaning more lofty than the immediate sense of the words guiding our thought to things more divine and incorporeal.*[234]

In contrast (and opposition) to the allegorical approach of Alexandria was the Catechetical School at Antioch. The Antiochene approach was founded on the principles of Artistotelian logic. The Antiochene approach insisted on the empirical and historical meaning in Scripture, i.e., the literal sense. Individuals such as Diodore and Theodore of Mopsuestia not only opposed the "spiritual first" approach of Alexandria, but actively combated allegorical interpretations. In their writings, they argued that allegory was nothing less than an imposition upon a biblical text. Moreover, they insisted that such allegorical conclusions distorted the plain, literal meaning intended by the biblical author. As such, the two schools developed a vigorous rivalry between one another.

Nevertheless, the Antiochene approach did not entirely restrict all meaning in Scripture to the literal sense. For example, the Antiochene adherents believed that the biblical prophecies of the Old Testament often contained a double meaning — the original intent of the passage and the fulfillment in the New Testament. Antioch also developed *theoria*, an approach that emphasized the literal but allowed for higher planes of contemplation, provided they did not abrogate the literal sense. One of the most well known figures and prolific commentators from the Antiochene approach was St. John Chrysostom (c. A.D. 347–407). Chrysostom's many commentaries begin with the literal interpretation of the passage. Yet, he did not altogether exclude *allegorisis* but preferred typology, at least, when he did make use of such methods.

The Synod frequently insisted on the need for a prayerful approach to the sacred text as a fundamental element in the spiritual life of every believer, in the various ministries and states in life, with particular reference to *lectio divina*.

— Pope Benedict XVI, *Verbum Domini* § 86

Medieval Interpretation and Other Developments Leading Up to the Enlightenment

In the post-Augustinian period, biblical exegetes were more concerned with supporting and defending theological positions than in biblical study for its own sake. While too often mischaracterized as the so-called "dark ages," the period from A.D. 500–1500 was a rich period of intellectual activity. Yet, in many ways, it was more a period of *consolidation* than of *creativity*. By the sixth century, the Church had become one of the primary (if not the primary) institutions in the world, and the heiress of the Roman Empire. Theology developed as the Queen of the Sciences. Cathedral schools developed and run by clergy flourished in this period. After A.D. 1000, some emerged as the great early universities of European history. Along with other monastic developments, beautiful liturgical editions of Sacred Scripture were produced at great cost. At this time, ***lectio divina*** emerged as a principle way of contemplating Scripture.

Lectio divina (Latin: "divine reading") is, in essence, "praying the Scriptures." It consists of a fourfold movement:

Lectio — **Read** and re-read a small passage of the Word of God, perhaps several times, in a slow, gradual and tranquil manner.

Meditatio — **Meditate** upon what was read, not in an analytic manner, or seeking knowledge; rather, allow the Spirit to explain what the Word is saying.

Oratio — **Pray** and *speak* to God about the light that you received from the reading and meditation.

Contempatio — **Contemplate** and continue praying, now in *silence*; receive God's love, draw close to Him.

The reader is urged — truly urged to "pray the Scriptures" and to develop a practice of spiritual and prayerful reading of Scripture.

Today, this medieval practice is experiencing something of a revival, but still, many people are unfamiliar with its benefits. Thanks in part to the emphasis Pope Benedict XVI has placed upon *lectio divina*, new generations of Christians are tapping into its riches. At a World Youth Day gathering, the pope explained "how it works" and encouraged young adults and everyone:

> A time-honored way to study and savor the word of God is *lectio divina* which constitutes a real and veritable spiritual journey marked out in stages. After the *lectio*, which consists of reading and re-reading a passage from Sacred Scripture and taking in the main elements, we proceed to *meditatio*. This is a moment of interior reflection in which the soul turns to God and tries to understand what his word is saying to us today. Then comes *oratio* in which we linger to talk with God directly. Finally we come to *contemplatio*. This helps us to keep our hearts attentive to the presence of Christ whose word is "a lamp shining in a dark place, until the day dawns and the morning star rises in your hearts" (2 *Pet* 1:19). Reading, study and meditation of the Word should then flow into a life of consistent fidelity to Christ and his teachings.[235]

The reader is urged — truly urged — to "pray the Scriptures" and to develop a practice of spiritual and prayerful reading of Scripture. Two important remarks about *lectio divina* should be added. First, for those who are newer to the practice, rest assured that it need not be a "long" process in terms of time spent doing it. Many have found *just a few minutes a day* a very helpful way to pray the Scriptures and meet the Lord in His word. (I suggest just seven minutes a day for those who are just beginning to discover this classical discipline.) Second, and I can't emphasize this enough: *don't worry if you are "doing it correctly."* The point is to encounter the Lord in His Word and to feel His loving presence as one prays the Scriptures. For those that want more "formal instruction" and guidance on the four movements of *Lection Divina*, several resources are listed at the end of this chapter.

Between Augustine and Aquinas, the two great ancient and medieval Doctors of the Church, spiritual exegesis of one sort or another flourished. For example, St. Bernard of Clairvaux produced *Eighty-six Homilies on the Canticle of Canticles*, and he concentrated on the union of the Divine logos and the soul of the Christian believer, as a kind of "spiritual marriage."

Some of the first "multi-author" biblical commentaries were produced shortly after the first millennium. Known as *Catenae* (Latin, "chain"), such works brought together a "chain of interpretation" from the earlier patristic era into a single volume of commentary. An excellent example of this is St. Thomas' *Catenae Aurea*, the "Golden Chain."

In Thomas Aquinas, however, a new watermark is reached in biblical interpretation. The earlier debates in the patristic era, concerning the literal versus the spiritual sense were definitively clarified and resolved by St. Thomas Aquinas. This is seen in three interrelated steps of Thomas.

First, Thomas advocated for "clarity" in Scripture. He insisted that *any given word in Scripture could only yield one sense*, so that there was no confusion.[236]

In articulating this position, Thomas was not denying the multiple senses found in Scripture overall; only that every word in Scripture would yield its proper meaning, so that there was no confusion. Second, and above all, Thomas insisted upon the literal sense as the foundation upon which all other interpretation is accomplished:

> In [Sacred Scripture] no confusion results, for *all the senses are founded on one — the literal — from which alone can any argument be drawn.*[237]

Finally, Thomas insists that from the literal sense, we can indeed derive spiritual meaning from Sacred Scripture, according to a fourfold division:

> So, whereas in every other science things are signified by words, this science has the property, that the things signified by the words have themselves also a signification. Therefore that first signification whereby words signify things belongs to the first sense, the historical or *literal*. That signification whereby things signified by words have themselves also a signification is called the spiritual sense, which is based on the literal, and presupposes it. Now this spiritual

sense has a threefold division ... Therefore, so far as the things of the Old Law signify the things of the New Law, there is the *allegorical* sense; so far as the things done in Christ, or so far as the things which signify Christ, are types of what we ought to do, there is the *moral* sense. But so far as they signify what relates to eternal glory, there is the *anagogical* sense.[238]

Following the medieval period, the Reformers — both Protestant and Catholic — sought to sharpen doctrinal positions *ad fontes*, going back to the original sources of Scripture and the early fathers. In terms of Catholic exegesis, some of the most significant developments of this period occur at the Council of Trent (1545–63), particularly the definitive declaration of the canon of Scripture (cf. Chapter 4) and the articulation of "divine revelation" as being comprised of both Sacred Scripture and Sacred Tradition. While Protestant developments operated in a similarly *ad fontes* fashion, with Luther and Calvin drawing upon Scripture (especially St. Paul) and St. Augustine, the key distinction from Catholic exegesis was a resolute conviction that "Scripture alone" (*sola Scriptura*) was the only inerrant source of divine revelation, and which was sufficient for the salvation of souls. As Martin Luther wrote in his German essay, "God's Word shall establish articles of faith, and no one else, not even an angel can do so."[239]

There are numerous issues with *sola Scriptura*; not least of which is its misunderstanding and abrogation of Tradition. This is all the more ironic when one recalls that Scripture itself is part of Tradition and that its canon was ratified through Tradition.

In his objection to *sola Scriptura* (and its primary "Scriptural proof" of 2 Tim 3:16), the soon to be canonized John Henry Newman wrote,

It is quite evident that this passage furnishes no argument whatever that the Sacred Scripture, without Tradition, is the *sole rule of faith*; for although Sacred Scripture is *profitable* for these four ends, still it is not said to be *sufficient*. The Apostle requires the aid of Tradition (2 Thess. 2:15). Moreover, the Apostle here refers to the Scriptures which Timothy was taught in his infancy. Now, a good part of the New Testament was not written in his boyhood: some of the Catholic Epistles were not written even when St. Paul wrote this, and none of the Books of the New Testament were then placed on the canon of the Scripture books. He refers, then, to the Scriptures of the Old Testament, and if the argument from the passage proved anything, it would prove too much, i.e., that the Scriptures of the New Testament were not necessary for a rule of faith.[240]

Conclusion

In this chapter, we were introduced to Principle #5, "God's Word Has Meanings." Fundamental to this principle is that God's Word has abundance of meaning(s), and from the ancient Jewish and earliest Christian interpreters, we can observe a number of approaches to the interpretation of a given passage of Scripture.

We discussed the two primary "senses" of Scripture (literal and spiritual) and discovered three aspects of the "spiritual sense" (allegorical, moral, anagogical — or "heavenly"). Related to this, we learned about "*sensus plenior*," the idea that a text can have a multiplicity of meanings, and given Divine authorship, a human author (and his original audience) may be unaware of a "deeper" meaning of a text, which becomes clear only at a later point in salvation history.

We then discussed some of the major figures and schools of interpretative thought in the ancient periods. We noted some of the vital contributions of individual patristic figures, such as Origen and Augustine. We compared and contrasted the Alexandrian (allegorical) and Antiochene (literal) approaches, and made similar observations about major figures and developments in the medieval period. Here, we familiarized ourselves with the medieval discipline of "praying the Scriptures," known as *lectio divina*, and strongly encouraged the reader to take up the practice.

This now takes us to our next chapter, where we will continue our discussion of Principle #5, and examine the search for meaning in God's Word — in the modern period.

Questions for Reflection

1. Has my own interpretation of Scripture taken into account the Four Senses of Scripture (Literal, Allegorical, Moral, Anagogical)? Have I given preference — knowingly or not — to one of these "over" the others? How can the four senses help me to appreciate the depth and unity of Scripture? What about *sensus*

plenior (Have I been aware of it, etc.)? What cautions are required with respect to both the four senses and *sensus plenior?*

2. Identify one fresh insight on reading Scripture from one of the Church fathers or medieval figures discussed in this chapter. Why is this insight particularly helpful in your own reading of Scripture?

3. What does my prayer life look like — and is their room within it to "pray the Scriptures?" How might *lectio divina* deepen my experience of Scripture? If I have done *lectio divina*, what have been some of the fruits? If it is something new, which passage of Scripture would I like to begin with? Why?

For Further Study

Aquinas, Thomas. *Catena Aurea: A Commentary on the Four Gospels Collected Out of the Works of the Fathers* (and edited by John Henry Newman). Southampton: Saint Austin Press, 1997.

―――. *Commentary on the Gospel of John 3 Volume Set* (Thomas Aquinas in Translation). James A. Weisheipl, Fabian Larcher, trans. Introduction and annotation by Matthew Levering and Daniel Keating. Washington, D.C.: CUA Press, 2010. A landmark commentary on the Fourth Gospel, these lectures were delivered to Dominican friars when Thomas Aquinas was at the height of his theological powers, when he was also composing the *Summa theologiae*. For numerous reasons, the *Summa* has received far more attention over the centuries than has his *Commentary on the Gospel of John*. However, scholars today recognize Aquinas's biblical commentaries as central sources for understanding his theological vision and for appreciating the scope of his *Summa theologiae*.

Brewer, D. Instone. *In Potipher's House: Techniques and Assumptions in Jewish Exegesis Before 70 C.E. TSAJ* 30. Tübingen: Mohr Siebeck, 1992.

Evans, C. A. and W. F. Stinesspring, eds. *Early Jewish and Christian Exegesis: Studies in Memory of William Hugh Brownlee.* Atlanta: Scholars Press, 1987.

Finan, Thomas and Vincent Twomey, eds. *Scriptural Interpretation in the Fathers: Letter and Spirit.* Dublin: Four Courts Press, 1995.

Fishbane, M. *Biblical Interpretation in Ancient Israel.* Oxford: Clarendon Press, 1985.

Gorday, Peter. *Principles of Patristic Exegesis.* Lewiston, NY: Edwin Mellen Press, 1983.

Froelich, Karlfried (ed.). *Biblical Interpretation in the Early Church.* Philadelphia: Fortress, 1984.

Oden, Thomas C. & Christopher H. Hall, eds. *The Ancient Christian Commentary on Scripture.* Downers Grove, IL: Intervarsity Press, 1998. This series revives the medieval tradition of biblical catenae, drawing upon the biblical text verse by verse, citing various Church fathers. Twenty-nine volumes on the Old and New Testament are now available.

O'Keefe, John and R.R. Reno. *Sanctified Vision: An Introduction to Early Christian Interpretation of the Bible.* Baltimore: Johns Hopkins, 2005.

Valkenberg, Wilhelm G. *"Did Not Our Hearts Burn?" The Place and Function of Holy Scripture in the Theology of St. Thomas Aquinas.* Utrecht: Thomas Instituut te Utrecht, 1990.

Wilken, Robert L. *The Spirit of Early Christian Thought: Seeking the Face of God.* New Haven: Yale University Press, 2003.

Simonetti, Manlio. *Biblical Interpretation in the Early Church: An Historical Introduction to Patristic Exegesis.* Edinburgh: T & T Clark, 1994.

Lectio Divina Resources

Binz, Stephen. *Conversing with God in Scripture: A Contemporary Appoach to Lectio Divina* (Frederick, MD: Word Among Us Press, 2008).

———. *Lectio Divina Bible Study: Learning to Pray in Scripture* (Huntington, IN: Our Sunday Visitor Press, 2009).

———. *Lectio Divina Bible Study: The Mass in Scripture* (Huntington, IN: Our Sunday Visitor Press, 2009).

———. *Lectio Divina Bible Study: The Sacraments in Scripture* (Huntington, IN: Our Sunday Visitor Press, 2009).

Gray, Timothy. *Praying Scripture for a Change: An Introduction to Lectio Divina* (West Chester, PA: Ascension Press, 2009).

Notes

206 *IBC*, III.C.1.a, b.

207 *IBC*, III.A.2.g.

208 Ibid.

209 CCC 115.

210 Ibid.

211 Ibid.

212 CCC 116; For a more detailed discussion cf. Thomas Aquinas, *Summa Theologica*, I, 1, 10, ad. I.

213 CCC 117.

214 Attributed to Augustine of Dacia, *Rotulus pugillaris*, I; cf. CCC 118.

215 *IBC*, II.B.c.

216 *IBC*, II.B.d.

217 *IBC*, II.B.1.c.

218 *IBC*, II.B.1.g.

219 *IBC*, II.B.2.b.

220   *IBC*, II.B.2.f.

221   *IBC*, II.B.2.f.

222   *IBC*, II.B.2.g.

223   *IBC*, II.B.3.a. Cf. R. E. Brown, *The Sensus Plenior of Sacred Scripture* (S.T.L. Diss.; St. Mary's Seminary & University, 1953; Baltimore, 1955).

224   *IBC*, II.B.3.b.

225   *IBC*, III.B.2.b; cf. *DAS* §28-30; *DV* §23.

226   An exquisitely rich example of this sort of argumentation from roughly the same period is from St. Melito of Sardis, in his *Peri tou Pascha* ("Concerning the Passover"). Every student of Scripture should be acquainted with this text, as a great example of this promise/fulfillment schema, and frankly, for its beauty.

227   Irenaeus, *Against Heresies*, 4.26.1. Commenting on his method, Mgr. Philippe Delhaye, former Secretary General of the International Theological Commission said, "St. Irenaeus was without doubt the first theologian to construct a system where the harmonization of the inspired written texts and the tradition of the Magisterium was explicitly and continually affirmed. For the Bishop of Lyon, it is the preaching of Christ which holds first place" (*L'Osservatore Romano*, 9 February 1987).

228   "Through none others do we know the disposition of our salvation, than those through whom the gospel came to us, first heralding it, then by the will of God delivering to us the Scriptures, which were to be the foundation and pillar of our faith … But … we challenge [the heretics regarding] … what that tradition is, which is from the Apostles, which is guarded by the succession of elders in the churches … they oppose themselves to tradition, saying that they are wiser, not only than those elders, but even than the Apostles. On the contrary, the Tradition of the Apostles, manifested in the whole world, is open in every Church to all who see the truth … And, since it is a long matter in a work like this to enumerate these successions, we will refute them by pointing to the tradition of that greatest and most ancient and universally known Church, founded and constituted at Rome by the two most glorious Apostles, Peter and Paul, a tradition which she has had and a faith which she proclaims to all men from those Apostles" (Irenaeus, *Against Heresies* 3,1-3).

229   "They endeavor to explain ambiguous passages of Scripture … they have constructed another god, weaving, as I said before, ropes of sand, and affixing a more important to a less important question. For no question can be solved by means of another which itself awaits solution; nor … can an ambiguity be explained by means of another ambiguity, or enigmas by means of another greater enigma, but things of such character receive their solution from those which are manifest, and consistent and clear" (Irenaeus, *Against Heresies*, 2.10.1).

230   "Moreover, the same holy council considering that not a little advantage will accrue to the Church of God if it be made known which of all the Latin editions of the sacred books now in circulation is to be regarded as authentic, ordains and declares that the old Latin Vulgate Edition, which, in use for so many hundred years, has been approved by the Church, be in public lectures, disputations, sermons and expositions held as authentic, and that no one dare or presume under any pretext whatsoever to reject it" (Council of Trent, *Decretum de Editione et Usu Sacrorum Librorum*, April 8th 1546).

231   Jerome, *Letter to Eustochius*, 22.

232   *Jerome, Letter to Rusticus*,125, 7, 3.

233   E.g., Augustine, *On Genesis: Against the Manichees*.

234   Gregory of Nyssa, *Commentary on the Song of Songs*, Preface.

235   Pope Benedict XVI, "Message to the Youth of the World on the Occasion of the 21st World Youth Day (April 9, 2006)." Available online: http://www.vatican.va/holy_father/ benedict_xvi/messages/youth/documents/hf_ben-xvi_mes_20060222_youth_en.html.

236   Aquinas, *Summa Theologica*, 1.1.10.

237   Aquinas, *Summa Theologica*, 1.1.10

238   Aquinas, *Summa Theologica*, 1.1.10.

239   Martin Luther, *Schmalkaldische Artikel*, II, 15.

240   John Henry Newman, *On the Inspiration of Scripture*, 131. Cf. *Not by Scripture Alone: A Catholic Critique of Sola Scriptura,* R. Sungenis, ed. (Mulvane, KS: Queenship Publishing), 1998.

CHAPTER 11

Modern Biblical Interpretation

There are numerous developments — monumental developments under the broader category of "modern" biblical interpretation. These developments are complex and involve many figures from philosophy[241] and biblical studies[242] and cannot be adequately (or even minimally) treated here. From Prussian philosopher Immanuel Kant (1724–1804), and his great questions, *"What can I know?"* and *"What must I do?;"* [243] to German philosopher Friedrich Nietzsche and his infamous quote, *"God is dead,"* [244] the Enlightenment project, which had begun in earnest in French and German philosophical quarters, soon spread to the world of biblical studies.

With respect to Scripture, the "first wave" of the Age of Reason (often at the expense of faith) hit Old Testament studies, with the biblical criticism of Julius Wellhausen (1844–1918)[245] and the Documentary Hypothesis supplanting the traditional view of Mosaic authorship[246] of the Pentateuch, which was universally accepted until the late 1600s. With the Documentary Hypothesis, scholars such as Wellhausen and others now proposed that at least four primary sources were involved in the composition of the Pentateuch, and that it was composed not in or at the time of Moses (c. 1300–1150 B.C.), but beginning in the post-Davidic kingdom and concluding during or after the exile to Babylon (587–539 B.C.), with the final redaction of it in the fourth century B.C. (Figure 1, above).

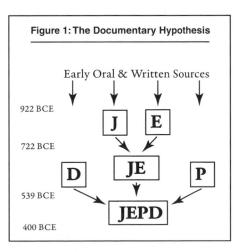

Figure 1: The Documentary Hypothesis

Early Oral & Written Sources

922 BCE — J E

722 BCE — JE

539 BCE — D P

400 BCE — JEPD

Another pioneer of this sort of scholarship was Hermann Gunkel (1862–1932), who, in the early twentieth century, undertook a critical treatment of Genesis[247] and the Psalms, examining the "forms" of the texts and their development.[248]

Such trends in the study of the Old Testament set the stage for New Testament criticism. Soon such historical-critical approaches were being applied to the texts of the New Testament as well. In his *Life of Jesus Critically Examined*,[249] David Fredrich Strauss (1808–74) argued that Jesus could not have been God incarnate. Rather, what was found in the gospels was not to be viewed as historical, but *myths* of the first followers of Christ. Strauss believed the first Christians composed miracle stories to explain what Jesus meant in various teachings, in language that would be intelligible to them.

Though not all early historical-critical scholars were as radical as Strauss in their conclusions, a thoroughgoing rational empiricism began to saturate biblical interpretation from this period onward. Not long after Strauss, H. J. Holtzmann (1832–1910) offered a portrait of Jesus as a teacher of timeless universal truths, and not a divine Son of God. (This line of reasoning was popular in 19th century Germany.) Holtzmann sought to resolve tensions between the Synoptic gospels (i.e., Matthew, Mark and Luke) to get back to the so-called "historical Jesus." His most significant work was *The Synoptic Gospels: Their Origin and Historical Character*.[250] In it, Holtzmann attempted to resolve tensions within the Synoptic gospels, the so-called Synoptic Problem." He proposed "Markan priority" over the traditional view, that Matthew was the first written gospel. It was Augustine who, in the early Church, first articulated a developed theory of the order of the Four Gospels, beginning with Matthew. The testimony of the early Church was unanimous as to Matthean priority, and the so-called Augustinian Hypothesis that postulated it lasted until the late nineteenth century.[251]

Holtzmann's work began to overturn the long-standing scholarly consensus, as he pioneered the Two Source Hypothesis. This hypothesis proposes that Mark and

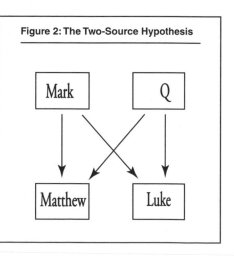

Figure 2: The Two-Source Hypothesis

Mark   Q

Matthew   Luke

another written source, now known as Q (German: *Quelle*, "source")[252] were the earliest Jesus traditions, and that each in turn influenced both Matthew and Luke in the composition of their own gospels. Today, despite many questions about the hypothetical Q source, the Two Source Hypothesis remains the dominant theory.

All of the above developments in modern biblical interpretation that we have quickly traced (Documentary Hypothesis, etc.), for all of their complexities, have something in common. Namely, all of these may be described as **diachronic** methods of exegesis. In Greek, *dia* carries the meaning of "through" and *chronos* of "time." Thus, diachronic methods of exegesis search for meaning by tracing a text's development as it passed through time, in various stages of editing and shaping. Some of the more influential diachronic methods include *source criticism*, *form criticism* and *redaction criticism*.

Source Criticism

The intent of source critics of the Bible is to attempt to identify the written (and oral) traditions that lay beneath or behind a text. Both the Documentary Hypothesis for the Old Testament (i.e., Pentateuch) and the Two Source Hypothesis for the New Testament (i.e., Synoptic gospels) are good examples of source criticism. Apparent contradictions in a book or passage of Scripture, along with doublets (i.e., "parallel literary narratives")[253] and other repetitions, shifts in style and/or vocabulary (e.g., *Elohim*, *Yahweh*), and other indications have led source critics to conclude that many biblical texts were not the product of a single author. Rather, such critics suggest that oral and literary traditions that were already in existence were integrated into the text, typically without any explicit indications by the author(s).

One of the significant contributions of source criticism is that it challenges us to be more observant to such literary patterns in Scripture, and to appreciate the complexity of the texts themselves. It also provides us with possibilities for resolving certain tensions and apparent discrepancies in Scripture and urges us to discover more about "the world behind the text," including potential sources (both oral and written).

On the other hand, we should note two key limitations of source criticism. First, source criticism often gives preference to hypothetical reconstructions of biblical texts and their history. Yet, too often, such reconstructions are based upon speculative theology rather than sound historical data.

This is, in our view, a particular weakness of both the Documentary Hypothesis and the Two Source Theory. For example, with respect to the latter, the alleged Q source has never been unearthed in any historical excavation. Rather, its existence is predicated upon its ability to "solve problems" in the Synoptic gospels. Thus, Q is a reconstructed text that can only be "seen" in light of the historical and living texts of Matthew, Mark and Luke.

A second and related difficulty is that by placing such emphasis on the traditions *behind the text,* what is often neglected in source critical approaches is any discussion of the text as a whole. As a result, one focuses on the potential "layers" of traditions that were brought together in the past rather than on the text in its final state. As a result, source critics tend to deemphasize any genuine commentary on what the text is saying in its canonical form.

Form Criticism

Like source criticism, form critics are involved in inquiries that look to "the world behind the text." Form criticism may be defined as the analysis of typical forms, particularly in a pre-literary state, such as legends, hymns, laments, and so on.[254] As such, form critics seek to identify the evolution of a tradition from its pre-literal or oral stage to its final stage in the written biblical text. A key presupposition in form critical approaches is that small units of text ("periscopes") had previously existed in smaller, oral forms which circulated as independent traditions. These traditions served a particular *Sitz im Leben* ("setting in life"), or social context, and were shaped and developed by various communities accordingly.

I often explain the dynamics of form criticism as follows. Think of your favorite Gospel passage. Now, imagine that that passage is a massive snowball, two or three feet in diameter. Form criticism essentially argues that that Gospel passage went through a number of stages of development before reaching its final form. Like a small snowball, several inches or so in diameter, it began to roll through time, perhaps decades, being shaped by the hill, which is the community over which it "rolls." As it does so, it expands, gaining mass, until finally it "stops" and reaches its final form, two or three feet across. Such is form criticism. The goal of the form critic then, is to attempt to re-trace the path of the snowball, as it were, "back up the hill" of its history. Only through this process of inquiry can the final structure, and more importantly, the "intention" of any biblical text be properly understood.

Thus, a text is classified according to its genre in its final form, e.g., a miracle story in the Gospel of Mark. (Other such forms could include parables, sayings of Jesus, dialogues, exorcisms, etc.) The miracle story is then deconstructed according to the form or forms that comprise it. As the layers of the larger snowball are removed through literary analysis, its history is uncovered. The smallest nub that remains is the original form; the largest one is the miracle story in its present form in the gospel. Through this type of analysis, the form critic hopes to uncover as much about the intentionality of a text from the miniscule snowball through the behemoth mass (suitable for making a snowman on the lawn).

One of the lasting contributions of form criticism is that it challenges us to be very discriminating when reading and studying Scripture. No longer should we breeze through passages or chapters of Scripture, giving attention only to whatever interests us along the way. Rather, we are urged ask specific questions as to the precise structure and composition of a particular passage.

Such investigation into the "form" of a text is crucial to our comprehension of meaning. If we are reading a passage from the Gospel, what kind of text is it: *A miracle story? A parable? A saying? What kind of miracle story is it: A healing? A nature miracle?* Additionally, such approaches have taught us to ask good questions based upon the genre of a text, such as: What purpose might this miracle story have had for the early Christian believers? In what way did it serve to form them in their understanding of who Jesus was? How did it impact their faith? What larger role might the text have played in their community? In other communities?

Yet, like source criticism, form criticism has its own set of limitations and weaknesses, too. First, like source criticism, it can tend to leave us hunting around in "the world behind the text" to the detriment to the text itself. One never gets on with the business of "making the snowman" and appreciating it because of a preoccupation with "pushing the large snowball" back up the hill, trying to de-layer it as one goes. Thus, the "history of the text" begins to take precedence over the final form of the text.

Second, some of the more radical critics, such as Rudolf Bultmann (1884–1776), sought to "demythologize" the gospels, yielding an existential and unhistorical Christ.[255] Additionally, Bultmann and other form critics of the mid-twentieth century often sought to explain the final written forms in Scripture according to non-Christian and non-Jewish sources, such as Greco-Roman religious and philosophical sources, and so on.

Third, and finally, form criticism's emphasis on the "life setting" of the passage is both a positive and a negative. Positively, it gets us asking the right questions, as noted above. However, genuine caution is required, lest we prematurely ascribe a definitive meaning to a text, based upon a presumed "history" and or "evolution" of the text over time. Can we really be quite certain that a text was shaped by a community according to their needs and, if so, what does this imply about the author of the text? Thus, we can better understand the concerns of the Church and its response in the crisis of interpretation in the early twentieth century. We now turn to one final and important diachronic method, redaction criticism.

Redaction Criticism

Redaction criticism developed in the mid-twentieth century and, in some sense, as a response to form criticism. It seeks to uncover the meaning of a biblical text by analyzing the editorial work at the final stage of the text's development. According to redaction critics, the form critics that preceded them too often treated the biblical authors as mere "collectors" of the gospel traditions, but prohibited any understanding of them as actual authors that shaped the text itself. Rather, they collected and assembled the traditions but played a minimal role, in terms of authorship.[256] For the redaction critic, the Gospel authors again become the emphasis of study — particularly at the final stage of composition. Redaction criticism presupposes an elongated "history of the text," in which the *final redactor* (or editor), as the "final hand" on the text, exerted the controlling view as to how the various traditions within the Gospel were to be employed, and understood by his audience. The "hand" of the redactor is especially evident, the redaction critic argues, in minute "seams" and "summaries," in which the author-redactor brought together these various traditions. Additionally, the redactor's inclusion, omission and re-arrangement of materials is said to reveal his theological motives.[257]

The lasting contribution of redaction criticism is difficult to measure. On the one hand, it serves as a much needed corrective to form criticism, which greatly diminished the role of the Evangelists as true authors. This is a positive solution to the form critical question. It causes us to compare and contrast the style and yes, the theological interests of one Gospel compared with another. On the other hand, redaction criticism makes particular judgments as to the intentions of a text, and locates the meaning at the final stage of development, in the hand of the redactor. The composers of the biblical texts are again "authors" — but to what end? Do the redactors' views override the earlier traditions and "voices" in the text? In a sense, they do, as they retain the "control" over them, according to the proponents of this method. Often then, the redaction critic tunes his ear to the tensions within the text, including what may be described as "competing forces" within the history of the community from which the document emerged. In a sense, the redactor is the final adjudicator of an array of interests which may be in tension or even conflict with one another. Despite what it offers us as a method of interpreting the meaning of Scripture, redaction criticism presents serious difficulties concerning the unity and coherence of the biblical texts. For example, were the biblical texts the products of *authors* or are they to be primarily understood as a tapestry of concerns (often in competition with one another) out of a particular *community*?

This concludes our look at three crucial diachronic methods of biblical interpretation, and takes us on to one final destination in our search for "meanings" in Scripture.

In the last quarter of the twentieth century, more attention has been given to **synchronic** methods of interpretation. Whereas diachronic methods examine the history of a text through time, i.e., "the world behind the text," synchronic methods place primary emphasis (and often exclusive emphasis) on the text as we have it *at one time*; asking us to examine closely "the world within the text" itself. As Pope Benedict remarked, "synchronic and diachronic methods of interpretation are increasingly recognized as equal in value."[258] Now, we turn to two key synchronic methods, *narrative criticism* and *canonical criticism*.

Narrative Criticism

Narrative criticism is less of a method than it is a perspective or focus brought to the biblical text.[259] Close attention is paid to the unity of the story, or narrative of the text itself. Emphasis is placed upon literary patterns in *the text* rather than historical developments *behind the text* (as in the various diachronic methods). Elements such as in Figure 3 are all considerations in narrative critical analysis.

Given such attention to narrative elements, students of Scripture must seek to encounter the real (historical) author of a text. Yet, in addition, an equal concern of the narrative critic is to discover the "implied author," which essentially amounts to the collective perspective revealed by the text itself. Narrative criticism concentrates on "the story being told,"[260] and the world behind the text, while not necessarily excluded, is nonetheless "bracketed off" from the space and time of the narrative itself.

While narrative criticism, as a discipline, is only a few decades old at this point, its contributions are clear. First, following several centuries of exegesis that has been preoccupied with the world behind the text, narrative approaches re-focus us on the text itself, and "the world within the story" itself. As noted above, a fair critique of diachronic methods is that the historical development and background is so emphasized that the narrative unity of the text is neglected. This approach reminds us that in addition to asking questions such as: "*What kind of pericope is this?*" and "*What is the history of this miracle story?*" we need to be asking, "*What is the story of John?*" and "*How is the plot of the crucifixion developed in Matthew?*" Second, and related to this, is the emphasis placed upon various narrative elements (e.g., repetition, irony, symbolism). such close attention as this brings us into a fresh encounter with the author, real and implied, that diachronic methods are not by nature capable of producing.

Figure 3: Ten Key Elements in Narrative Criticism

Plot

Repetition

Irony

Comparison & Contrast

Mood

Chiasm

Point of view

Characterization

Symbolism

Setting

However, we can also note several limitations and weaknesses of narrative critical approaches. First, since by its nature it does not seek to put us in touch with "the world behind the text," the historical horizon is less in view. That is not to say the historical horizon is not available at all, as most narrative critics are all for some discussion of historical dimensions of the text. However, those committed to a narrative critical approach would do well to at least consult other sources which put one in closer proximity to the historical background of the text itself.

A second critique is this: some have charged narrative critics with "exporting" modern categories back onto the ancient world. In one sense, this is a fair assessment, as narrative critics themselves are quick to point out that the approach makes use of the conventions used by modern literary criticism, such as the analysis of plot, character, etc. What is debatable is whether or not such analysis is guilty of "exporting" something back onto the text that does not belong there. On the one hand, the literary analysis is modern; but on the other hand, the "biblical story" from Genesis to Revelation is, for the most part, in a *narrative form.* As one of the leading narrative critics, Robert Alter suggests that what we need to better understand is that:

> The religious vision of the Bible is given depth and subtlety by being conveyed through the most sophisticated resources of prose fiction … Almost the whole range of biblical narrative … embodies the basic perception that man must live before God, in the transforming medium of time, incessantly and perplexingly in relation with others; and a literary perspective on the operations of narrative may help us more than another to see how this perception was translated into stories that have had such a powerful, enduring hold on the imagination.[261]

The Catholic exegete should be aware of this rich tapestry of interpretative approaches, seeking to know as much as possible about each one — its contributions and achievements, as well as its limitations and even "blind spots."

Provided one is aware of the literary lens through which the narrative critic "looks" at Scripture (just as the other methods do), it can be a valuable tool for the biblical student. However, we can never neglect the historical horizon, as Christianity is anything but fiction. Some (but certainly not all) narrative critics do not make such judgments. Each interpretation must be assessed upon its own merits and characteristics, and the above cautions are not meant to steer the Catholic exegete from this newer approach. In the hands of someone with a hermeneutic of faith and a sincere interest in the historical horizon, this method can be a powerful and illuminating tool.

Canonical Criticism

One other type of approach to deriving meaning from Scripture is *canonical* criticism. In the modern era, the approach is most associated with Brevard Childs (1923–2007) and James A. Sanders (1927–).[262] This method is characterized by a particular interest in the meaning of a text first within the book in which it is located and second, within the larger context of the whole canon of Scripture to which it belongs.[263] As such, this approach emphasizes the unity of the whole canon, despite the various books and texts that comprise it. Additionally, canonical criticism examines biblical texts as "sacred" and "authoritative." From the perspective of Catholic biblical interpretation, this method may seem anything but new; from the apostles and the early fathers onward, there has existed in Christian exegesis a concern for the whole of Scripture. However, as a modern discipline, canonical *criticism* is a new (and welcome) development in biblical interpretation. Those critical of the approach suggest that like narrative criticism, this synchronic approach does not give due attention to questions of history, authorship and the development of the text. Sanders and Childs have responded to such critiques and have suggested that canonical criticism — though it does give preference to the final literary stage — is indeed interested in the developmental process that gave shape to the canonical form of the text.

FOR REFLECTION

"The contemplation of God's face is a never-ending journey toward Him accomplished by following right behind the Word … The Bridegroom passes by and the bride exits; she no longer remains in the place where she had been, but touches the Word who leads her on."

— *Gregory of Nyssa,* Homily on the Song of Songs *12 (Trans. by C. McCambley.* Saint Gregory of Nyssa. Commentary on the Song of Songs. *Brookline, MS: Hellenic College Press, 1987), 219.*

Windows, Mirrors, Helicopters

Today, more than ever before, there is an appreciation for a wide array of methodologies, including ancient and medieval approaches (e.g., allegorical) as well as modern methods; especially historical-critical methods (e.g., form, source, redaction criticism), but also newer methods (e.g., narrative and canonical criticism). The Catholic exegete should be aware of this rich tapestry of interpretative approaches, seeking to know as much as possible about each one — its contributions and achievements, as well as its limitations and even "blind spots."

Form, source and redaction criticism are methods capable of opening up "the world behind the text." Narrative criticism can bring the story of Scripture into sharper focus, and helps the exegete encounter not only the text; but through such engagement of the text, he can encounter himself in a new way. Finally, canonical criticism challenges us to interpret the text in light of the whole of Scripture.

In your imagination, picture your favorite biblical passage. Think about the very words of the text. Now, imagine these biblical words are no longer printed on the page, but inscribed on a window pane. You stand on one side of the window pane, looking "at the text" on clear glass. On the other side of the window pane is the dusty biblical world, as it really was. This is, at best, the great value of form, source, and redaction criticism in that they ask us to look at the text in such a way, as on a clear pane, through which we see not only the text, but the world behind it as well.

Similarly, imagine that the text of your favorite Bible story is written not on a window pane, but on a mirror. As you gaze at the text, you are aware not only of the Scriptural words, but at the same time, you are aware of your own reflection "in the text." This is, at best, the great value of narrative criticism.

Finally, imagine one more scene. Now however, instead of the Word of God being inscribed on a window or a mirror, visualize the text as if it were written over an entire landscape, i.e., "printed" and overlaid on a pasture, rolling hills, and so on. In order to see the "text" in this way, you would really have to soar above it. In a helicopter, you could "hover" over a particular text and inspect it up close. You could also soar up high in the air and look at the entire landscape, and compare different texts with one another, in light of the whole. This is, at best, the great value of canonical criticism.

All of these "scenes" help to illustrate the various advantages of different methods of interpreting Scripture. Yet, we should be aware of their limitations as well. In each of these imaginary scenes, the greatest danger is perhaps the most obvious, but the one that happens the most: *losing sight of the text itself.*

In an effort to get in touch with the world behind the text, one gazes so intently at the window that one no longer sees *the text on the window* but is preoccupied only by the world moving in the background. Now, when one does "return to the text," one's perspective is distorted and cannot really focus on the "closeness" of the text itself. Such is the danger with the historical-critical methods. Likewise, seeking to understand one's own "place" in the text, in narrative criticism one studies Scripture as if it were written on a mirror. Here, it is possible to lose sight of the biblical words and instead, focus on the reflection. Such is the danger of this method of approach. Finally, even canonical criticism can fall prey to such risks. If one is moving about indiscriminately or without a proper map (to extend the metaphor), one may lose sight of where one took off or needs to land. That is, one does not land a helicopter on a whole landscape, but in one particular spot. The place where one took off and needs to again land is the spot where the specific text is being studied. The danger then, in canonical criticism, is losing the trees for the forest.

The wise Catholic exegete will be aware of the advantages of these various ways of "seeing" Sacred Scripture, and make use of them accordingly. He will also be aware of the inherent risks in each of these ways of looking at the biblical text. Though various cautions could be articulated about the risks of each type of approach, the larger one, as seen through the above illustrations, is simply and plainly, *never lose sight of the biblical text itself.* That is always, always your first priority.

That said, the wise Catholic student of Scripture will become aware of *all of the major methods*, and not give undue preference to any one way of "seeing," despite what it may yield. Rather, the Catholic Bible student may involve himself in looking at Scripture through all of these lenses — and still others that have not been mentioned here. This will surely involve hard work. Yet, since God's Word is expressed in human language and human writing, such rigor and commitment are vital. Therefore, the wise exegete should be open to exploring biblical texts from a variety of vantage points in search of meaning, and be prayerful and discerning as one looks at Scripture. Whatever the method, remember: your main goal is to "see" the Word, both the written Word and the Living Word — Jesus. When we stop seeing the Word, and only see other things, we need to adjust our focus, or if necessary, find another lens.

Conclusion

All of the discussions of various senses and approaches to Scripture — from the ancient period to the present day — underscore the necessity of Principle #5: ("God's Word is Rich in Meaning"). Therefore, we must "put out into the deep" (Luke 5:4) and do our best to uncover as much meaning as we can, even knowing that we may never mine the depths of the wisdom of the Word of God exhaustively. Now, we move to our discussion of the final two principles.

A Final Note: Some familiarity with major figures in modern biblical interpretation can be a helpful thing. While a comprehensive review of modern biblical scholars is beyond the scope of this book, a brief sketch of a dozen and a half of some of the more influential scholars can be found in **Appendix B.** Included are both "rationalist" scholars (e.g., Rudolf Bultmann, Albert Schweitzer) and Catholic/Christian scholars (e.g., Raymond Brown, N. T. Wright).

FOR REFLECTION

Spend some time in *meditating on* the following passage:

The beginning of wisdom is the most sincere desire for instruction, and concern for instruction is love of her, and love of her is the keeping of her laws, and giving heed to her laws is assurance of immortality, and immortality brings one near to God. (Wis 6:17–19)

Questions for Reflection

1. With regard to modern biblical interpretation, which word(s) best fits my perspective: "Curious," "Interested," "Cautious," "Intimidated," "Eager," "Turned off." Why?
2. Which "ism" (Form, Source, Redaction, etc.) do I have the most difficulty with? Why?
3. How is it that the canonical approach, while being a modern development in the twentieth century, has an "ancient ring" to it?
4. Do I understand the difference between diachronic and synchronic approaches to Scripture?

5. What is narrative criticism — and what sort of 'categories' does it rely upon. How is this a valuable development? What cautions are necessary?

For Further Study

Alter, Robert. *The Art of Biblical Narrative.* New York: Basic Books, 1981.

De Lubac, Henri. *Medieval Exegesis*, Volume I. Grand Rapids, MI: Eerdmans, 1998.

———. *Scripture in the Tradition, trans.* L. O'Neil. Chestnut Ridge, NY: Crossroad, 1997.

De Margerie, Bertrand. *An Introduction to the History of Exegesis.* 3 vols. Petersham, MA: Saint Bede's Publications, 1993–95.

McKnight, Edgar. *What is Form Criticism?* Eugene, OR; Wipf & Stock, 1997.

Montague, G. *Understanding the Bible.* Mahwah, NJ: Paulist Press, 2000.

Nichols, Aidan. "The Interpretation of Scripture: The Letter," *The Shape of Catholic Theology: An Introduction to its Sources, Principles and History*, 141–53. San Francisco: Ignatius Press, 1991.

Perrin, Norman. *What is Redaction Criticism?* Eugene, OR: Wipf & Stock, 2002.

Powell, Mark Allan. *What is Narrative Criticism?* Minneapolis: Fortress Press, 1990

Reventlow, Hans. *The Authority of the Bible and the Rise of the Modern World.* London: SCM Press, 1985.

Robinson, Robert B. *Roman Catholic Exegesis Since Divino Afflante Spiritu.* Atlanta: Scholars Press, 1988.

Soulen, R. N. and R. K. Soulen. *Handbook of Biblical Criticism*, 3rd ed. London: Westminster John Knox Press, 2001.

Vanhoozer, Kevin. *Is There a Meaning in the Text?* Grand Rapids: Zondervan, 1998. A conservative, erudite Evangelical scholar discusses the question of "meaning" in biblical texts, and critiques some of the more radical post-modern biblical critics.

Williamson, Peter. *Catholic Principles for Interpreting Scripture: A Study of the Pontifical Biblical Commission's The Interpretation of the Bible in the Church.* Pontificia Università Gregoriana, 2000, Subsidia Biblica 22. Rome: Pontificio Istituto biblico, 2001. Williamson's thesis at the Gregorian University in Rome was particularly influential for this book. Whereas seven principles of Catholic Biblical interpretation are presented here.

Notes

241   For a very basic introduction to philosophical movements, and their importance for the biblical exegete, cf. Peter Hicks, *The Journey Thus Far: Philosophy through the Ages* (Grand Rapids: Zondervan, 2006). For more philosophical and intricate treatments of the topic, cf. Etienne Gilson, *Christian Philosophy* (Durham: Pontifical Institute for Medieval Philosophy, 1993); *God and Philosophy* (New Haven, CT: Yale University Press, 2002); Jacques Maratain, *Introduction to Philosophy* (Lanham, MD: Rowman and Littlefield Publishers,

2005).**242**   For a summary of major figures in modern biblical interpretation, see Appendix B.

243   Cf. Immanuel Kant, *The Critique of Pure Reason* (1781; revised significantly in 1787).

244   Friedrich Nietzsche, *The Gay Science* (1882). "Where has God gone?" he cried. "I shall tell you. We have killed him - you and I. We are his murderers ... God remains dead. And we have killed him" (*The Gay Science,* §125).

245   J. Wellhausen, *Prolegomena To The History Of Israel* (Berlin, 1882).

246   In numerous passages, the biblical texts themselves presume Moses as author of Genesis-Deuteronomy: Exod 17:14; 34:27; Lev 1:1; 6:8; 31:9; Num 33:1-2; Deut 31:9; Josh 1:7-8; 8:31-34; Judg 3:4; 1 Ki 2:3; 2 Ki 14:6; 21:8; 2 Chr 34:14; 35:12; Ezra 6:18; Neh 13:1; Dan 9:11-13; Mal 4:4; Matt 19:7-8; 22:24; Mark 7:10; 12:24; Luke 24:44, etc.

247   Hermann Gunkel, *Genesis*. Translated by Mark E. Biddle (Macon, GA: Mercer University Press, 1997; German ed. 1910).

248   Hermann Gunkel, *The Psalms: A Form-Critical Introduction*. Introduction by James Muilenburg. Translated by T. M. Horner (Philadelphia: Fortress Press, 1967; German ed. 1927).

249   Cf. David Friedrich Strauss, *The Life of Jesus Critically Examined*, Peter C. Hodgson, ed. and trans. George Eliot (Philadelphia: Fortress Press, 1972).

250   Heinrich Julius Holtzmann, *Die Synoptischen Evangelien: Ihr Ursprung und ihr geschichtlicher Charakter* [The Synoptic Gospels: Their Origin and their Historical Character] (Leipzig, 1863).

251   For example, Irenaeus writes: "Matthew brought out a written Gospel among the Jews in their own tongue, when Peter and Paul were preaching the Gospel at Rome and founding the Church. But after their demise, Mark himself the disciple and recorder of Peter, has also handed on to us in writing what had been proclaimed by Peter. And Luke too, the follower of Paul, put down in a book the Gospel which was being preached by him. Later on too, John, the disciple of the Lord, who had even reclined on his bosom, he too brought out a Gospel while he was dwelling in Ephesus of Asia" (*Against Heresies*, 3.1.1). Likewise, the Church historian Eusebius: "So then Matthew wrote the oracles in the Hebrew language, and every one interpreted them as he was able" (*Ecclesiastical History*, 3.39).

252   Cf. David Catchpole, *The Quest for Q* (Edinburgh: T & T Clark, 1993); John Kloppenborg Verbin, *Excavating Q: The History and Setting of the Sayings Gospel* (Minneapolis: Fortress Press, 2000).

253   Cf. Gen 12:10-13, 20:1-18, 26:6-11; Exod 20:1-17, 34:10-28; Mark 6:35-44, 8:1-9.

254   Cf. "Form Criticism," in *Handbook of Biblical Criticism*. R. N. Soulen and R. K. Soulen, eds. (Louisville: Westminster John Knox, 2001), 61-65; M. J. Buss, *Biblical Form Criticism in Its Context*. Journal for the Study of the Old Testament, 274 (Sheffield: Sheffield Press, 1999).

255   Cf. Rudolf Bultmann, *History of the Synoptic Tradition* (Harper San Francisco, 1976; German original, 1921); *The New Testament and Mythology and Other Basic Writings* (Minneapolis: Augsburg Fortress Publishers, 1984); *The Gospel of John: A Commentary* (Louisville: Westminster John Knox Press, 1971; German original, 1941).

256   Cf. "Redaction Criticism," in Soulen and Soulen, *Handbook of Biblical Criticism*, 158-60; Norman Perrin, *What is Redaction Criticism?* (Philadelphia: Fortress Press, 1969).

257   Soulen and Soulen, *Handbook of Biblical Criticism*, 159. The authors give a number of examples, including: Why does Luke (presumably) alter Mark's account of John the Baptist as Elijah (cf. Mark 6:15-16 with Luke 9:7-9)? Why is Satan presented only at the beginning and end of Luke's Gospel but not during it (cf. Luke 4:1-13; 22:3)?

258   Cardinal Joseph Ratzinger, "The Catechism's Use of Scripture," in *On the Way to Jesus Christ*, Michael J. Miller, trans. (San Francisco: Ignatius Press, 2005), 152.

259   Cf. "Narrative Criticism," in Soulen and Soulen, *Handbook of Biblical Criticism*, 119-20; Mark Allan Powell, *What is Narrative Criticism?* (Minneapolis: Fortress Press, 1990).

260   Soulen and Soulen, *Handbook of Biblical Criticism*, 120.

261   Robert Alter, *The Art of Biblical Narrative* (New York: Basic Books, 1981), 23. Cf. Ch. 1 ("A Literary Approach to the Bible," 2-23). More recently, Alter has published a translation of the Pentateuch in which he pays close attention to the rhythm in the original Hebrew. While it would not be recommended to use Alter's translation as a "replacement" of a more formal translation, such as the Revised Standard Version, such work is valuable in that it brings us to the text in a fresh way, with due attention to the force, beauty, and style of the original Hebrew. Cf. Alter, *The Five Books of Moses: A Translation with Commentary* (New York: W. W. Norton, 2008).

262   Cf. Brevard Childs, *Old Testament Theology in a Canonical Context* (Philadelphia: Fortress, 1984, 1994); *The New Testament as Canon: An Introduction* (Philadelphia: Fortress, 1994); James A. Sanders, *Torah and Canon* (Philadelphia: Fortress, 1972); *Canon and Community: A Guide to Canonical Criticism* (Philadelphia: Fortress, 1984); *From Sacred Story to Sacred Text* (Philadelphia: Fortress, 1987). While Sanders is attributed with coining the term "canonical criticism," Childs is the figure most associated with this approach.

263   Cf. "Canonical Criticism," in Soulen and Soulen, *Handbook of Biblical Criticism*, 29-30.

> Truth is power, but only
> when one has patience
> and requires of it no
> immediate effect. And
> one must have no specific
> aims. Somehow, lack of
> an agenda is the greatest
> power. Sometimes it is
> better not to think in terms
> of plans; here months
> may mean nothing, and
> also years. Truth must be
> sought for its own sake,
> its holy, divine greatness.
>
> — *Romano Guradini,*
> Precursor to the Vatican

Principle 6
God's Word Requires Sound, Balanced, Methodological Analysis

Our sequential investigation into the seven principles of Catholic biblical interpretation of principles may be summarized as follows:

Principle #1: If God is the ultimate author of Scripture, and if He simultaneously guides the human authors in expressing His message in human language …

Principle #2: Then He does so in and through actual history, and we must learn to uncover the original meaning, as best as we can, using sound historical and theological inquiry …

Principle #3: Furthermore, this "divine word in history" was first apprehended by Christ's apostles, and preserved for all people in both written and unwritten forms (Scripture and Tradition). Moreover, it was the Church that recognized this revelation as "from God" and so developed the canon of Scripture.

Principle #4: The Tradition of the Church and the development of the biblical canon reflect the inherent unity and coherence that exist between the Old and New Testament. This is especially seen in and through the theme of covenant, continually re-emerging in new ways until it leads to Christ and the New Covenant. Additionally, biblical typology and "recapitulation" deepen our awareness to this unitive pattern in Scripture.

Principle #5: As a result of this unity and coherence of the whole, we can exclaim that indeed Scripture is meaningful in all of its books and words that comprise it. There is literal as well as spiritual meaning. From ancient times until the present day, there are available to us a wide array of interpretative approaches that help us uncover the multiplicity of meanings in Scripture.

This leads us to a new and important plateau. In examining the last two principles that remain, we begin the crucial work of *analysis of God's Word* ... and *application of God's word*. These final principles are the most "intimate," in that they call for our personal response to Scripture in conspicuous and functional ways, as balanced students of Scripture (Principle #6) and, as we will see in the following chapter, as bold proclaimers of God's Word (Principle #7).

Principle #6: Catholic biblical interpretation requires sound and balanced analysis. In the end, all analysis should be based upon excellence in scholarship, encountered from a robust Christian faith, and reflect pastoral concern and the needs of God's people. Three essential criteria for ensuring such control in one's exegesis of Sacred Scripture:
> *1. Attention to the content and unity of the Bible.*
> *2. Reading all of Scripture within the living Tradition of the Church*
> *3. Reference to the analogy (or rule) of faith.*

From the Heart of the Church

All of the work that we did in the last chapter, of "putting out into the deep" in search of various interpretative methods is absolutely crucial. But now we must ask some very important questions. Questions such as the following:

- *As Catholic students of Scripture, how can we as make sense of all of these various manners of interpreting Scripture?*
- *By what means can we know that a biblical scholar is standing firm ground in making an assertion about a biblical passage?*

Only where both methodological levels, the historical-critical and the theological, are respected, can one speak of a theological exegesis, an exegesis worthy of this book.

— Pope Benedict XVI, *Verbum Domini* § 34

In short, such questions coalesce around the topic of building a "sound and balanced" approach to Scripture from a genuinely Catholic point of view. By a "Catholic point of view," I mean one that is from the heart of the Church (*ex corde ecclesia*); wholly orthodox and in keeping with the teachings and Tradition of the Church.

At the same time, this Catholic point of view is one that is both: (a) truly engaged with historic scholarship, old and new; and (b) "intellectually sophisticated," inasmuch as it is open and unafraid of insights from a variety of perspectives. It is to this end that Principle # 6 is dedicated: we are called to a vigorous engagement of both the world of Scripture and the world of biblical criticism in search of "explaining God's Word." All of our explanations must be sound and balanced explanations and truly Catholic explanations of the Word.

The Essential Marriage of Biblical Exegesis and Biblical Theology

Questions such as these demand answers; Catholic exegesis is not simply a matter of research, i.e., reading commentaries until we feel as though we've found "a workable answer." Nor is it a matter of endless labor and searching. Most of all, Catholic exegesis is not — repeat, not a matter of "guesswork." Earnest questions such as the above demand answers — and the good news is that the Church does offer faithful, clear and concrete guidance toward developing our own "sound and balanced" approach to biblical interpretation. It is toward this end our principle aims: as we strive to explain God's Word. The remainder of this chapter will discuss three crucial criteria to ensure exactly that — that all of our labors in searching for meaning *meets a fruitful, spiritual end,* for the sake of the Kingdom of God. This is the goal of Principle #6.

Before we can enter into a discussion of these criteria and how they can assist us, we must pause at this stage and ask ourselves a very important question about the entire interpretative process we are involved in. Make no mistake: our answer is critical; if we miss the mark here, not only will our "search for meaning" be jeopardized, but quite likely, the whole process of interpreting the Word. The question is this: *What is the relationship between biblical exegesis and biblical theology?*

The primary setting for scriptural interpretation is the life of the Church.

— Pope Benedict XVI, *Verbum Domini* § 29

As we know, biblical exegesis seeks to explain or interpret the Scriptures. It often involves close scrutiny of a biblical passage — perhaps six or seven verses at most, oft times a single verse or single word. This is important work — yet it cannot produce the rich fruit of true interpretation. The last few centuries of interpretation have made this all too clear; many have poured themselves out in the work of exegesis — only to produce commentaries, monographs and opinions that at worse distort the truth and at best, offer mere hypotheses and guesses at what God's Word means. On its own, biblical exegesis is a science — a necessary science — but a science and intensive labor that closely analyzes the data in, behind and around the world of the Bible so that questions about a given passage can be answered and an interpretation offered.

If biblical exegesis is best understood as a *science*, then biblical theology is, in a manner of speaking, an art. Like exegesis, it focuses on the biblical Word, but goes *beyond analysis to synthesis*. And not just "any" synthesis, no. Rather, Catholic biblical theology takes the results of exegesis and ponders them with and from the heart of the Church. Biblical exegesis is the "micro" — and biblical theology is the "macro" of interpretation. We have not arrived at meaning, truly Catholic meaning, until we sufficiently engage in both endeavors — in an integrative fashion. Exegetes, be prepared to be wise theologians! Theologians: your work must rest upon the fruit of biblical exegesis! "*The primary setting for scriptural interpretation is the life of the Church.*"[264]

Consider the following metaphor. The biblical exegete relies upon a magnifying glass to do his work, closely examining the minutiae, typically in a small passage. In contrast, the biblical theologian uses a large light board, looking at the passage in the broader context of the canon. He asks questions such as these: "*How does my exegesis square with the whole of Scripture?*" "*What light does the Creed shed upon this passage?*" "*What do the Church fathers, mystics and saints have to say as to this or that theme in the passage?*" "*How do my results illuminate the mystery of salvation, the mysteries of Christ?*"

So, we could say that the science of biblical exegesis is the first step in the process of arriving at a truly Catholic interpretation of Scripture. The next step involves the art of biblical theology, where the exegetical bud can potentially bloom into a beautiful flower worth gazing at! *Only when there is a healthy "marriage" between biblical exegesis and biblical theology do we experience the fruit of Catholic biblical interpretation.*[265]

A theology which no longer draws its life-breath from faith ceases to be theology ... but where theology is practiced on bended knee, it will prove fruitful for the Church.

— Pope Benedict XVI

Three Vital Criteria for Sound and Balanced Exegesis

The *Catechism* and *Dei Verbum* provide three criteria for a fundamentally sound and balanced exegesis of Scripture that can properly be called Catholic biblical interpretation.[266] The *Catechism* discusses each criterion as follows:

Criterion #1

> Be especially attentive "*to the content and unity of the whole Scripture.*" Different as the books which compose it may be, Scripture is a unity by reason of the unity of God's plan, of which Christ Jesus is the center and heart, open since his Passover.[267]

As the *Catechism* explains, following His Resurrection it was Jesus himself who so instructed His disciples as to the meaning of His life, ministry and Passion: This is evident in the encounter of Christ by the disciples on the Emmaus Road, as recorded by St. Luke in his Gospel (cf. Luke 24:13–34).

> And he said to them, "O foolish men, and slow of heart to believe all that the prophets have spoken! Was it not necessary that the Christ should suffer these things and enter into his glory?" And beginning with Moses and all the prophets, he interpreted to them in all the scriptures the things concerning himself. (Luke 24:25–27)
>
> Then he said to them, "These are my words which I spoke to you, while I was still with you, that everything written about me in the Law of Moses and the prophets and the psalms must be fulfilled." Then he opened their minds to understand the scriptures, and said to them, "Thus it is written, that the Christ should suffer and on the third day rise from the dead, and that repentance and forgiveness of sins should be preached in his name to all nations, beginning from Jerusalem. You are witnesses of these things. And behold, I send the promise of my Father upon you; but stay in the city, until you are clothed with power from on high." (Luke 24:44–49)

Sacred Scripture is written in the heart of the Church before being written on material instruments.

— Origen

This action, of Christ's opening up the mysteries of His life for His disciples, along with His blessing upon them (v. 50), are the last recorded words and deeds of Christ in Luke's Gospel, prior to His glorious Ascension (v. 51). This "divine catechesis" of Christ to His apostles caused them to proclaim, "Did not our hearts burn within us while he talked to us on the road, while he opened to us the scriptures?" (Luke 24:32) As I like to joke with my seminarians, "How would you like to have been a part of *that Bible study?!*" The truth is that we are a part of that "breaking open" of Christ's life according to Scripture: every time we open the gospels. For the Apostles took this knowledge from Christ and from the Spirit by which He guided them "into all truth" (John 16:13), and composed the gospels so that all men at all times and in all places might have their hearts burn within them:

> In His gracious goodness, God has seen to it that what He had revealed for the salvation of all nations would abide perpetually in its full integrity and be handed on to all generations. Therefore Christ the Lord in whom the full revelation of the supreme God is brought to completion, commissioned the Apostles to preach to all men that Gospel which is the source of all saving truth and moral teaching, and to impart to them heavenly gifts. This Gospel had been promised in former times through the prophets, and Christ Himself had fulfilled it and promulgated it with His lips. This commission was faithfully fulfilled by the Apostles who, by their oral preaching, by example, and by observances handed on what they had received from the lips of Christ, from living with Him, and from what He did, or what they had learned through the prompting of the Holy Spirit. The commission was fulfilled, too, by those Apostles and apostolic men who under the inspiration of the same Holy Spirit committed the message of salvation to writing.[268]

An authentic interpretation of the Bible must always be in harmony with the faith of the Catholic Church.

— Pope Benedict XVI, *Verbum Domini* § 30

Through Jesus and His apostles (and their successors the bishops) we have this deposit of faith, which leads to the knowledge of Christ and salvation. As Catholic students of the Bible, we must be ever mindful of the content and unity of all of Scripture, and here, the contribution of canonical criticism as an interpretative approach is especially clear. This leads us to the second of the three criteria:

Criterion #2

> Read the Scripture within "the living Tradition of the whole Church." According to a saying of the Fathers, Sacred Scripture is written principally in the Church's heart rather than in documents and records, for the Church carries in her Tradition the living memorial of God's Word, and it is the Holy Spirit who gives her the spiritual interpretation of the Scripture ("… according to the spiritual meaning which the Spirit grants to the Church").[269]

This second measurement of biblical interpretation leaves no doubt that Catholic exegetes labor not merely "to satisfy their curiosity, or to provide them with material for study and research," but in service to the Church and the proclamation of Jesus Christ for the salvation of souls, so that every member of the Church might be "equipped" to do the work of God (2 Tim 3:16–17).[270] In the early Church, the unique and privileged position of the Church in receiving and proclaiming the Scriptures was continually and loudly proclaimed. Origen expressed this well when he wrote, "Sacred Scripture is written in the heart of the Church before being written on material instruments."[271]

Pope Paul VI expressed this need for Catholic scholars to do exegesis accordingly, since the Church, as he puts it, is the "womb of the Holy Scriptures,"[272] that gave us the Bible in the first place:

You are aware that Holy Scripture, and in particular the New Testament, took shape within the community of the people of God, of the Church gathered around the apostles. It was the latter who, formed in the school of Jesus and having become witnesses of his Resurrection, transmitted his actions and his teachings, explaining the salvific meaning of the events they had witnessed. It is right to say, therefore, that if it was the Word of God that summoned and brought forth the Church, it was the Church, for its part, that was in a certain way, the womb of the Holy Scriptures, that Church which in those Scriptures expressed and recognized, for all future generations, her faith, her hope, her rule of life in this world.[273]

*The texts inspired by God were entrusted in the first place to the commu-
nity of believers, to Christ's Church, to nourish the life of faith and to guide
the life of charity.*
— Pope Benedict XVI

Criterion #3

> Be attentive to the analogy of faith. By "analogy of faith," we mean
> the coherence of the truths of faith among themselves and within
> the whole plan of Revelation.[274]

In a recent address to the Pontifical Biblical Commission, Pope
Benedict XVI described the *analogy of faith* as "the consistence of the
individual truths of faith with one another and with the overall plan of
the Revelation and the fullness of the divine economy contained in it."[275]

The analogy of faith (*regula fidei*) challenges us to interpret any individual text in the full context of all of Scripture (i.e., canonical criticism), but also within the overall plan of salvation. The pope says that
no discovery of a truth is to be examined remotely, but in light of the
full deposit of faith. Such a holistic approach to interpretation not only
guards us from the dangers of "eisegesis" (i.e., reading into the text), but
further unites us with God more deeply, and with one another:

> The truth possesses in itself a unifying force. It frees men from isola-
> tion and the oppositions in which they have been trapped by igno-
> rance of the truth. And as it opens the way to God, it, at the same
> time, unites them to each other.[276]

What is involved in adhering to the *Rule of Faith*?[277] How do we appropriate it? I suggest at least four things should be kept in mind by the
Catholic student of Scripture at all times.

1) Robust Mining of the Word of God

Above all else, we look to the whole canon of Scripture, to bring about
what Paul calls the *hupakone pisteuo*, "the obedience of faith" (Rom 1:5,
16:26). As Pope Leo III eloquently summarized, "Most desirable is it,
and most essential, that the whole teaching of theology should be per-
vaded and animated by the use of the divine Word of God."[278] However,
unlike those who hold to *Sola scriptura* ("Scripture alone") we look beyond Scripture to Sacred Tradition, and thus drink from the one divine

wellspring from which they both flow, "and in a certain way merge into a unity and tend toward the same end."[279] Those who reject Tradition in favor of "Scripture alone" may fail to realize that what stands in place of Tradition in such adjudications of Scripture are the "private judgments" of the individual as he so determines "in his heart." Embracing the analogy of faith, among other things, guards us against such an individuation and privatization of the Word.

FOR REFLECTION	*To what degree does my praying of the Liturgy of the Hours and/or of the Holy Mass draw me deeper into the mysteries of the Scriptures? To what extent is the reverse true for me — that my study, in particular, of the Sacred Scriptures draws me deeper into the liturgy and worship of the Church?*

2) Prayerful Reflection Upon Sacred Tradition — Especially the Liturgy

Primarily, Tradition is the *unwritten* expression of divine faith in the life of the Church. As such, when we enter the mysteries of the liturgy, we are aware that we are in the presence of Truth itself, in the Holy Eucharist:

> To accomplish so great a work, Christ is always present in His Church, especially in her liturgical celebrations. He is present in the sacrifice of the Mass, not only in the person of His minister ... but especially under the Eucharistic species ... He is present in His word, since it is He Himself who speaks when the holy scriptures are read in the Church.[280]

As much as it is important to search the great Tradition for truths that inform our exegesis of Scripture, we are reminded that *Truth has searched for us* and we have been found.

3) Illumination from Scholarly and Wise Theologians

In addition to the body of Sacred Tradition, we look to individual theologians who, while adhering to the faith, make exceptional use of their intellectual faculties and illuminate texts. Thus, the Church encourages us to consult "judicious theologians and commentators ... as to what is the true or most probable meaning of the passage in discussion."[281] This could (and should) include ancient and medieval exegesis, as well as modern and more recent biblical scholarship. Above all, however, we remember that the Holy Prophets, the Apostles and Saints — and most especially, our blessed Mother, Our Lady of Good Counsel are the best theologians of all. Moreover, they point us to the source of all truth, Jesus, who is Wisdom Incarnate.

4) Prudent for Reflection of Faith and Reason

Finally, our commitment to interpreting the Word in light of the analogy of faith is animated by Reason, which permits us to turn our natural intellectual capacities heavenward: Nevertheless, "Those who devote themselves to the study of Sacred Scripture should always remember that the various hermeneutical approaches have their own philosophical underpinnings, which need to be carefully evaluated before they are applied to the sacred texts."[282] Ultimately, reason and philosophical inquiry point us back to Scripture, if they are to be of greater value: "The fundamental conviction of the 'philosophy' found in the Bible is that the world and human life do have a meaning and look towards their fulfillment, which comes in Jesus Christ."[283]

In his address to the PBC on April 23, 2009, Pope Benedict reiterated the importance of the above three criteria discussed in this chapter. After explaining each of them as "norms" from which all biblical exegesis should spring, he added this:

> The task of researchers who study Sacred Scripture with different methods is to contribute in accordance with the above-mentioned principles to the deepest possible knowledge and explanation of the meaning of Sacred Scripture. The scientific study of the sacred texts is important but is not sufficient in itself because it would respect only the human dimension. To respect the coherence of the Church's faith, the Catholic exegete must be attentive to perceiving the Word of God in these texts, within the faith of the Church herself.[284]

When exegesis is done with disregard for these criteria — all three working together — it reflects a blind spot on the part of the interpreter, at best, or at worst, some sort of "secularization of the text" that only shows concern for the human, and not the divine dimension of the text, as the pope writes.

In the end, John Paul II reminds us that with respect to the analogy of faith, we are not left to our own devices in interpreting Scripture soundly. Rather, it is the in *the threefold unity of Scripture, Tradition and Magisterium* that we find true north with clarity and precision; and it is in this direction that we are called to journey in all of our exegetical work:

> Scripture, therefore, is not the Church's sole point of reference. The "supreme rule of her faith" derives from the unity which the Spirit has created between Sacred Tradition, Sacred Scripture and the Magisterium of the Church in a reciprocity which means that none of the three can survive without the others.[285]

Having these three criteria can make all the difference in the world. In closing, let us raise two challenges that arise from our discussion of them.

1. Commit all of your Scripture study to the scrutiny of these criteria.

Stated succinctly, the first challenge for the biblical student is this: live by these criteria! Commit yourself to assessing your study and your conclusions accordingly. You may have already been familiar with them prior to reading this chapter; yet, do not dismiss them as "basic." The challenge for many is not, as I suspect, awareness of these norms, but rather, "taking them seriously" and engaging them again and again in the process of biblical exegesis.

Don't let these criteria fool you! Their beauty is their clarity and simplicity. However, their simplicity of expression does not limit their usefulness. To the contrary: these are deep principles and if we embrace them and allow them to, they will carry us over unfathomable depths and turbulent seas of various interpretative waters.

The criteria are articulated in condensed form in the *Catechism* and I recommend committing them to memory — period. In addition, one might place them on a sticky note inside of one's Bible or on a desk where biblical study is often done. Place them in some prominent visual location, so as to continually remind yourself of the *evaluative process* that the criteria call us to engage in, which is anything but simple.

2. Scrutinize the biblical scholarship you read in light of the criteria.

A second and equally important challenge is to apply these standards to the biblical scholarship that we are interacting with, i.e., the exegesis of others. These criteria can brightly illuminate biblical conclusions and, importantly, the process by which scholars reach them. The criteria enable us to read biblical interpretations thoughtfully, critically and with greater objectivity.

Several decades ago, Pope Benedict XVI (then Cardinal Ratzinger) delivered a now famous address on various challenges presented by biblical criticism today. The address (part of the Erasmus lecture series), was titled "Biblical Interpretation in Crisis," but is often referred to as his "critique of (biblical) criticism."[286] It is an excellent evaluation of both the strengths and weaknesses of historical-critical approaches and how Catholic scholars can integrate such methods and scholarly insights into their own work in a sensible way. As he rightly observes, "In the last hundred years, exegesis has had many great achievements, but it has brought forth great errors as well."[287]

Near the end of the address, Ratzinger offers "five hopes" for biblical scholarship in the near future. As we end this chapter, these "hopes" will be re-stated and summarized as our final recommendations for adhering to Principle #6 — with respect to both self-evaluation and our assessment of the work of other biblical scholars.

1. Develop sound methods of biblical exegesis. It is not sufficient to simply "do research" and present one's opinions as facts. As Ratzinger urges, the time has come for "a new and thorough reflection on exegetical method."[288] We ought to ask what method or methods a scholar has employed in arriving at a particular conclusion. Biblical exegetes (as well as those who read their work) must realize that all conclusions, even those that claim to be "scientific" in approach, have philosophical underpinnings. What are they? If the philosophical framework is not readily apparent from the work itself, are there reliable critiques of the work (such as in other commentaries, monographs or articles that interact with it)? Finally, remember to apply the three criteria to the work — and conduct your own evaluation.

2. Exegesis must be historically situated. Of course, this point echoes what was previously articulated in our discussion of Principle #2 (above). Unless the exegesis is adequately rooted in "history" — both biblical history and the history of exegesis, a scholar's work can slip into arbitrary preferences, even as it passes on its findings as "certain."

3. Patristic and medieval exegesis should be considered. Ratzinger correctly points out that too often contemporary scholarship is disinterested in conclusions of biblical thinkers — many of them giants — that precede the modern era. As a result, their scholarship is disconnected from the wisdom of the past and often prejudices all previous conclusions as "pre-modern" and less relevant. As Ratzinger sums up,

> "It is not sufficient to scan simply the last one hundred and fifty years. The great outlines of patristic and medieval thought must also be brought into the discussion. It is equally indispensable to reflect on the fundamental judgments made by the Reformers and the critical importance they have had in the history of exegesis."[289]

4. Biblical exegetes should avoid hypotheses as much as possible. To be sure, it is right to refrain from speaking with a tone of certainty unless such is warranted. Conclusions should be based on prudential judgments, only after all relevant data have been thoroughly scrutinized. Here, Ratzinger is asking biblical theologians to do the work of biblical theology (in contrast to systematic theology), and focus on the text as much as possible. This is not at all to diminish the value of systematic theology. In fact, Ratzinger sees a return to the text as paving the way to "a new and fruitful collaboration":

> What we need now are not new hypotheses … What we do need is a critical look at the exegetical landscape we now have, so that we may return to the text and distinguish between those hypotheses which are helpful and those which are not. Only under these conditions can a new and fruitful collaboration between exegesis and systematic theology begin. And only in this way will exegesis be of real help in understanding the Bible.[290]

5. Biblical exegetes must always engage Scripture as a student of history and a servant of the Church. The biblical exegete should understand his position in context of two thousand years of inquiry — and as a subject of the Church. As Ratzinger concludes,

> The exegete must realize that he does not stand in some neutral area, above or outside history and the Church. Such a presumed immediacy regarding the purely historical can only lead to dead ends. The first presupposition of all exegesis is that it accepts the Bible as a book. In so doing, it has already chosen a place for itself which does not simply follow from the study of literature. It has identified *this particular literature* as the product of a coherent history, and this history as the proper space for coming to understanding.[291]

Clearly, the implementation of these "five hopes" in biblical exegesis is a pressing need. They provide further wisdom for the biblical exegete.

The hopes laid out in his now famous address describe practical rules for sound methodological analysis of Scripture. They are equally applicable to any interpretative approach — providing substantial guidance for the narrative critic as well as adherent of form criticism. Yet, these five hopes are especially pertinent to historical-critical approaches to Scripture. In this way, the hopes are more than mere suggestions for "today's exegete;" they offer this, yes, but more than this, they establish important norms for what historical-critical approaches *can become* in the near future, if historical-criticism is to yield what was promised by its early proponents, centuries ago: a clearer portrait of the Jesus of history. Provided we remember that the Jesus of history is the same as the Christ of faith, and provided we take seriously Ratzinger's hopes, we can be increasingly optimistic as to the usefulness of such methods in the years ahead.

Conclusion

Where do we stand in our larger discussion of Catholic biblical principles?

In the present chapter, we explored a vital principle of Catholic biblical interpretation: all exegesis must be sound and balanced. Adhering to this principle does not limit our freedom as interpreters; to the contrary, it anchors us in the unity of Scripture and the unity of our Faith. By being well-grounded in truth, we are free to think, study, pray and respond to Scripture. The principle provides us with an assessment tool; a set of controls for evaluating or measuring good Catholic exegesis, just as it establishes controls for directing our work as students.

Questions for Reflection

1. How familiar am I with what the Catechism teaches on Scripture? Do I generally rely upon the Catechism as a primary source of guidance for understanding and living my Christian faith? (What sections am I most conversant with; which ones would be helpful for me to review?)

   a. More specifically, what role do the three criteria (CCC 111–19) have in my own biblical interpretation? Do I understand each of them? Could I articulate them clearly to a family member or parishioner?

   b. Why is the "unity and coherence" of Scripture an essential norm for biblical interpretation Criterion #1?

   c. In what ways is Criterion #2 both a simple and a complex norm? List three reasons why this criterion is essential for the biblical interpreter.

2. What is the "analogy of faith"? How exactly should biblical exegesis be accountable to the analogy of faith? What dangers are present for those who ignore or overlook this criterion?

3. Which of Ratzinger's "five hopes" is most relevant to my experience? Why?

4. How can we grow spiritually through the work of biblical exegesis?

For Further Study

Brown, Raymond E. *Biblical Exegesis and Church Doctrine*. Mahwah: Paulist Press, 1985. Brown discusses the relationship between Catholic exegetes and the Church. To some degree, his analysis of "Liberal Analysis of Church Dogma" (cf. Ch. 3 of his book) is eye-opening and worth reading. On the other hand, in his call for a "properly nuanced" (p. 65) understanding of Church teaching, Brown often seems petrified of "ultraconservative" Catholic exegesis.

Granados, Jose, ed. *Opening Up the Scriptures: Joseph Ratzinger and the Foundations of Biblical Interpretation*. Grand Rapids: Eerdmans, 2008.

Hahn, S. W. *Covenant and Communion: The Biblical Theology of Pope Benedict*. Ada, MI: Brazos Press, 2009.

Neuhaus, Richard J., ed. *Biblical Interpretation in Crisis: The Ratzinger Conference on Bible and Church*. Grand Rapids: Eerdmans, 1989. Note: Cardinal Ratzinger's address, found within this volume, is must reading for seminarians. It is also available online at: www.christendom-awake.org/pages/ratzinger/biblical-crisis.htm.

Ratzinger, Joseph Cardinal (Pope Benedict XVI). *God's Word: Scripture — Tradition — Office*. San Francisco: Ignatius Press, 2008.

———. *Jesus of Nazareth*. San Francisco: Ignatius Press, 2007. Ratzinger's first full volume in his papal role is stellar on many accounts. Not only is the life of Jesus in the Gospels well explained, but also, the reader will come away with a better understanding of various problems in biblical exegesis.

———. "Reflections by Cardinal Ratzinger: The Relationship Between Magisterium and Exegetes" (May 10, 2003). Available online at: www.vatican.va/roman_curia/congregations/cfaith/pcb_documents/rc_con_cfaith_doc_20030510_ratzinger-comm-bible_en.html.

Stuhlmacher, Peter. *Historical Criticism and Theological Interpretation*. Philadelphia: Fortress Press, 1977. The author advocates an approach that engages history seriously and, at the same time, is open to the transcendent.

Notes

264   §*VD* 29.

265   Cf. Principle #7 below.

266   Cf. CCC 111; *DV* §12.

267   CCC 112.

268   *DV* §7.

269   CCC 113.

270   *PD* §49.

271   Origin, *Homilae in Leviticum*, 5,5.

272   Paul VI, "Address to the Pontifical Biblical Commission," March 14, 1974 (*L'Osservatore Romano*, April 18, 1974).

273   Paul VI, "Address to the Pontifical Biblical Commission," (emphasis added).

274   CCC 114.

275   Benedict XVI, "Address to the Pontifical Biblical Commission," April 23, 2009.

276   Congregation for the Doctrine of the Faith, "Instruction on the Ecclesial Vocation of the Theologian," May 24, 1990 (in *L'Osservatore Romano*, July 2, 1990).

277   Cf. Paul M. Blowers, "The Regula Fidei and the Narrative Character of the Early Christian Faith," in *Pro Ecclesia* 6 (1997), 199-228.

278   *PD* §16.

279   *DV* §9.

280   *Sacrosanctum Conciliam* §7. (Vatican II, "Constitution on the Sacred Liturgy," 1963.)

281   *PD* §23.

282   *Fides et Ratio*, §55.

283   *Fides et Ratio*, §55. Cf. §18-23, which talks beautifully of the role of wisdom, with many examples given from the Wisdom books of the Old Testament, as well as the Gospels and Paul's epistles. As a biblical scholar, this is one of my favorite sections of the encyclical!

284   Benedict XVI, "Address to the Pontifical Biblical Commission," April 23, 2009.

285   *Fides et Ratio*, §80.

286   Joseph Cardinal Ratzinger, "Biblical Interpretation in Crisis: On the Question of the Foundations and Approaches of Exegesis Today." (Rockford, IL: Rockford Institute, 1988). Every year the Institute on Religion and Public Life (publisher of First Things), sponsors the Erasmus Lecture in New York City. In 1988, that lecture was delivered by Joseph Cardinal Ratzinger at St. Paul's Church. It has since been published by the Rockford Institute (Rockford, IL) and is widely available in print (i.e., various collections of his addresses) as well as on various websites.

287   Ratzinger, "Biblical Interpretation in Crisis."

288   Ibid.

289   Ibid.

290   Ibid.

291   Ibid.

> These gliding and glittering lights of God's Word which sparkle over the eyes of the soul ... now let what we hear from Elijah rise up to our soul and would that our thoughts, too, might be snatched up into the fiery chariot ... so we would not have to abandon hope of drawing close to these stars, by which I mean the thoughts of God.
>
> *Gregory of Nyssa,* Homily X

Principle 7
God's Word Is Life-giving and Active!

After much effort, we have arrived at our final principle of Catholic biblical interpretation:

Principle #7: God's inspired word fulfills a life-giving, foundational, and authoritative role in the life of the Church. Thus, Catholic biblical interpretation does not conclude with an understanding of words, concepts and events. It must seek to arrive at the reality of which the language speaks, a transcendent reality, communication with God.

The Church is called to continually actualize the ancient texts as the Word for today, and embody it in all situations and cultures. To this end, the Catholic student of Scripture must have competence in all of the previous principles so that he/she can read, study, pray and proclaim Scripture faithfully and clearly with full confidence in their transformative power.

From Inspiration to Application

You are now well-acquainted with principles for Catholic Scripture study, beginning with Principle #1, which states that God's Word is "God's words in human language."

From that foundational platform, we launched into a study of six other principles. We described Principle #2 ("God's Word is discovered in history") as closely related to Principle #1 The divine author breathes His truth into the human language of the biblical author in history. As such, all of the written Word is understood just as the Christ, the Living Word is: *Incarnationally.*

Principle #1 (Inspiration) and Principle #2 (Incarnation) represent a kind of "marriage" from which our other principles are born. Collectively, they form a "family" of interpretive principles.

Care must be taken to ensure that the study of sacred Scripture is truly the soul of theology inasmuch as it is acknowledged as the word of God addressed to today's world, to the Church and to each of us personally.

— Pope Benedict, *Verbum Domini* § 47

Principle #3 states that God's Word subsists both in Sacred Tradition and in Sacred Scripture. Thus, we can only speak of a canon and the canonization of Scripture in light of the incarnation of God's inspired Word in the Church.

The unity of the Word, in both the Old and New Testament constitutes Principle #4. The "unitive pattern" in the Word of God is a result of both the inspired Author who oversaw all of its writing and its deeper unity and the human authors who composed these books in history.

Principle #5 holds that this divine and human Word has been shown throughout history to be rich in "meanings." With prayer and study, the student of the Word can "put out into the deep" of history and gather many possible methods and senses by which Scripture can be interpreted. And in our consideration of Principle #6 we saw that the Church offers maternal guidance in interpreting this inspired and incarnate Word in the form of three essential criteria in the *Catechism*. such norms assure that the Inspired and Incarnate Word is grounded and balanced from a historic Catholic perspective.

Living in Front of the Text

Now, one final principle remains.

As Catholic students of the Bible, Principles 1–6 move us along a circuit; but our ultimate pathway does not end with "exegesis of the text." All of our historical methods — as crucial as they are to the work of exegesis — can only indicate *the world behind the text* and literary methods can only explain *the world behind and or within the text*.

Exegesis is not enough.

History is not enough.

Even when exegesis begins from and is grounded in an inspiration-al-incarnational framework, *there is more to say.* Even when exegesis is mindful of crucial links: between Scripture and Tradition, between Old and New Testament, and between exegete and Magisterium, *there is more to say.* Even when exegesis pays attention to the various senses of Scrip-tural passage, and when it draws out a plethora of meanings from it, *there is more to say.* Even when, in the final analysis, a biblical interpretation can be properly described as "sound and balanced" exegesis, *there is still more to say.*

Even when, in the final analysis, a biblical interpretation can be prop-erly described as "sound and balanced" exegesis, there is still more to say.

As Pope Benedict XVI recently observed, "An authentic process of interpretation *is never purely an intellectual process but also a lived one,* demanding full engagement in the life of the Church, which is life "ac-cording to the Spirit."[292]

For Christians, the Bible is the word of God for all succeeding ages. That means that we live, as it were, in *the world in front of the text.* Thus, there is the absolute necessity of a hermeneutic that integrates the word behind and within the text with the world in front of the text, i.e., that operates within a broader interpretive framework which bridges the past with the present.[293]

The letter needs to be transcended: the word of God can never simply be equated with the letter of the text. To attain to it involves a progres-sion and a process of understanding guided by the inner movement of the whole corpus, and hence it also has to become a vital process.

— Pope Benedict XVI, *Verbum Domini* § 38

Hence, reason alone is not able to fully comprehend the events and the message recounted in the Bible. In order to truly understand the Bi-ble one must welcome the meaning given in the events, above all, in the person of Jesus Christ.[294] Because the Bible is the word of God, it must be approached in the light of faith in order to be properly understood. Therefore, exegesis is a theological discipline. The light of the Holy Spirit is needed to interpret Scripture correctly. As someone grows in the life of the Spirit, his or her capacity to understand the realities of which the Bible speaks also grows.[295]

Our pathway is from *inspiration* to *application*. We always begin with the reality of Scripture as an inspired Word. But our destination is not merely the *explanation* of the biblical Word, but the *actualization* of it. This is at the core of Principle #7.

Holiness: Actualization of the Word

To "actualize" something, whether a goal or objective, is to make it real, to make it happen. In a war game, a soldier must acquire his target before he pulls the trigger on his paint gun. But it is only when his buddy is covered in bright pink or green paint that the "kill" was actualized.

In modern psychology, some experts talk about "self-actualization."[296]

In the pyramid of human needs, there are the essential *physiological* needs, such as air, food, water, and sleep. Without such basic needs being met, most other human activity or aspirations are senseless (cf. Figure 4). Building upon the physiological are the needs of *safety* (e.g., physical, economic security), *love/belonging* (e.g., family, friendship) and *esteem* (e.g., self-confidence, respect of others). Yet, beyond these needs is "self-actualization," in which our moral and creative choices lie. Here, we attempt to solve problems, develop our personality, and embrace (or reject) ideas and truths. Whatever one thinks of the categories, it is an interesting way of delineating between various needs.

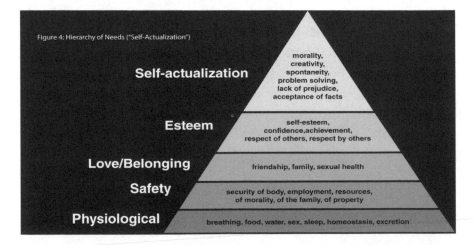

Figure 4: Hierarchy of Needs ("Self-Actualization")

Self-actualization: morality, creativity, spontaneity, problem solving, lack of prejudice, acceptance of facts

Esteem: self-esteem, confidence, achievement, respect of others, respect by others

Love/Belonging: friendship, family, sexual health

Safety: security of body, employment, resources, of morality, of the family, of property

Physiological: breathing, food, water, sex, sleep, homeostasis, excretion

More importantly, there is a parallel between this concept from psychology and what Vatican II referred to as the "universal call to holiness."[297] In this field of psychology, the person is considered in light of their overall progress and in discovering their "full human potential."

Yet, for the Christian, *this pyramid, while helpful in some ways, is insufficient in others.* This hierarchy indicates no explicit awareness of God. A purely physiological or psychological explanation of "needs" does not account for our deepest and greatest necessity — God, who is love (cf. 1 John 4:16). As the opening paragraph of the *Catechism* summarizes,

> God, infinitely perfect and blessed in himself, in a plan of sheer goodness freely created man to make him share in his own blessed life. For this reason, at every time and in every place, God draws close to man. He calls man to seek him, to know him, to love him with all his strength. He calls together all men, scattered and divided by sin, into the unity of his family, the Church. To accomplish this, when the fullness of time had come, God sent his Son as Redeemer and Savior. In his Son and through him, he invites men to become, in the Holy Spirit, his adopted children and thus heirs of his blessed life.[298]

We are all called to this deeper human potential, not mere "self-actualization." We are called to the actualization of *Christ's virtues.* The Church therefore summons us to this true purpose of life.

A purely physiological or psychological explanation of "needs" does not account for our deepest and greatest necessity — God, who is love.

It is an awakening and an invitation; and an invitation to the blessed life of God is one of holiness:

> Therefore in the Church, everyone, whether belonging to the hierarchy or being cared for by it, is called to holiness ... In order that the faithful may reach this perfection, they must use their strength accordingly as they have received it, as a gift from Christ. They must follow in His footsteps and conform themselves to His image seeking the will of the Father in all things. They must devote themselves with all their being to the glory of God and the service of their

neighbor. In this way, the holiness of the People of God will grow into an abundant harvest of good, as is admirably shown by the life of so many saints in Church history. [299]

Whether we are a Bishop or priest, consecrated religious, a mom or dad, a sister or brother, we are all called to a life of holiness. As Jesus himself taught us in His Sermon on the Mount, "Be ye therefore perfect, even as your Father which is in heaven is perfect" (Matt 5:48, KJV). As *Lumen Gentium* teaches us,

> *This call is truly universal ...*
> The classes and duties of life are many, but holiness is one — that sanctity which is cultivated by all who are moved by the Spirit of God, and who obey the voice of the Father and worship God the Father in spirit and in truth.[300]

> *... and must become truly active:*
> They must follow in His footsteps and conform themselves to His image seeking the will of the Father in all things. They must devote themselves with all their being to the glory of God and the service of their neighbor. In this way, the holiness of the People of God will grow into an abundant harvest of good, as is admirably shown by the life of so many saints in Church history.[301]

We must help the people of God actualize this Word in their hearts and in their lives, and so help everyone lead lives of holiness on their journey to Christ.

Completing the Work of Exegesis

Given this universal and active call to holiness, we come back to the issue at hand: it is not enough merely to study the Word of God soundly. This is the essence of our final principle, and this is what is meant by engaging in the work of "actualizing" the Word.

And the first work of actualizing Scripture is simply, receiving the Word in our own heart. In the call to holiness, above all, the Christian looks to Mary, the Mother of our Lord, who received the Living Word in her heart. As Pope John Paul II reminded us,

The followers of Christ still strive to increase in holiness by conquering sin, and so they raise their eyes to Mary, who shines forth to the whole community of the elect as a model of the virtues.[302]

We are called to "magnify" Christ in our hearts, as Mary, our Blessed Mother taught us through her life, which was wholly at the service of the Redeemer. It is through the school of Mary that we grow in holiness. As we live out this call, we realize the next stage in actualizing the Word is witnessing to its transformative power through our actions and our words. By "magnifying" Christ in our own lives, and contemplating the many ways Christ has been and is being magnified in His saints, we are able to "complete the work of exegesis." In a word, Mary is the "more" in "there is more to say" in exegesis. Mary is the ultimate actualization of the Word — she proclaims Christ unceasingly:

> Mary, whom tradition is wont to call the "new Eve" and the true "Mother of the living," *boldly proclaims* the undimmed truth about God: the holy and almighty God, who from the beginning is the source of all gifts, he who "has done great things" in her, as well as in the whole universe.[303]

FOR REFLECTION

"Love the Lord thy God with the entire and full affection of the heart; love Him with the vigilance and foresight of reason; love Him with the full strength and vigor of the soul, so that His love for you would not fear even to die; as it is written in a verse of this Canticle, 'Love is strong as death.'" (Song of Songs 8:6)
— St. Bernard of Clairvaux, Sermon XX on the Song of Songs (From Sermons on the Song of Songs, Mahwah, NJ: Paulist Press, 1987)

We too are called to "boldly proclaim" the great things Christ has done and is doing in us and through His Bride, the Church. Thus, as in all other areas of our lives, the Mother of God ought to guide us in the study of Scripture. She is the portrait of "complete openness to the person of Christ, to his whole work, to his whole mission."[304]

The Ecclesial Context of Scripture

Given this, our biblical knowledge cannot stop short at an understanding of words, concepts and events. It must seek to arrive at the reality of which the language speaks, a transcendent reality, communication with God.[305] Scripture does not merely explain events of the past, it is always "living and active" (Heb 4:12).

Importantly then, the meaning of a text can be fully grasped only as it is *actualized* in the lives of readers who appropriate it:

> Beginning with their situation, they are summoned to uncover new meanings, along the fundamental line of meaning indicated by the text. Biblical knowledge should not stop short at language; it must seek to arrive at the reality of which the language speaks.[306]

Yet, we must remember that while we are indeed "summoned to uncover new meanings," we need to do so from the heart of the Church. We must always keep our other principles before us in this work of actualization. In seeking to arrive at "the reality" of the text for God's people today, we cannot and must not exploit the Word for the sake of some ideological opinion:

> Actualization, therefore, cannot mean manipulation of the text. It is not a matter of projecting novel opinions or ideologies upon the biblical writings, but of sincerely seeking to discover what the text has to say at the present time. The text of the Bible has authority over the Christian church at all times, and, although centuries have passed since the time of its composition, the text retains its role of privileged guide not open to manipulation.[307]

Unless we acknowledge the Lord's real presence in the Eucharist, our understanding of Scripture remains imperfect.

— Pope Benedict XVI, *Verbum Domini* § 54

All actualization of the Word — whether in prayerful and devotional reading of Scripture, in the sacred liturgy, as the "end" of scholarly exegesis and study, or in teaching and proclaiming it — is towards an ecclesial "target." Accordingly, the first objective of the biblical student is to "lock on" to this target in all of our activity. Do we have the Church always "in our sites" when we're handling Scripture? Along the same lines, the second objective of actualization is to "pull the trigger," that is, to connect our exegesis of Scripture with the life of the Church. Until we do so, we are only dealing with the "historical" horizon of the ancient world.

We must connect it properly with the "living horizon," bringing forward the message for the Church today, in various situations.

As Pope Benedict XVI urges,

> *The ecclesial context alone* enables Sacred Scripture to be understood as an authentic Word of God which makes itself the guide, norm and rule for the life of the Church and the spiritual growth of believers.[308]

The following four areas are ways in which Scripture has been and must always be directed for the good of the Church.

1) In the Sacred Liturgy

As we enter into the Sacred Liturgy, we are reminded of the close connection between Word and Sacrament. This has always been the case, from the very beginnings of the Church (and before its birth, in the ancient Jewish liturgies):[309]

> From the earliest days of the church, the reading of Scripture has been an integral part of the Christian liturgy, an inheritance to some extent from the liturgy of the synagogue. Today, too, it is above all through the liturgy that Christians come into contact with Scripture, particularly during the Sunday celebration of the Eucharist.

Yet, as Pope Benedict XVI recently reminded us,

> *A faith-filled understanding of sacred Scripture must always refer back to the liturgy*, in which the word of God is celebrated as a timely and living word: "In the liturgy the Church faithfully adheres to the way Christ himself read and explained the sacred Scriptures, beginning with his coming forth in the synagogue and urging all to search the Scriptures."[310]

The ecclesial context alone enables Sacred Scripture to be understood as an authentic Word of God which makes itself the guide, norm and rule for the life of the Church and the spiritual growth of believers.

— Pope Benedict XVI

There is a reciprocal role between the Word of God and the Holy Eucharist. Hearing the Scriptures devoutly prepares us for the mysteries of the Eucharist — and in turn, the Holy Sacrament deepens our understanding of Scriptures and Christ's love for us revealed within them.[311]

Likewise, as the IBC document reminds us, it is in the context of the Holy Eucharist that we come face to face with the "perfect actualization" of the Word, as we gaze upon the Living Word, our Lord Jesus.[312]

Peter Williamson offers another vital reason: "The liturgy is still the primary place where most Catholic Christians encounter Scripture."[313]

Scripture must not only be the starting point, but also the foundation and norm for all catechesis.

---

2) In the Work of Catechesis

As the *IBC* document thoughtfully states, the heart and soul of all true Catholic catechesis is to be the Word of God:

> The explanation of the Word of God in catechesis has Sacred Scripture as first source. Explained in the context of the Tradition, Scripture provides the starting point, foundation and norm of catechetical teaching. One of the goals of catechesis should be to initiate a person in correct understanding and fruitful reading of the Bible. This will bring about the discovery of the divine truth it contains and evoke as generous a response as is possible to the message God addresses through his word to the whole human race.[314]

Four things are to be noted here.

First and foremost, Scripture is to be the origin of our catechesis. Catechetical workbooks and textbooks are fine, provided that they faithfully teach the Catholic faith. Here it must be asked, *"Are we grounding our catechesis in Holy Scripture?"* There are certainly some good catechetical resources available today, but there are unfortunately some weak, lukewarm ones as well. Some of these display little regard for Scripture at all. All of this calls for greater scrutiny: pastors and directors of religious education programs— will you commit yourselves to identify and make use of catechetical resources that are rooted in Scripture? It is not adequate to say, "This is what we've always used here, etc." The people of God and their children need to meet Jesus Christ through his Word! Second, and along these same lines, Scripture must not only be the "starting point," but also the "foundation and norm" for all catechesis.

Catechesis should communicate in a lively way the history of salvation and the content of the Church's faith, and so enable every member of the faithful to realize that this history is also part of his or her own life.

— Pope Benedict XVI, *Verbum Domini* § 74

Get rid of textbooks that prop up some ideological point of view that is not consistent with the teachings of the Church. If necessary, use age-appropriate catechisms and lessons from the Bible itself. Third, note the insistence on explaining Scripture in the context of Sacred Tradition. Often today, I hear of catechesis that is biblical, but often reflects Protestant sensibilities rather than the fullness of Catholic Tradition. Fourth and finally, the *IBC* document sets as one of the essential goals of all catechesis, "to initiate a person in correct understanding and fruitful reading of the Bible." As such, all programs should be measured with this critical goal in mind; rather than dumping information on them that they may or may not remember in three months' time, the goal is to teach them "how to fish" in the written Word.

FOR REFLECTION

> *"Let no day pass without reading some portion of the Sacred Scriptures and giving some space to meditation; for nothing feeds the soul so well as these sacred studies do."*
>
> — *Theonas of Alexandria (c. A.D. 300)*
> Epistle of Theonas

3) Through Pastoral Ministry

Three particular groups of people require special care with respect to Scripture: young adults; the poor, sick and elderly, and those with special needs; and engaged couples.

First, many young adults in the Church today have little connection with Sacred Scripture. As *Verbum Domini* reminds us, "Young people need witnesses and teachers who can walk with them, *teaching them to love the Gospel and to share it*, especially with their peers, and thus to become authentic and credible messengers."[315]

Today, far too many teens and young adults have been poorly or improperly catechized. In some instances, such malnourishment on the "true bread" (John 6:32) which gives "life to the world" (v. 33) has had a drastic and sad consequence for them — and for the Church. Many have left the Church altogether, in search of "spiritual food" elsewhere (e.g., Evangelicalism, other religions). The data (and my own personal experience) indicates that often such "seeking" occurs during the high school/college years or shortly thereafter.

Both my wife and I grew up Catholic, though our internal experience of Scripture and the Faith waned in our teens. We left the Church for a period — she after high school, I after college. We later met one another through a young adult ministry in a highly influential Evangelical "seeker" church near Chicago called Willow Creek. We spent a number of years in this mega-church before returning to our Catholic roots. As an aspiring leader at the church, I sought to help many people "convert to Christ." Willow Creek is a particularly interesting case, since nearly *seventy-five percent* of its members were baptized Catholics. Looking back on these years, I now see and regret that I failed to recognize Christ in these young adults. Like me, many of these young adults were former Catholics who were at Willow Creek in part because the roots of their faith had not gone deep enough. Sadly, we were hungering for Christ, but felt that we were not "being fed" in the Church. Regardless of the "fault," one thing is clear: *this should not be.*

There may be plenty of "blame" to throw around for the large number of persons who have left the Catholic Church for such reasons: the individuals themselves who decided to leave, lukewarm/uncatechized parents, busy/ill-equipped priests/parish staff, over-zealous evangelists who prey upon the vulnerable. Yet, pointing fingers or wringing our hands does not address the problem. In fact, it can distract us from a more urgent need: *inviting them back* to be fed upon Christ in Word — and in Sacrament.

We must boldly challenge young adults to discover their vocation in life. And whether it is to the priesthood, married life, or some other call, we should not be afraid to help them encounter Christ in Scripture!

It is in times of pain that the ultimate questions about the meaning of one's life make themselves acutely felt. If human words seem to fall silent before the mystery of evil and suffering, and if our society appears to value life only when it corresponds to certain standards of efficiency and well-being, the word of God makes us see that even these moments are mysteriously "embraced" by God's love.

— Pope Benedict XVI, *Verbum Domini* § 106

Whether through parish Bible studies, apologetics groups, service trips, or engaging speakers, we ought to prayerfully consider how the pirit desires to penetrate and transform the hearts of young men and women. We must ask God to penetrate our parishes with truth and love. Make a commitment to seek ideas from interested young adults as to ways to reach them with the Gospel.

Aside from young adults, there are an array of diverse individuals and groups that desperately need to hear the Scriptures afresh: the poor, sick (and terminally ill), the elderly, those with disabilities and special needs. How will you reach them with God's Word?

While each category presents its own challenges, a few points must be mentioned.

First, those with special burdens are frequently not in the place where they are most likely to hear the Scriptures — the Church. Therefore, we must take the Word of God to them in their situation. Perhaps some of the poor in your community are not proficient in speaking or reading English. Can your parish provide Bibles in *Spanish* (or other languages) to such families or groups? Better yet, can you invite such groups to the parish for a dinner and fellowship, and have a presentation on the Scriptures in their language? Obviously, the Church is engaged in all kinds of ministry to the sick — whether hospitalized or homebound. Sacramental and pastoral visits are most common; but are there opportunities to reach the sick with the healing power of the Scriptures. What are some of the passages that would be most encouraging to someone who is ill? Can you *memorize* some of these so that you can recount such passages at a moment's notice?

In the face of widespread confusion in the sphere of affectivity, and the rise of ways of thinking which trivialize the human body and sexual differentiation, the word of God re-affirms the original goodness of the human being, created as man and woman and called to a love which is faithful, reciprocal and fruitful.

— Pope Benedict XVI, *Verbum Domini* § 85

Similarly, the elderly and others with special needs may be stricken with physical, mental emotional (or other) challenges that prevent them from receiving God's Word in a meaningful way. What are some of the challenges that come to mind? How could you and your parish connect with such persons so that they too encounter the Lord, who is our "common salvation" (Jude 3)?

Another group of persons that is in particular need of a fresh encounter with Scripture are engaged couples. For several years, I had the privilege of working with thousands of couples preparing for the Sacrament of Marriage in the Archdiocese of New York. That experience was incredible, and taught me at least three things. First, do not assume that otherwise intelligent Catholic adults have any real understanding of Scripture. Many today are getting engaged later in life. In my own experience, I encountered countless couples that had advanced degrees in engineering, medicine, business, law and finance — with the equivalent of a sixth grade education in Sacred Scripture! Second, do not presume — even if they do attend Mass with some regularity that they have ever really thought about Jesus: who He is, their relationship with Him, and what impact He could have on their marriage and family. Thus, pre-marital meetings with the priest are wonderful opportunities for re-evangelization. Additionally, marriage preparation (Pre-Cana) classes can be excellent times for sharing the Good News with these couples.

4) In Evangelization

Proclaiming the Gospel is something that we are *all* called to; it does not matter whether we are a bishop, priest, deacon, college student, married couple or senior. We are *all* called to proclaim Christ everywhere and in all ways. On the first pages of the *Catechism*, we read,

> All Christ's faithful are called to hand it on from generation to generation, by professing the faith, by living it in fraternal sharing, and by celebrating it in liturgy and prayer.[316]

In my experience, many Catholics today are less comfortable than we should be in sharing the Gospel with others. Fortunately, that seems to be changing for the better, as many young people have a renewed dedication and a robust attitude towards evangelization.

St. Francis is to have said, *"Preach the Gospel in all the world; if necessary, use words."* This is a beautiful expression. His words reflect the holistic, Catholic ethos with respect to the proclamation of the Gospel and the work of evangelization. Through acts of charity, great or small, the Gospel is preached; in compassion, love and true justice, Christ is proclaimed. This is very true. It is also true that often, we identify our Protestant brothers and sisters as those Christians who tend to "use words" while we Catholics prefer to share Christ "through our actions." However, this is a false dichotomy! Indeed, we must avoid proselytizing tactics, or pressuring attitudes or haranguing behavior — for this is <u>not</u> reflective of Jesus Christ. That said, it is incumbent upon all of us to allow the Gospel of Jesus Christ to permeate all of our actions — and be reflected in all of our words. As Pope John Paul II famously said,

> Do not be afraid to go out on the streets and into public places like the first apostles, who preached Christ and the good news of salvation in the squares of cities, towns and villages. *This is no time to be ashamed of the Gospel* (cf. Rom 1: 16). *It is the time to preach it from the rooftops* (cf. Matt 10:27). Do not be afraid to break out of comfortable and routine modes of living in order to take up the challenge of making Christ known in the modern "metropolis." It is you who must "go out into the byroads" (Matt 22:9) and invite everyone you meet to the banquet which God has prepared for his people. The Gospel must not be kept hidden because of fear or indifference. *It was never meant to be hidden away in private.* It has to be put on a stand so that people may see its light and give praise to our heavenly Father (cf. Matt 5:15–16).[317]

Recently, some of my own seminarians have gone to the "byroads" of nearby university campuses through our New Evangelization Club. Those who did so sacrificed much needed rest and time with their own families to participate in such events over fall and/or spring break periods. Their mission was clear: to proclaim the Good News of Jesus Christ — with boldness, but also with great respect and gentleness. After these events, I was greatly encouraged to hear report after report of wonderful conversations between our seminarians and students of many diverse backgrounds. In recalling the evangelization event, I heard phrases like "it was incredible" and "I'm so glad I went" many times over. I listened with delight to numerous stories like the following: "He was an agnostic guy, but really open. We talked for an hour, and he had sincere questions. He was really interested in knowing what I believed ..." And the graces were twofold, as our seminarians were as blessed as those who discovered new things about God, Holy Scripture and the Church. As dramatic as it may sound, I suspect that many of our seminarians — many who beforehand may have thought, "I just can't do this" — are not only glad that they "stepped out," but eagerly look forward to more of these respectful and exciting conversations. The point seems clear enough: evangelization (with or without Scripture) can be scary — but also richly rewarding for all involved.

Among the new forms of mass communication, nowadays we need to recognize the increased role of the internet, which represents a new forum for making the Gospel heard. Yet we also need to be aware that the virtual world will never be able to replace the real world, and that evangelization will be able to make use of the virtual world offered by the new media in order to create meaningful relationships only if it is able to offer the personal contact which remains indispensable.

— Pope Benedict XVI, *Verbum Domini* § 113

More recently, Pope Benedict XVI called for a renewed awakening to the importance of "witness" with respect to the proclamation of God's Word:

> The immense horizons of the Church's mission and the complexity of today's situation call for new ways of effectively communicating the word of God. The Holy Spirit, the protagonist of all evangelization, will never fail to guide Christ's Church in this activity. Yet it is important that every form of proclamation keep in mind, first of all, the intrinsic relationship between *the communication of God's word* and *Christian witness*. The very credibility of our proclamation depends on this. On the one hand, the word must communicate everything that the Lord himself has told us. On the other hand, it is indispensable, through witness, to make this word credible, lest it appear merely as a beautiful philosophy or utopia, rather than a reality that can be lived and itself give life. This reciprocity between word and witness reflects the way in which God himself communicated through the incarnation of his Word. The word of God reaches men and women "through an encounter with witnesses who make it present and alive."[318]

Enact the Gospel

In his second encyclical, Pope Benedict XVI talks about Christian hope and in his discussion of the Gospel, makes an important distinction:

> So now we can say: Christianity was not only "good news"—the communication of a hitherto unknown content. In our language we would say: the Christian message was not only "informative"

but "performative." That means: the Gospel is not merely a communication of things that can be known—it is one that makes things happen and is life-changing. The dark door of time, of the future, has been thrown open. The one who has hope lives differently; the one who hopes has been granted the gift of a new life.[319]

According to Pope Benedict, we must not think of Scripture as a "Word of the past," as *informative* only. Rather, the Gospel has always been — and always will be a *performative* Word. As he says, it "makes things happen and is life-changing."

FOR REFLECTION | *The Christian message was not only informative but performative. The Gospel is not merely a communication of things that can be known—it is one that makes things happen and is life-changing.*
— Pope Benedict XVI

Similarly, in his monumental work, *Theo-Drama*, Von Balthasar writes of the creative and redemptive actions of God in history; and describes those divine actions as a "theo-drama" that the Church is caught up in. For Von Balthasar, each believer plays a role in this *theo-drama*, each of us is an actor in this great divine plot, and, to use Von Balthasar's terminology, each of us in the actions of our own lives must "substantiate" the truth of the *theo-drama* that we are caught up in.[320] This is because the drama of Christ is not fantasy, but the deepest and truest reality that man participates in. The Gospel is "the greatest drama ever staged ... *a terrifying drama of which God is the victim and the hero.*"[321] Because of this, the life of every baptized Christian is dramatically lived with Christ and enacts His Gospel in our lives. Apprehended in this way, evangelization consists of a "For Reflection" of actions and words, body and spirit, mind and heart, towards the work of the Spirit. Thus, the contemplative-pastoral priest is called to a participation in the Spirit, an enacting of the Scriptures across his entire life, so that the people of God move towards this kind of participation and action in their lives as well.

In no way can the Church restrict her pastoral work to the "ordinary maintenance" of those who already know the Gospel of Christ ... The Church must go out to meet each person in the strength of the Spirit.

— Pope Benedict XVI, *Verbum Domini* § 95

As we take our place in the drama of salvation, with Christ, and immersed in His Word of life, we are reminded of the greatest human "actor" — the Blessed Virgin Mary — whose actions and words were so beautifully integrated within her, that she was and is a living Scripture:

> From the Cross you received a new mission. From the Cross you became a mother in a new way: the mother of all those who believe in your Son Jesus and wish to follow him. The sword of sorrow pierced your heart. Did hope die? Did the world remain definitively without light, and life without purpose? At that moment, deep down, you probably listened again to the word spoken by the angel in answer to your fear at the time of the Annunciation: "Do not be afraid, Mary!" (Luke 1:30). How many times had the Lord, your Son, said the same thing to his disciples: do not be afraid! In your heart, you heard this word again during the night of Golgotha. Before the hour of his betrayal he had said to his disciples: "Be of good cheer, I have overcome the world" (John 16:33). "Let not your hearts be troubled, neither let them be afraid" (John 14:27).
>
> "Do not be afraid, Mary!" In that hour at Nazareth the angel had also said to you: "Of his kingdom there will be no end" (Luke 1:33). Could it have ended before it began? No, at the foot of the Cross, on the strength of Jesus' own word, you became the mother of believers. In this faith, which even in the darkness of Holy Saturday bore the certitude of hope, you made your way towards Easter morning. The joy of the Resurrection touched your heart and united you in a new way to the disciples, destined to become the family of Jesus through faith. In this way you were in the midst of the community of believers, who in the days following the Ascension prayed with one voice for the gift of the Holy Spirit (cf. Acts 1:14) and then received that gift on the day of Pentecost. The "Kingdom" of Jesus was not as might have been imagined. It began in that hour, and of this "Kingdom" there will be no end. Thus you remain in the midst of the disciples as their Mother, as the Mother of hope. *Holy Mary, Mother of God, our Mother, teach us to believe, to hope, to love with you. Show us the way to his Kingdom! Star of the Sea, shine upon us and guide us on our way!*[322]

Mary, he reminds us, has the quintessential role in this drama, and is continually our "acting coach" for our own part on this stage. This is because she is the *Ecclesia Immaculata,* "the heavenly Church who is perfected in advance."[323] As Pope Benedict XVI reflects, "[Mary] discovered the profound bond which unites, in God's great plan, apparently disparate events, actions and things."[324]

Draw near to Mary in your study and proclamation of Scripture. Pray that the Blessed Virgin accompany you in the hard but rewarding work ahead: it is in her that the Incarnate Word comes to us. She models for us *receptivity to the Word,* and we cannot "actualize" the Word of God unless we continually receive the Word made flesh. But whereas she received Him perfectly and wholly as the *Ecclesia Immaculata,* we as imperfect and sinful members of the Body must receive Him again and again, eucharistically.[325] Thus, it is she that stands behind us and "completes our imperfect assent."[326]

To whom should we entrust all of our Scriptural work other than Mary? Her "actualization of the Word" is pure, complete, life giving. She takes no credit for herself, but perpetually points us on to her beloved son, Jesus Christ, conceived by the Holy Spirit: "He who is mighty has done great things for me, and holy is His name" (Luke 1:49). Let us then draw near to Mary, the one in whom there is a pure and perfect correspondence between "gift and self-giving, reception and thanksgiving."[327] For the Blessed Virgin, who bore the Living Word in her womb, "keeps no grace for herself; she receives grace in order to transmit it. This is what a mother does."[328]

Conclusion

Scripture fulfills a life-giving, foundational and authoritative role in the life of the Church.[329] Scripture does not merely trace Salvation history of the "past," it communicates life and is perpetually relevant to all people at all times. The Church must continually actualize the Word for today, and embody it in all situations and cultures. We are called to receive this Word, and allow it to permeate all of our lives and ministry, for the Word is ever new (Rev 21:5). Especially in the sacred liturgy, in catechesis, in pastoral ministry and the work of evangelization, to which we are all called, Scripture plays a transformative and life-changing role in all of our lives (Rom 12:2). As such, we are called to continually "proclaim the Gospel" in all situations and to all people, just as Mary "performed" the Gospel in an integrated and truly human fashion.

Questions for Reflection

1. How would I summarize Principle #7? Principle #1 was called the "foundational" principle … in what way is Principle #7 the "capstone" principle?

2. How can we make the truths of God's Word accessible to contemporary culture?

3. Biblical interpretation does not stop with "exegesis alone." Explain.

4. What lessons can the biblical student take from modern psychology with respect to the "actualization" of Scripture? In what ways does the analogy from psychology fall short?

5. Having completed The Word of the Lord, spend some time reviewing the book. (As a help, refer to the summary of all seven principles in Appendix I, as well as the conclusions at the end of each chapter.)

   a. How has this overall study impacted your view of Scripture? What challenges remain? How will you meet those challenges?

   b. Finally, spend some time in prayer, thanking God for His Word, and ask Him to help you grow, especially in the ways that are most important for you.

For Further Study

Anderson, Carl. *A Civilization of Love: What Every Catholic Can Do to Transform the World.* New York: HarperOne, 2008.

Aumann, J. *Christian Spirituality in the Catholic Tradition.* San Francisco: Ignatius Press, 1985.

Balthasar, Hans Urs von. *The Threefold Garland.* San Francisco: Ignatius Press, 1982.

Bartholomew, Craig and Michael W. Goheen, *The Drama of Scripture: Finding Our Place in the Biblical Story.* Grand Rapids: Baker Academic, 2004.

Chesteron, G. K. *What's Wrong with the World.* San Francisco: Ignatius Press, 1994, reprint.

Danielou, Jean. *The Bible and the Liturgy.* Notre Dame, IN: University of Notre Dame Press, 1956.

John Paul II. *Christifideles Laci.* Post-Synodal Apostolic Exhortation, "On the Vocation and the Mission of the Lay Faithful in the Church and in the World (1988). Available online: http://www.vatican.va/holy_father/john_paul_ii/apost_exhortations/documents/hf_jp-ii_exh_30121988_christifideles-laici_en.html.

——. *Letter to Families.* St. Paul, MN: Pauline Books and Media, 1994.

————. *Redemptoris Mater.* Encyclical letter, "On the Blessed Virgin Mary in the Life of the Pilgrim Church" (1987). Available online: http://www.vatican.va/holy_father/john_paul_ii/encyclicals/documents/hf_jp-ii_enc_25031987_redemptoris-mater_en.html.

Martin, Ralph and Peter Williamson, eds. *John Paul II and the New Evangelization: How You Can Bring the Good News to Others.* Cincinnati: Servant Books, 2006.

Nichols, Aidan. *Christendom Awake: On Reenergizing the Church in Culture.* Grand Rapids: Eerdmans, 1999.

Niehbur, H. R. *Christ and Culture.* New York: Harper, 1951.

Ratzinger, Joseph Cardinal (Pope Benedict XVI). *Christianity and the Crisis of Cultures.* San Francisco: Ignatius Press, 2006.

————. *Christocentric Preaching,* in *The Word Toward a Theology of the Word.* New York: J.P. Kennedy & Sons, 1961.

————*Dogma and Preaching.* San Francisco: Ignatius Press, 1983.

————. *God is Near Us: The Eucharist, the Heart of Life.* San Francisco: Ignatius Press, 2003.

————. *Ministers of Your Joy: Scriptural Meditation of Priestly Spirituality.* Ann Arbor: Servant Publications, 1989.

————. *Spe Salvi.* Encyclical letter, "On Christian Hope" (2007). Available online at: www.vatican.va/holy_father/benedict_xvi/encyclicals/index_en.htm.

————. *Truth and Tolerance.* San Francisco: Ignatius Press, 2004.

Vanhoozer, Kevin. *The Drama of Doctrine: A Canonical-Linguistic Approach to Christian Theology.* Louisville: Westminster John Knox, 2005.

Notes

292 Pope Benedict XVI, *Verbum Domini* §38.

293 Cf. *IBC,* II.A.2.a.

294 Cf. *IBC,* II.A.2.d.

295 Cf. *IBC,* II.A.2.f.

296 The so-called "hierarchy of needs," proposed in 1943 by Abraham Maslow. Cf. A.H. Maslow, "A Theory of Human Motivation," in *Psychological Review* 50(4) (1943), 370-96.

297 Cf. *LG* §39-42.

298 CCC 1.

299 *LG* §39, 40.

300 *LG* §39.

301 *LG* §40.

302 John Paul II, *Redemptoris Mater* §6. (Encyclical "On the Blessed Virgin Mary in the Life of the Pilgrim Church,"1987).

303 *Redemptoris Mater* §37. Concerning the New Eve, cf. Irenaeus, *Against Heresies,* III.22; concerning the Mother of all the living, cf. Epiphanius, *Panarion,* III, 2.

304 *Redemptoris Mater* §37; cf. *Ad Caeli Reginam,* §37-39.

305   *IBC,* II.A.1.d.

306   *IBC,* II.A.1.d.

307   *IBC,* II.A.1.e.

308   Benedict XVI, Address to the Participants in the Plenary Assembly of the Pontifical Biblical Commission.

309   *IBC* IV.C.1.

310   Pope Benedict XVI, *Verbum Domini* §52.

311   Cf. Pope Benedict XVI, *Verbum Domini* §54.

312   *IBC* IV.C.2; cf. *Sacrosanctum Concilium* §7.

313   Williamson, *Catholic Principles for Interpreting Scripture*, 313.

314   *IBC* IV.C.3.b.

315   Benedict XVI, *Verbum Domini* §97.

316   CCC 3.

317   John Paul II, "Address at World Youth Day," (World Youth Day VIII, 1993), emphasis mine.

318   Pope Benedict, *Verbum Domini* §97.

319   Benedict XVI, *Spe Salvi* §2; cf. §4, 10.

320   Hans Urs von Balthasar, *Theo-Drama*, vol. 1, *Prolegomena* (San Francisco: Ignatius Press, 1988), 288.

321   Dorothy Sayers, *Creed or Chaos?* (New York: Harcourt, Brace and Co., 1949), 1.

322   Benedict XVI, *Spe Salvi* §50.

323   Hans Urs von Balthasar, *The Threefold Garland* (San Francisco: Ignatius Press, 1982), 103. Translated from the German original, *Der Driefache Kranz* (1978) by Erasmo Leiva-Merikakis.

324   Pope benedict XVI, *Verbum Domini* §87.

325   Ibid, 34.

326   Ibid.

327   Ibid, 137.

328   Ibid.

329   Cf. *DV* §21.

APPENDIX A

The 7 Principles of Catholic Biblical Interpretation in Summary Form

Principle #1: **God's Word: divine words in human language.**

Catholic Biblical Interpretation is governed by the firm belief that Scripture is the inspired word of God, expressed in human language. God's Word was written under the direction and inspiration of the Holy Spirit and — at the same time — was written by true human authors with their intellectual capacities and limitations. The thought and the words belong both to God and to human beings in such a way that the whole Bible comes simultaneously from God and from the inspired human authors.

Principle #2: **God's Word is revealed in history.**

Catholic Biblical Interpretation is profoundly concerned with history because of the nature of biblical revelation and the Living Word who revealed himself to humanity in history (John 1:14). Yet, Scripture can never be reduced to the natural order but fully affirms the supernatural and God's intervention in history. Interpretation of a biblical text must be consistent with the meaning expressed by the human authors. Thus, Catholic exegetes must place biblical texts in their ancient contexts, helping to clarify the meaning of the biblical authors' message for their original audience and for the contemporary reader.

Principle #3: **God's Word: Sacred Tradition and Sacred Scripture.**

Catholic Biblical Interpretation is grounded in the firm belief that there is one source of Divine revelation: Sacred Scripture and Sacred Tradition. The living presence of God's Word in the Church's life through time "flow from the same one divine wellspring" (DV §9) and "form one sacred deposit of the word of God" (DV §10). It was by the apostolic Tradition that the Church discerned which writings are to be included in the biblical canon (DV §8) and it is above all Sacred Tradition that helps us to truly and properly understand the Word of God.

Principle #4: **God's Word: revealed in the unity of the Old and New Testaments.**

Catholic biblical interpretation insists upon the unity and coherence of the whole canon of Scripture, both Old and New Testaments. This unitive dimension of the Word of God is evident in many ways; Catholic exegetes should be particularly aware of three:

- The Theme of Covenant
- Biblical Typology
- Recapitulation in Christ

In these and other ways, we affirm Augustine's conclusion: "The New Testament lies hidden in the Old and the Old Testament is unveiled in the New."

Principle #5: God's Word has meaning(s).

Catholic Biblical interpretation affirms that God's Word is rich in meaning and a multiplicity of approaches can assist the exegete in explaining texts. No one sense of Scripture or method of interpretation is adequate in itself to plumb the depths of Scripture. Catholic exegetes thus benefit from exploration of various methods, including ancient, medieval, and modern biblical scholarship. Such an array of approaches can cast valuable light on the Sacred Page, provided one "reads" them within the tradition of the Church and according to the hermeneutics of faith.

Principle #6: God's Word requires sound, balanced, methodological analysis.

Catholic biblical interpretation requires sound and balanced analysis. In the end, all analysis should be based upon excellence in scholarship, encountered from a robust Christian faith, and reflect pastoral concern and the needs of God's people. Three essential criteria for ensuring such control in one's exegesis of Sacred Scripture:

1) Attention to the content and unity of the Bible.
2) Reading all of Scripture within the living Tradition of the Church
3) Reference to the analogy (or rule) of faith.

Principle #7: God's Word Is life-giving and actve!

God's inspired word fulfills a life-giving, foundational, and authoritative role in the life of the Church. Thus, Catholic biblical interpretation does not conclude with an understanding of words, concepts and events. It must seek to arrive at the reality of which the language speaks, a transcendent reality, communication with God. The Church is called to continually actualize the ancient texts as the Word for today, and embody it in all situations and cultures. To this end, the Catholic student of Scripture must have competence in all of the previous principles so that he/she can ready, study, pray and proclaim Scripture faithfully and clearly with full confidence in their transformative power.

APPENDIX B

Modern Biblical Scholars

Part I: Meet the Rationalists: Six Influential Academic/ Secular Biblical Scholars

1. **Julius Wellhausen** (1844–1918) Considered the father of modern source criticism of the Bible, and particularly OT **source criticism**. His major contribution is known as the **Documentary Hypothesis** (DH). With it, Wellhausen posits four primary written sources behind the books of the Pentateuch as we now have them. These sources are identified as the Yahwist, the Elohist, the Deuteronomist and the Priestly source (J-E-D-P). While many facets of the DH are still debated, today, his contributions set the tone for the study of the Pentateuch for two centuries.

2. **Heinrich Holtzmann** (1832–1910) German liberal scholar who proposed "Markan priority," which argues that Mark (not Matthew) was the earliest gospel. His conclusions helped overturn the traditional consensus. This gave way in the early twentieth century to more speculative theories about the Gospels, notably the **'Q'** source. Since no historical or archeological evidence is available, 'Q' remains a hypothesis and can only be accessed by comparing gospel parallel passages, where Q represents the common material in Matthew and Luke (but absent in Mark). As such, Holtzmann is credited with the beginnings of modern Gospel research.

3. **Albert Schweitzer** (1875–1965) Franco-German scholar, physician and humanitarian with doctorates in theology, philosophy and music. In *The Quest for the Historical Jesus*, he skillfully critiqued two centuries of Jesus scholarship. Yet, he replaced them with his own problematic theory, in which Jesus was a **failed apocalyptic prophet**. According to Schweitzer, Jesus anticipated the **end of the world** and awaited the **Son of Man** — but did <u>not</u> recognize Himself as this figure. He once wrote that Jesus "*threw himself on the wheel of history and was crushed by it.*" Many people were influenced by Schweitzer's work — and many questioned their Christian faith as a result.

4. **Rudolph Bultmann** (1884–1976) Lutheran pastor and one of the most influential historical-critical scholars of the twentieth century. In *Jesus Christ and Mythology*, he argued that Evangelists drew upon motifs from Hellenism, and imported myths into the Jesus tradition. Despite this, Bultmann considered himself a "believer" who respected Jesus' wisdom and believed he was doing a great service to historic Christianity by "*de-mythologizing*" the Jesus of the gospels so that the "true" nature of his message of an existential Christianity could be realized in the life of his disciples.

5. **John Dominic Crossan** (1934–) Former Catholic priest who co-founded *The Jesus Seminar* (1980s), a skeptical think-tank which cast ballots to determine the

veracity of Gospel passages. The failed results of *The Jesus Seminar* is the full flowering of two centuries of rationalism and anti-supernatural bias. Crossan writes, "Jesus' strategy was a combination of free healing and common eating that negated the hierarchical norms of *Jewish religion* and *Roman power.* He was neither broker nor mediator but *the announcer that neither should exist between humanity and divinity or humanity and itself."*

6. **Bart Ehrman** (1955–) Former fundamentalist Christian, now secular theologian and popular author. Ehrman sees little reason to trust the Bible, or its message, given that it is a "corrupt" text. His sensationalistic titles and dramatic remarks often land him on cable television documentaries. Interestingly, Ehrman grew up in fundamentalist Christian environments — but eventually rejected its "easy-believism" and developed into a skeptic.

Part II: Ten Significant Catholic/Christian Scholars of the Modern Era

[Note: Scholars are listed alphabetically. C = Catholic; P = Protestant/Evangelical.]

1. **Richard Bauckham** [P] (1946–) Contemporary Anglican scholar with expertise in early Judaism and the Gospels. His *Jesus and the Eyewitnesses* examines the Four Gospels as **eye-witness testimony**, and he mounts considerable data to support his positive claims. *Jesus and the Eyewitnesses* is arguably one of the most important gospel studies in the early twenty-first century.

2. **Gregory Beale** [P] (1949–) Contemporary Evangelical noted for his work in OT/NT and early Jewish studies. Strong advocate of biblical inerrancy and authority. Beale's *Temple and the Church's Mission* is an excellent example of his inter-textual mastery and contributes to a deeper understanding of the **Jerusalem Temple** of the OT and Jesus Christ in the NT. More recently, his work on *The Commentary of the NT Use of the OT* has become a very respected resource for OT/NT study.

3. **Raymond E. Brown** [C] (1928–1998) Roman Catholic priest of the Sulpician order and the most recognized Catholic biblical scholar of the twentieth century. Brown was one of the earliest modern Catholic scholars to work in the H-C method. He co-edited the ***New Jerome Biblical Commentary***, a classic biblical commentary. His two-volume commentary on ***The Gospel of John*** is the single most influential modern work on the Gospel. Other well-known studies include: ***The Birth of the Messiah*** and ***The Death of the Messiah.*** Brown's passion for ecumenical progress sometimes landed him in trouble, often from conservative Catholics, who believed his positions undercut various teachings of the Church.

4. **Alfred Edersheim** [P] (1825–1889) Born of Jewish parents in Vienna, Edersheim converted to Christianity and later taught and preached at Oxford. His most important works are *The Temple and Its Ministry and Services at the Time of Jesus Christ* and *The Life and Times of Jesus the Messiah.* Edersheim' s keen understanding of **early Judaism**, its worship, institutions, literature, etc. was unparalleled in his time. Like-

wise, his erudition and attention to historical detail in the study of the gospels was remarkable, especially for his day. His study of the life of Jesus remains a treasury of information and is a masterpiece in early twentieth century NT studies. Regrettably, his work has been dismissed as out of date scholarship.

5. **André Feuillet** [C] (1909–1998) French biblical scholar and Sulpician priest. An under-appreciated yet very important **pre-Vatican II Catholic scholar**. The prolific list of monographs and essays demonstrates his tireless efforts for the Church — and his interest in deepening the faith of others. Though scientifically rigorous, all of his work is permeated by **magisterial adherence** and supreme **confidence in the biblical Word**. Although much of his work precedes the Council, in many ways it anticipates its vision and 'follows' its mandates. A good example of this is Feuillet's *Interpreting the Scriptures*, completed before Vatican II.

6. **Joseph Fitzmyer** [C] (1920–) American Jesuit who, along with **Raymond Brown** was one of the earliest Catholic scholars to produce commentaries after *Divino Afflante Spiritu* (1943) using H-C methods. Fitzmyer's major works include commentaries on: *The Gospel of Luke* (2 vols), *Acts of the Apostles* and *Romans*. As a member of the **Pontifical Biblical Commission**, Fitzmyer penned a number of works that advocate a particularly historical approach to biblical topics. Such views often conflicted with Magisterial teaching (E.g., Mary's perpetual virginity is not a matter of historical veracity; James was "brother" of Jesus.)

7. **Luke Timothy Johnson** [C] (1943–) Catholic scholar who focuses on Jewish and Greco-Roman influences on early Christianity. On the one hand, he is very adept at critiquing the fallacies of modern Jesus research and in their place, arguing positively for the historical reliability of the New Testament (see: *The Real Jesus: The Misguided Quest for the Historical Jesus and the Truth of the Traditional Gospels*). On the other hand, Johnson stands opposed to particular Church teachings and is a notable advocate for women's ordination. Though most of his NT work is absent of such opinions, it is more evident in works like *The Creed: What Christians Believe and Why it Matters*.

8. **John Meier** (1942–) [C] Important Catholic scholar of the late twentieth/ early twenty-first centuries, known for his four-volume magnum opus, ***A Marginal Jew: Rethinking the Historical Jesus.*** Using methods of empirical research, he attempts to reconstruct the historical Jesus and find common ground among Catholics, Protestants, Jews (and agnostics), as to the question, "who Jesus was and what he intended." In *Vol I (The Roots of the Problem and the Person)*, he establishes and tests criteria toward that end. In *Vol II (Mentor, Message, Miracles)*, he focuses on Jesus' relationship with John the Baptist, his announcement of the Kingdom and His miracles. In *Vol III (Companions and Competitors)*, he examines the Twelve as well as the Pharisees, Sadducees, etc. In *Vol IV (Law and Love)*, he examines Jesus' moral teachings in light of the Law of Moses.

9. **Joseph Cardinal Ratzinger/Pope Benedict XVI** [C] (1927–) Never in the history of the papacy has there been a biblical theologian in the Chair of Peter such

as Joseph Ratzinger. As priest, professor, bishop and now pope, it is hard to find a work of his not distinguished by his grand biblical vision. His thought is marked by a "**hermeneutic of faith**," resting on the witness of the Apostles — and the biblical worldview of the early Fathers. Despite varied interests pertaining to Scripture (criticism, sacraments, typology, Tradition, etc.), it is his biblical Christology which ties everything together. Articulating the Living Word within the Written Word is at the heart of his thought. In *Jesus of Nazareth* (two vols.) he helps the reader encounter "**the face of the Lord**" in fresh ways, re-uniting: **faith and reason, exegesis and theology**, and **Word and Sacrament**.

10. **N. T. Wright** [P] (1948–) Among the most influential of today's biblical scholars. Wright is respected for his works on the historical Jesus and the Apostle Paul. He has been very critical of and has confronted the conclusions of "The Jesus Seminar" and frequently engages in lively (and friendly) debate with liberal scholars. Wright is an expert on Jesus' **Resurrection** and **the reliability of the Gospels**. His major work is a three-volume series: *Vol I* (*The New Testament and the People of God*); *Vol II* (*Jesus and the Victory of God*); and *Vol III* (*The Resurrection of the Son of God*). More recently, Wright has written a series of books that are aimed at more of a popular audience. The better of these include his "For Everyone" NT commentary series (e.g., *John for Everyone*) and *How God Became King: The Forgotten Story of the Gospels*. **Note:** Not all of Wright's work "fits" with a Catholic and Sacramental approach. Nevertheless, his grand biblical worldview, his critique of empty rationalism, and his confidence in the Gospels, specifically in the believability and meaning of the Resurrection, are all reasons that make it worthwhile to read him — and a good note to end on.

APPENDIX C

Biblical Resources

Selecting Biblical Software

I am often asked by seminarians and others, "Is Bible software helpful, and should I invest in it? If so, which is the best platform?" The short answer is, yes, biblical software programs can be very helpful for both beginners as well as more advanced students of Scripture. I recommend their use.

A slightly longer answer is as follows. First, biblical software is not absolutely "necessary" to study the Bible well. Obviously, people have done so for centuries without it. At the same time, the better programs allow the student to study the Word in some new and unimaginably fast ways. For example, one can quickly ascertain the occurrence of a particular word in Scripture. The program I use reported that the name "Solomon" occurs 315 times in 215 verses in Scripture (and 3 additional verses in 1, 2 Esdras and 4 Maccabees). And it yielded that information in 1.51 seconds! Additionally, it lists the verses so that I can bring them up, compare them, etc.

The truth is, that is a basic function of such programs. Beyond such "speed searches," today's programs are quite advanced. The better programs contain dozens of translations of the Bible (English and numerous other languages), they include the ancient languages of the Bible (Hebrew, Greek, Aramaic; even Coptic and Syriac). Translations can be quickly compared; Greek words can be parsed, and so on.

For many, however, the real payoff is in all of the tools that such programs often include: passage analysis; interactive maps; extra-biblical texts (Apocrypha, Josephus, Church fathers, etc.) as well as scholarly commentaries — all fully "searchable." And much more.

Depending upon features, the cost of such packages range from several hundred to a thousand dollars (for all of the "bells and whistles.") Some advice: talk with someone who uses such programs. (E.g., "What do you like/dislike about the program, and why did you purchase this program over that one? Would they buy this one again? Why/why not? Etc.)

Two of the more popular programs are as follows:

• ***BibleWorks***© *is sort of an "all in one" program that can do a lot of essential tasks lightning fast. It contains a number of helpful reference tools, original language tools, etc. There are really no additional modules to buy, and as such, the package is a good value under $300 at present. (www.bibleworks.com)*

• *Logos© is similar to BibleWorks,© but offers about six levels of the product, from basic Bible student to advanced scholars packages. It is also an expandable program; meaning, there are now thousands of electronic books that are available as modules — from single monographs to full commentary sets, such as Anchor Bible, Ancient*

Christian, and the others listed below. It is a dynamic program that could be a fine long-term investment, provided one has the funds.

* One additional remark on Logos Bible Software: until the past year or two, most of the electronic titles offered were of a Protestant origin. More recently, Logos has invested in more Catholic resources and, in fact, has a full-time Catholic products specialist. Presently, Logos offers three base packages specifically designed for Catholic Scripture study: (i) **Catholic Foundations Library***; (ii)* **Catholic Scripture Study Library***; and (iii)* **Catholic Scholars Library***. All three packages are designed "from the ground up" with a Catholic user in mind. All three packages (and optional modules) offer hundreds of essential texts and reference materials, from Catholic Bible translations, to the Church fathers, to the Summa Theologica and much more. A "Ratzinger collection" is available, as is a fully-searchable Catechism of the Catholic Church. (www.logos.com)*

Selecting Biblical Commentaries

Q: Which commentaries should I read/buy?

In many ways, this is a personal decision, and a number of factors may be involved: purpose, frequency of use, budget, etc. On the one hand, I am inclined to not point to any one commentary series, and encourage each reader to make appropriate selections based upon the above factors and/or other factors.

On the other hand, I recognize some readers are looking for specific recommendations. With this in mind, the following commentaries are recommended as a starting point; these resources generally have proved helpful in the past. As you make your own selections, hopefully the seven principles of Catholic biblical interpretation will help guide you towards an appropriate resource.

1. If you are not in need of a biblical commentary, but are perhaps just looking for a reliable one-volume reference work on Scripture, I recommend: **Catholic Bible Dictionary** (CBD), Scott W. Hahn, ed., New York: Doubleday, 2009. In this dictionary, you will find hundreds of dictionary length articles on the persons, places, things and institutions in Sacred Scripture. Importantly, every book of the Old Testament is featured in its own article. Though the articles range from a few paragraphs to a few pages, they are packed with salient information and analysis. Additionally, there are some longer essays in CBD that treat key themes in biblical theology in a bit more depth ("Biblical Interpretation," "Covenant," "Sacrifice," "Priesthood," "Sin," etc.) The CBD is a "required text" in my Scripture classes and many students have indicated that they have found it to be quite useful.

2. If you are looking for a distinctively Catholic commentary, and/or need only one or two volumes on a favorite biblical book, or for a Bible study, etc., then

I recommend: ***Catholic Commentary on Sacred Scripture*** (CCSS), Grand Rapids, MI: Baker Academic Press.

This new and much needed series seeks to integrate solid biblical scholarship "with lively faith to help Catholics interpret Scripture and apply it to Christian life today."[330] This series is highly recommended to Catholic students of Scripture. Those studying the principles studied in the present book will feel "at home" in these commentaries:

> Central to the commentary's approach are the theological principles taught by Vatican II for interpreting Scripture 'in accord with the same Spirit by which it was written' — that is, interpreting Scripture in its canonical context and in the light of Catholic tradition and the analogy of faith (*Dei Verbum*, §12). The CCSS helps readers grasp the meaning of texts both in their historical and literary context and in their relationship to Catholic doctrine and life in the present.[331]

Some of the particular features are as follows:[332]

- Written in an engaging style that can be read for personal study and spiritual nourishment as well as referenced for exegetical information
- Distinguished by a theological and pastoral hermeneutic rather than a focus on technical questions that legitimately interest scholars but have less relevance for Christian life
- Interprets the canonical form of the text in light of the whole of Scripture and the Church's faith
- Shows the relationship between Scripture and Catholic doctrine, worship, and daily life
- Aims to serve readers across a spectrum of Catholic opinion while remaining faithful to Church teaching
- Applies the theological principles taught by Vatican II for interpreting Scripture "in accord with the same Spirit by which it was written.

Seventeen New Testament volumes are planned, and at present, approximately half are in print. Others will follow. The editors may offer an Old Testament series in the future, however, at present all volumes are exclusively for the books of the New Testament. For more information and availability of volumes, see: **www.catholicscripturecommentary.com**.

Other Recommended Commentaries

Anchor Bible Commentary (AB), New York: Doubleday Press

This critical commentary series tends to highlight historical and linguistic background information. In addition to detailed analysis of the text, each volume contains an introduction, a translation by the author and numerous exegetical notes. *AB* is a classic commentary series that is worth consulting, even if one occasionally disagrees with the author. The volumes on John and the Johannine Epistles (both by Raymond Brown) are particularly noteworthy. Joseph Fitzmyer's volumes on Luke and Acts are widely recognized; I also recommend Fitzmyer's volume on Romans, for which his massive, historical bibliography on the epistle is worth the price alone. Joseph Blenkinsopp's three volumes of Isaiah reflect the "source critical" orientation of the entire series. A final note: *AB* includes volumes on all of the deuterocanonical books (of which the ones on Sirach and Wisdom of Solomon are particularly good). (New York: Doubleday, edited by William Foxwell Albright and David Noel Freedman.)

Ancient Christian Commentary on Scripture (ACC) (Downers Grove, IL: Inter-Varsity press, Thomas Oden, general editor)

The *ACC* series consists of twenty-nine volumes. It provides select quotations from the early Church fathers on all of the books of the Bible. This is a refreshing addition to the plethora of modern commentaries (of which only a select few are mentioned here.) In the style of medieval catenae, each volume provides patristic commentary on the passage in view. Scores of ancient authors are used across the entire series. Until recently this series, from the Protestant publisher InterVarsity, excluded the deuterocanonical books. In the Spring of 2010, a volume on the "Apocrypha" (i.e., deuterocanonicals) was published.

Opening the Scriptures, Huntington, IN: Our Sunday Visitor

A series of expositions on the Gospels by George Martin, the founding editor of *God's Word Today* magazine: *Bringing the Gospel of Mark to Life*; *Bringing the Gospel of Matthew to Life*, and *Bringing the Gospel of Luke to Life*, all published by Our Sunday Visitor. Daniel J. Harrington, S.J., says that "these expositions of the Gospels are written with admirable clarity. They interpret each Gospel in its first-century context, convey the best insights of modern scholars, and challenge the readers to apply the text to their own lives."

New International Commentary on the Old Testament (NICOT) and *New International Commentary on the New Testament* (NICNT), Grand Rapids: Eerdmans

This Old Testament — and corresponding New Testament commentary series reflects conservative Protestant scholarship. These series address exegetical and theological issues in a scholarly manner, while seeking to be useful to the interested lay person. As such, technical details are relegated to footnotes and appendixes. That said, some knowledge of Hebrew, Greek, and Latin is helpful. (NICOT: Grand Rapids: Eerdmans, R. K. Harrison, general editor; NICNT: Grand Rapids: Eerdmans F. F. Bruce, general editor.)

Navarre Biblical Commentary, New York: Four Courts/Scepter Press

The Navarre Bible Commentary is a compilation of resources: the complete biblical text, according to the RSV; the New Vulgate version, and brief commentary on the text. The editors of the series are from the University of Navarre (Spain) and examine the text from the point of view of their founder, St. Josemaría Escrivá. Particular preference is given to official Church documents and interpretations from the fathers and doctors of the Church. Each volume in the series (also "bundled together," i.e., "Pentateuch," "Gospels," etc.) contain introductions to each Biblical book, maps and textual notes. The individual volumes can be excellent resources for spiritual and ecclesial perspectives on the biblical text.

Word Biblical Commentary **(WBC)**, *Nashville, TN*

This commentary series addresses both exegetical and literary-critical concerns; scholarship is generally from an informed Evangelical point of view. Similar to the style of the *Anchor Bible* commentary series, *WBC* series includes detailed analysis of the text, an introduction, translation by the author and a considerable number of ex-egetical notes. Attention to the original languages is emphasized; as is the "structural" dimension of biblical texts. (Waco, TX: Word Books, David A. Hubbard and Glen W. Barker, general editors.)

Notes

330   Source: http://www.catholicscripturecommentary.com.

331   Ibid.

332   Ibid. The features listed here are all from the Catholic Commentary on Sacred Scripture website.

AN INDEXED BIBLIOGRAPHY

The following is a selection of texts that bear on the discussions in The Word of the Lord to one degree or another. A number of the resources are accompanied by some annotation as to their usefulness, relevance, etc. This bibliography is somewhat unique in that each volume is indexed to the corresponding principles (1–7).

Achtemeier, Paul J. *Inspiration and Authority: Nature and Function of Christian Scripture.* Peabody, MA: Hendrickson, 1999. (Principle #1.)

Aland, K. *The Text of the New Testament.* Grand Rapids: Eerdmans, 1987. (Principle #2.)

Alter, Robert. *The Art of Biblical Narrative.* New York: Basic Books, 1981. A seminal work of "narrative criticism." (Principle #5.)

Anderson, Carl. *A Civilization of Love: What Every Catholic Can Do to Transform the World.* New York: HarperOne, 2008. (Principle #7.)

Anderson, N., Felix Just, S.J., and Tom Thatcher, eds. *John, Jesus, and History, Volume 1: Critical Appraisals of Critical Views.* Atlanta: SBL, 2007. (Principle #2.)

Aquinas, Thomas. *Catena Aurea: A Commentary on the Four Gospels Collected Out of the Works of the Fathers* (and edited by John Henry Newman). Southampton: Saint Austin Press, 1997.

———. *Commentary on the Gospel of John 3 Volume Set* (Thomas Aquinas in Translation). James A. Weisheipl, Fabian Larcher, trans. Introduction and annotation by Matthew Levering and Daniel Keating. Washington, D.C.: CUA Press, 2010. A landmark commentary on the Fourth Gospel, these lectures were delivered to Dominican friars when Thomas Aquinas was at the height of his theological powers, when he was also composing the *Summa theologiae.* For numerous reasons, the *Summa* has received far more attention over the centuries than has his *Commentary on the Gospel of John.* However, scholars today recognize Aquinas's biblical commentaries as central sources for understanding his theological vision and for appreciating the scope of his *Summa theologiae.*

Athanasius, Saint. *On the Incarnation.* Crestwood, NY: St. Vladimir's Seminary Press, 1996. (Principle #2.)

Aumann, J. *Christian Spirituality in the Catholic Tradition.* San Francisco: Ignatius Press, 1985. (Principle #7.)

Balthasar, Hans Urs von. *The Office of Peter and the Structure of the Church.* San Francisco: Ignatius Press, 1986. (Principle #3.)

———. *The Threefold Garland.* San Francisco: Ignatius Press, 1982. Beautiful Marian reflection and a very pastoral work by Balthasar (Principle #7.)

———. *Theo-Drama*, vol. 1, *Prolegomena.* San Francisco: Ignatius Press, 1988. (Principle #2, 7.)

Barbeau, J. W. "Newman and the Interpretation of Inspired Scripture," *Theological Studies,* 63 no 1 (2002), 53-67. (Principle #5.)

Bartholomew, Craig. *"Behind" the Text: History and Biblical Interpretation.* Scripture and Hermeneutics Series. Grand Rapids: Eerdmans, 2003. (Principle #5.)

Bartholomew, Craig and Michael W. Goheen, *The Drama of Scripture: Finding Our Place in the Biblical Story.* Grand Rapids: Baker Academic, 2004. (Principle #7.)

Bauckham, Richard. *Jesus and the Eyewitnesses.* Grand Rapids: Eerdmans, 2006. A fresh study of the gospels as the product of "individual eye-witnesses." (Principles #2, 3, 6.)

———. *Testimony of the Beloved Disciple: Narrative, History, and Theology in the Gospel of John.* Grand Rapids: Eerdmans, 2007. (Principle #5.)

Beale, Gregory and D. A. Carson, eds. *Commentary on the New Testament Use of the Old Testament.* Grand Rapids: Baker Academic, 2007. A very unique commentary in which the books of the New Testament are scrutinized, chapter by chapter, with an eye to their use of Old testament texts and motifs. Highly recommended; perhaps one of the most important biblical reference works in recent decades and a very fine example of Principle #4 at work!

Béchard, Dean, ed. and trans. *The Scripture Documents: An Anthology of Official Catholic Teachings.* Collegeville, MN: Liturgical Press, 2002. Collection of magisterial and ecclesial documents on Sacred Scripture, e.g., *Providentissimus Deus, Dei Verbum, Interpretation of the Bible in the Church.* (Principle #2.)

Benoit, Pierre. *Aspects of Biblical Inspiration.* Chicago: Priory Press, 1965. (Principle #1.)

Bouyer, Louis. *The Meaning of Sacred Scripture.* Notre Dame, IN: University of Notre Dame Press, 1958. (Principle #5.)

Brewer, D. Instone. *In Potiphar's House: Techniques and Assumptions in Jewish Exegesis Before 70 C.E. TSAJ* 30. Tübingen: Mohr Siebeck, 1992. (Principle #5.)

Brown, Raymond E. *Biblical Exegesis and Church Doctrine.* Mahwah: Paulist Press, 1985. (Principle #5, 6.)

———. *The Critical Meaning of the Bible.* Ramsey, NJ: Paulist Press, 1981. (Principle #5, 6.)

———. *The Gospel according to John.* 2 vols. Anchor Bible 29-29A. Garden City, NY: Doubleday, 1966-1970. Landmark study of The Gospel of John from one of the leading Catholic biblical scholars of the twentieth century. (Principle #2, 3, 5, 6.)

———. *The Sensus Plenior of Sacred Scripture.* S.T.L. Diss.; St. Mary's Seminary & University, 1953; Baltimore, 1955. (Principle #5.)

Brown, Raymond E., Joseph A. Fitzmyer and Roland E. Murphy, eds. *The New Jerome Bible Handbook.* Collegeville, MN: Liturgical Press, 1992. Mentioned in the Introduction. (Principle #5.)

Bultmann, Rudolf. *The Gospel of John: A Commentary.* Louisville: Westminster John Knox Press, 1971; German original, 1941. (Principle #5, 6.)

———. *History of the Synoptic Tradition.* Harper San Francisco, 1976; German original, 1921. (Principle #5, 6.)

———. *The New Testament and Mythology and Other Basic Writings.* Minneapolis: Augsburg Fortress Publishers, 1984. (Principle #5, 6.)

Burtchaell, J. T. *Catholic Theories of Biblical Inspiration Since 1810: A Review and Critique.* Cambridge: Cambridge University Press, 1969. (Principle #5, 6.)

Butler, B. C. *The Church and Infallability.* London, Sheed and Ward, 1954. (Principle #3.)

Catchpole, David. *The Quest for Q.* Edinburgh: T & T Clark, 1993. (Principle #5, 6.)

Cavadini, John C. "The Use of Scripture in the Catechism of the Catholic Church," *Letter & Spirit* 2 (2006), 43-54. (Principle #3, 5.)

Charlesworth, James ed. *The Old Testament Pseudepigrapha,* 2 Vols. New Haven, CT: Yale Univ. Press, 1983, 1985. (Principle #5.)

Childs, Brevard. *Introduction to the Old Testament as Scripture.* Philadelphia: Fortress Press, 1979. A canonical approach to the Bible. (See Principle #5.)

———. *The New Testament as Canon: An Introduction.* Philadelphia: Fortress Press, 1984. (Principle #3; Excursus on the Canon.)

Chesteron, G. K. *What's Wrong with the World.* San Francisco: Ignatius Press, 1994, reprint. (Principle #7.)

Congar, Yves. *Tradition and Traditions.* London: Burn and Oates, 1966. (Principle #3.)

Congar, Yves and Avery Dulles. *The Meaning of Tradition.* San Francisco: Ignatius Press, 2004. (Principle #3.)

Danielou, Jean. *The Bible and the Liturgy*. Notre Dame, IN: University of Notre Dame Press, 1956. (Principle #7.)

————. *From Shadows to Reality: Studies in the Biblical Typology of the Fathers*. London: Burns & Oates, 1960. (Principle #4.)

De Lubac, Henri. *Medieval Exegesis*, Volume I. Grand Rapids, MI: Eerdmans, 1998. (Principle #5.)

————. *Scripture in the Tradition*, trans. L. O'Neil. Chestnut Ridge, NY: Crossroad, 1997. (Principle #5.)

De Margerie, Bertrand. *An Introduction to the History of Exegesis*. 3 vols. Petersham, MA: Saint Bede's Publications, 1993-95. (Principle #5.)

Dulles, Avery. *Models of Revelation*. Dublin: Knopf Doubleday, 1983. (Principle #3.)

Ehrman, Bart. *Misquoting Jesus: The Story behind Who Changed the Bible and Why*. San Francisco: HarperSanFrancisco, 2005.

Evans, Craig. *Fabricating Jesus: How Modern Scholars Distort the Gospels*. Downers Grove, IL: InterVarsity Press, 2006. Helpful volume for beginning students interested in "the search for the historical Jesus" from the point of view of an Evangelical scholar. Evans studied under some of the most significant scholars in the "Jesus Seminar" movement, and offers a fair and reasoned critique of such approaches. (Principle #6.)

————. *Life of Jesus Research: An Annotated Bibliography*. Rev. ed. New Testament Tools and Studies 24. Leiden: E.J. Brill, 1996. (Principle #5.)

Evans, C. A. and W. F. Stinesspring, eds. *Early Jewish and Christian Exegesis: Studies in Memory of William Hugh Brownlee*. Atlanta: Scholars Press, 1987. (Principle #5.)

Farmer, William R. *The Synoptic* Problem. Dillsboro, NC: Western North Carolina Press, 1976. (Principle #6.)

————. *The Gospel of Jesus: The Pastoral Relevance of the Synoptic Problem*. Louisville: Westminster/John Knox, 1994. Helpful and clear guide to some of the issues related to the "Two-Source" gospel theory, from the perspective of a former proponent of the hypothesis. In this pastorally motivated volume, which follows up the excellent work in *The Synoptic Problem*, Farmer lays out a number of problems with an uncritical reception of "Q" as more than a construct. (Principle #6.)

Farmer, William R. and D. Farkasfalvy. *The Formation of the New Testament Canon*. New York: Paulist, 1983. (Principle #3; Excursus on the Canon.)

Finan, Thomas and Vincent Twomey, eds. *Scriptural Interpretation in the Fathers: Letter and Spirit*. Dublin: Four Courts Press, 1995. (Principle #3, 5.)

Fitzgerald, Sally, ed. *The Habit of Being: Letters of Flannery O'Conner*. New York: Farrar, Strauss, Giroux, 1979. (Principle #7.)

Fishbane, M. *Biblical Interpretation in Ancient Israel*. Oxford: Clarendon Press, 1985. (Principle #5.)

France, R. T. *Jesus and the Old Testament*. Vancover: Regent College Publishing, 1992. (Principle #4.)

Gilson, Etienne. *Christian Philosophy*. Durham: Pontifical Institute for Medieval Philosophy, 1993. (Principle #5.)

————. *God and Philosophy*. New Haven, CT: Yale University Press, 2002. (Principle #5.)

Goodacre, Mark. "A Monopoly on Markan Priority? Fallacies at the Heart of Q," *Society of Biblical Literature Seminar Papers 2000*. Atlanta: Society of Biblical Literature, 2000. (Principle #6.)

————. *The Synoptic Problem: A Way Through the Maze*. London: Sheffield, 2001. (Principle #5, 6.)

Gorday, Peter. *Principles of Patristic Exegesis*. Lewiston, NY: Edwin Mellen Press, 1983. (Principle #3, 5.)

Finan, Thomas and Vincent Twomey (eds.), *Scriptural Interpretation in the Fathers: Letter and Spirit*. Dublin: Four Courts Press, 1995. (Principle #3, 5.)

Froelich, Karlfried (ed.). *Biblical Interpretation in the Early Church*. Philadelphia: Fortress, 1984. . (Principle #3, 5.)

Granados, Jose, ed. *Opening Up the Scriptures: Joseph Ratzinger and the Foundations of Biblical Interpretation*. Grand Rapids: Eerdmans, 2008. (Principle #5, 6.)

Gray, Tim. *Praying Scripture for a Change: An Introduction to Lectio Divina*. Wes Chester, PA: Ascension Press, 2009. An excellent companion *to this entire volume* and its larger goal of studying Scripture as a mystic, and yet as a contemplative that is rooted in action. (Principle #7.)

Grillmeier, A. "Dogmatic Constitution on Divine Revelation, Chapter III," *Commentary on the Documents of Vatican II*, ed. H. Vorgrimler, 199-215. New York: Crossroads, 1969. (Principle #2, 6.)

Gunkel, Hermann. *Genesis*. Translated by Mark E. Biddle (Macon, GA: Mercer University Press, 1997; German ed. 1910. (Principle #5.)

————. *The Psalms: A Form-Critical Introduction*. Introduction by James Muilenburg. Trans. T. M. Horner. Philadelphia: Fortress Press, 1967; German original 1927. Crucial development in the study of the Psalms under the broader category of historical-critical methodology (Principles #2, 5).

Hagerty, C. *The Authenticity of Sacred Scripture*. Houston, TX: Lumen Christi Press, 1969. (Principle #1.)

Hahn, Scott. W. *Covenant and Communion: The Biblical Theology of Pope Benedict*. Ada, MI: Brazos Press, 2009. (Principle #4, 6.)

————. *A Father Who Keeps His Promises: God's Covenant Love in Scripture*. Cincinnati: Servant Books, 1998. A straightforward and fairly simple approach to the theme of "covenant" in Scripture. For a more in-depth study, see *Kinship by Covenant* (below).

————. *Kinship by Covenant: A Canonical Approach to the Fulfillment of God's Saving Promises*. The Anchor Yale Bible Reference Library. New Haven, CT: Yale University Press, 2009. (Principle #4.)

————. "Inspiration," *Catholic Bible Dictionary*, ed. Scott W. Hahn, 384. New York: Doubleday, 2009. (Fine summary of essential information regarding Principle #1.)

————. *Letter and Spirit: From Written Text to Living Word in the Liturgy*. New York: Doubleday, 2005. (Principle #1, 6, 7.)

————. *Scripture Matters: Essays on Reading the Bible from the Heart of the Church*. Steubenville, OH: Emmaus Road, 2003. (Principle #1-7.)

Healy, Mary. "Inspiration and Incarnation: The Christological Analogy and the Hermeneutics of Faith," *Letter & Spirit* 2 (2006), 27-41. (An important essay that addresses issues and concern relevant to the study of Principle #1 and #2.)

Johnson, Luke Timothy. *The Real Jesus: the Misguided Quest for the Historical Jesus and the Truth of the Traditional Gospels*. San Francisco: HarperSanFrancisco, 1995.

Keener, Craig. *The Historical Jesus of the Gospels: Jesus in Historical Context*. Grand Rapids: Eerdmans, 2009. An excellent synthesis of the most important results of historical critical scholarship as it pertains to "the historical Jesus" (Principle #2) and at the same time, an important critique of deficiencies within some of the findings within this larger field of biblical study. (Principle #6.)

————. *The Gospel of John: A Commentary*, 2 Vols. Peabody, MA: Hendrickson, 2003. Keener places particular emphasis on Jewish underpinnings on the gospel -while not ignoring other possible influences. (Principle #5, 6.)

Kloppenborg Verbin, John. *Excavating Q: The History and Setting of the Sayings Gospel* Minneapolis: Fortress Press, 2000. (Principle #5, 6.)

Komoszewski, J. Ed., M. James Sawyer, Daniel B. Wallace. *Reinventing Jesus.* Grand Rapids: Kregel, 2006. (Principle #6.)

Lienhard, Joseph T. *The Bible, the Church, and Authority: The Canon of the Christian Bible in History and Theology.* Collegeville, MN: Liturgical Press, 1995. (Principle #3; Excursus on the canon.)

Maritain, Jacques. *Introduction to Philosophy.* Lanham, MD: Rowman and Littlefield Publishers, 2005. (Principle #5.)

Mariano, Magrassi. *Praying the Bible: An Introduction to Lectio Divina,* trans. Edward Hagman. Collegeville, MN: Liturgical press, 1988. (Principle #7.)

Martin, Ralph and Peter Williamson, eds. *John Paul II and the New Evangelization: How You Can Bring the Good News to Others.* Cincinnati: Servant Books, 2006. (Principle #7.)

McDonald, L. M and J. A. Sanders. *The Canon Debate.* Peabody, MA: Hendrickson, 2002. (Principle #3; Excursus on the canon.)

McGowan, A.T.B. "The Divine Spiration of Scripture," *Scottish Bulletin of Evangelical Theology* 21 no 2 (2003), 199-217. (Principle #1.)

McKnight, Edgar. *What is Form Criticism?* Eugene, OR; Wipf & Stock, 1997. (Principle #5.)

Metzger, Bruce. *The Canon of the New Testament: Its Origin, Development, and Significance.* Oxford: Oxford University Press, 1997. (Principle #3; Excursus on the canon.)

———. *New Testament: Its Background, Growth and Content.* Nashville: Abingdon Press, 2003. (Principle #5; Excursus on the canon.)

Montague, G. *Understanding the Bible.* Mahwah, NJ: Paulist Press, 2000. (Principle #4, 5.)

Murphy, Dennis J., ed. *The Church and the Bible: Official Documents of the Catholic Church.* Rev. second ed. Saint Paul: Alba House, 2007. At over a thousand pages, this volume is one of the most inclusive collections to date. (Principle #2.)

Neuhaus, Richard J., ed. *Biblical Interpretation in Crisis: The Ratzinger Conference on Bible and Church.* Grand Rapids: Eerdmans, 1989. (Principle #6.)

Neusner, Jacob. *A Rabbi Talks with Jesus.* Montreal: McGill-Queen's University Press, 2000. (Principle #5.)

———. *Judaism and Christianity in the Age of Constantine: History, Messiah, Israel, and the Initial Confrontation.* Chicago Studies in the History of Judaism. Chicago: University of Chicago Press, 1987. (Principle #2.)

Newman, John Henry. *On the Inspiration of Scripture,* ed. J. D. Holmes, J.D. and R. Murray. London: Chapman, 1967. (Principle #1.)

Nichols, Aidan. *Christendom Awake: On Reenergizing the Church in Culture.* Grand Rapids: Eerdmans, 1999. (Principle #1, 2, 3, 6.)

———. *Epiphany: A Theological Introduction to Catholicism.* Collegeville, MN: Michael Glazier Press, 1996. (Principle #1, 2, 7.)

———. "Imagination and Revelation: The Face of Christ in the Old Testament," *The Way* 21 (1981) 270-77. (Principle #4, 7.)

———. *Lovely Like Jerusalem: The Fulfillment of the Old Testament in Christ and the Church.* San Francisco: Ignatius Press, 2007. An incredibly rich theological reflection on the relevance of the Old Testament in light of the New. Nichols handles the topic of biblical typology with particular craftsmanship. (Principle #4, 7.)

———. *The Shape of Catholic Theology: An Introduction to its Sources, Principles and History.* San Francisco: Ignatius Press, 1991. (Principle #1-6.)

———. *The Splendour of Doctrine: The Catechism of the Catholic Church on Christian Believing.* Edinburgh: T & T Clark, 1995. (Principle #3.)

Niehbur, H. R. *Christ and Culture.* New York: Harper, 1951. (Principle #7.)

Noth, M. *A History of the Pentateuchal Traditions.* B. W. Anderson, trans. Englewood Cliffs: Prentice-Hall, 1972; German original 1948. (Principle #5.)

Oden, Thomas C. & Christopher H. Hall, eds. *The Ancient Christian Commentary on Scripture.* 29 vols. Downers Grove, IL: Intervarsity Press, 1998-. (Principle #5.)

O'Keefe, John and R.R. Reno. *Sanctified Vision: An Introduction to Early Christian Interpretation of the Bible.* Baltimore: Johns Hopkins, 2005. (Principle #5.)

Orchard, Bernard J.and Harold Riley. *The Order of the Synoptics: Why Three Synoptic Gospels?* Macon, GA: Mercer University Press, 1987. (Principle #5, 6.)

Perrin, Norman. *What is Redaction Criticism?* Eugene, OR: Wipf & Stock, 2002. (Principle #5.)

Pitre, Brant. *Jesus, the Tribulation, and the End of the Exile: Restoration Eschatology and the Origin of the Atonement.* Grand Rapids: Baker Academic, 2005. Excellent example of a recent Catholic biblical exegete who operates within a "Principle #6" (balanced) framework, drawing upon insights from ancient, medieval and modern scholarship (Principle #5) in a fresh way, always leading towards a rich pastoral application of the text (Principle #7).

Powell, Mark Allan. *What is Narrative Criticism?* Minneapolis: Fortress Press, 1990. (Principle #5.)

Rad, Gerhard von. *The Problem of the Hexateuch and Other Essays.* E. W. Trueman Dicken, trans. Edinburgh: Oliver and Boyd, 1966; German original 1938. (Principle #5.)

Rahner, K. *Inspiration in the Bible. Quaestiones Disputatae*, Vol. 1. New York: Herder & Herder, 1966. (Principle #1.)

Ratzinger, Joseph Cardinal (Pope Benedict XVI). *Christianity and the Crisis of Cultures.* San Francisco: Ignatius Press, 2006. (Principle #1-7.)

––––––. *Christocentric Preaching*, in *The Word Toward a Theology of the Word.* New York: J.P. Kenedy & Sons, 1961. (Principle #1, 2, 7.)

––––––. *Dogma and Preaching.* San Francisco: Ignatius Press, 1983. (Principle #7.)

––––––. *God is Near Us: The Eucharist, the Heart of Life.* San Francisco: Ignatius Press, 2003. (Principle #1, 3, 7.)

––––––. *God's Word: Scripture — Tradition — Office.* San Francisco: Ignatius Press, 2008. (Principle #2, 3, 4.)

––––––. *Gospel, Catechesis, Catechism. Sidelights on the Catechism of the Catholic Church.* San Francisco: Ignatius Press, 1997. (Principle #3, 4.)

––––––. *In the Beginning: A Catholic Understanding of the Story of Creation and the Fall.* Grand Rapids: Eerdmans, 1986. (Principle #5.)

––––––. *Jesus of Nazareth.* San Francisco: Ignatius Press, 2007. (Principle #1-7.)

––––––. *Ministers of Your Joy: Scriptural Meditation of Priestly Spirituality.* Ann Arbor: Servant Publications, 1989. (Principle #7.)

––––––. *Many Religions One Covenant: Israel, the Church and the World.* San Francisco, CA: Ignatius Press, 1999 (Principle #4).

––––––. *On the Way to Jesus Christ*, trans. Michael J. Miller. San Francisco, 2005. (Principle #4, 7.)

––––––. "Reflections by Cardinal Ratzinger: The Relationship Between Magisterium and Exegetes" (May 10, 2003). Available online at: www.vatican.va/roman_curia/congregations/cfaith/pcb_documents/rc_con_cfaith_doc_20030510_ratzinger-comm-bible_en.html. (Principle #6.)

––––––. *Spe Salvi.* Encyclical letter, "On Christian Hope" (2007). Available online at: www.vatican.va/holy_father/benedict_xvi/encyclicals/index_en.htm. (Principle #7.)

––––––. *The Spirit of the Liturgy.* San Francisco: Ignatius Press, 2000. (Principle #3, 7.)

————. *To Look on Christ: Exercises in Faith, Hope, and Love.* New York: Crossroad Publishing Co., 1991. (Principle #7.)

————. *Truth and Tolerance.* San Francisco: Ignatius Press, 2004. (Principle #6, 7.)

Rendtorff, R. *The Problem of the Process of the Transmission of the Pentateuch.* Trans. J. J. Scullion. Sheffield: JSOT Press, 1990; German original, 1977. (Principle #2, 5.)

Reventlow, Hans. *The Authority of the Bible and the Rise of the Modern World.* London: SCM Press, 1985. (Principle #1, 6.)

Robinson, Robert B. *Roman Catholic Exegesis Since Divino Afflante Spiritu.* Atlanta: Scholars Press, 1988. (Principle #1, 2, 5.)

Rofe, A. *Introduction to the Composition of the Pentateuch.* Sheffield: Sheffield Academic Press, 1999. (Principle #5.)

Sanders, James A. *From Sacred Story to Sacred Text.* Philadelphia: Fortress Press, 1987. (Principle #7.)

Sayers, Dorothy. *Creed or Chaos?* New York: Harcourt, Brace and Co., 1949. (Principle #7.)

Schönborn, Christoph. *Living the Catechism of the Catholic Church (Volume I: The Creed),* trans. David Kipp. San Francisco: Ignatius Press, 1995. (Principle #3, 7.)

Schuler, P. *A Genre for the Gospels: The Biographical Character of Matthew.* Philadelphia: Fortress Press, 1982. (Principle #5.)

Seeters, John van. *Prologue to History: The Yahwist as Historian in Genesis.* Louisville: Westminster/John Knox, 1992. (Principle #5.)

Simonetti, Manlio. *Biblical Interpretation in the Early Church: An Historical Introduction to Patristic Exegesis.* Edinburgh: T & T Clark, 1994.

Soulen, R. N. and R. K. Soulen. *Handbook of Biblical Criticism,* 3rd ed. London: Westminster John Knox Press, 2001. Good reference work that defines and summarizes many types of biblical methodology, persons, etc. (Principle #5.)

Stein, Robert H. *The Synoptic Problem: An Introduction.* Grand Rapids: Baker Books, 1987. (Principle #5.)

Stendhal, Krister. *Paul Among Jews and Gentiles.* Philadelphia: Augsburg Press, 1976. (Principle #5.)

Stewart, Robert B. ed. *The Resurrection of Jesus: John Dominic Crossan and N. T. Wright in Dialogue.* Philadelphia: Augsburg Fortress, 2005. Spirited debate among Jesus scholars from two disparate points of view. (Principle #1, 2, 6.)

Strauss, David Friedrich. *The Life of Jesus Critically Examined.* Ed. and trans. Peter C. Hodgson. Philadelphia: Fortress Press, 1972. (Principle #6.)

Streeter, B. H. *The Four Gospels: A Study of Origins.* London: Macmillan, 1924; 2nd ed., 1926. (Principle #5.)

Stuhlmacher, Peter. *Historical Criticism and Theological Interpretation.* Philadelphia: Fortress Press, 1977. (Principle #5.)

Sullivan, F. A. *Magisterium: Teaching Authority in the Catholic Church.* New York: Paulist Press, 1985. (Principle #3.)

Sundberg, A.C. "The Old Testament: A Christian Canon," *Catholic Biblical Quarterly* 30 (1968), 143-55. (Principle #3, 4; Excursus on the canon.)

Sungenis, R. ed. *Not by Scripture Alone: A Catholic Critique of Sola Scriptura.* Mulvane, KS: Queenship Publishing, 1998. (Principle #1, 2, 6.)

Tov, Emmanuel. *Exploring the Origins of the Bible: Canon Formation in Historical, Literary, and Theological Perspective.* Grand Rapids: Baker Academic, 2008. (Principle #3; Excursus on the canon.)

Trembath, Kern Robert. *Evangelical Theories of Biblical Inspiration: A Review and Proposal.* Oxford: Oxford University Press, 1987. (Principle #1.)

Tuckett, C. M. *The Revival of the Griesbach Hypothesis*. Cambridge: Cambridge Univ. Press, 1983. (Principle #5.)

Turo, J.C. and R. E. Brown. "Canonicity," *The New Jerome Biblical* Commentary, ed. R. E. Brown, J. A. Fitzmyer and R. E. Murphy, 515-34. Prentice Hall, NJ: Prentice Hall, 1969. (Principle #3; Excursus on the canon.)

Valkenberg, Wilhelm G. *"Did Not Our Hearts Burn?" The Place and Function of Holy Scripture in the Theology of St. Thomas Aquinas*. Utrecht: Thomas Instituut te Utrecht, 1990. (Principle #3,5.)

VanderKam, James C. *An Introduction to Early Judaism*. Grand Rapids: Eerdmans, 2000. (Principle #5.)

Vanhoozer, Kevin. Vanhoozer, Kevin. *The Drama of Doctrine: A Canonical-Linguistic Approach to Christian Theology*. Louisville: Westminster John Knox, 2005. (Principle #1, 2, 5, 6, 7.)

———. *Is There a Meaning in the Text?* Grand Rapids: Zondervan, 1998. A conservative, erudite Evangelical scholar discusses the question of "meaning" in biblical texts, and critiques some of the more radical post-modern biblical critics. (Principle #2, 6.)

Vawter, Bruce. *Biblical Inspiration: Theological Resources*. London: Westminster, 1972. (Principle #1.)

Wenham, Gordon. "Pondering the Pentateuch: the Search for a New Paradigm," *The Face of Old Testament Studies: A Survey of Contemporary Approaches*. D. W. Baker and B. T. Arnold, eds. Grand Rapids: Baker Book House, 1999, 116-44. (Principle #4.)

Wilken, Robert L. *The Spirit of Early Christian Thought: Seeking the Face of God*. New Haven: Yale University Press, 2003. (Principle #5.)

Williamson, Peter. *Catholic Principles for Interpreting Scripture: A Study of the Pontifical Biblical Commission's The Interpretation of the Bible in the Church*. Pontificia Università Gregoriana, 2000, Subsidia Biblica 22. Rome: Pontificio Istituto biblico, 2001.

Wojtyla, Karol (Pope John Paul II). *Christifideles Laici*. Post-Synodal Apostolic Exhortation, "On the Vocation and the Mission of the Lay Faithful in the Church and in the World (1988). Available online at: http://www.vatican.va/holy_father/john_paul_ii/apost_exhortations/documents/hf_jp-ii_exh_30121988_christifideles-laici_en.html. (Principle #7.)

———. *Letter to Families*. St. Paul, MN: Pauline Books and Media, 1994. (Principle #7.)

———. *Redemptoris Mater*. Encyclical letter, "On the Blessed Virgin Mary in the Life of the Pilgrim Church" (1987). Available online: http://www.vatican.va/holy_father/john_paul_ii/encyclicals/documents/hf_jp-ii_enc_25031987_redemptoris-mater_en.html. (Principle #7.)

———. *Sources of Renewal: The Implementation of Vatican II*. Trans. P. S. Falla. San Francisco: Harper & Row, 1972. (Principle #1-7.)

Wright, Christopher. *Knowing Jesus Through the Old Testament*. Downers Grove, IL: InterVarsity Press, 1995. (Principle #4, 7.)

Wright, N. T. *The Challenge of Jesus: Rediscovering Who Jesus Was and Is*. Downers Grove, IL: InterVarsity Press, 1999. (Principle #2, 6, 7.)

———. *The Contemporary Quest for Jesus*. Minneapolis: Fortress Press, 2002. (Principle #5, 6.)

———. *Jesus and the Victory of God: Christian Origins and the Question of God*, Volume 2, Philadelphia: Augsburg Fortress, 1996. (Principle #2, 5, 6.)

Wright, N.T and Stephen Neill. *The Interpretation of the New Testament 1816-1986*. Oxford: Oxford University Press, 1988. (Principle #4, 5.)

ABOUT THE AUTHOR

Dr. Steven Smith is Assistant Professor of Sacred Scripture at Mount St. Mary's Seminary in Emmitsburg, Maryland. He completed his Master's Degree in Theology from Wheaton College Graduate School and earned his doctorate in New Testament and Early Christianity from Loyola University of Chicago. He has authored numerous articles on Scripture and Catholic theology, appeared on television and radio programs and spoken at conferences and parishes across North America. He and his wife Elizabeth have been married twelve years and God has blessed them with two beautiful daughters, Isabelle Marie and Olivia Marie.

INVITE DR. STEVEN SMITH TO YOUR PARISH, CONFERENCE OR EVENT!

Steven Smith is a very energetic, insightful and faithful speaker on Sacred Scripture and the Catholic faith. He is available for speaking engagements such as conferences and parish events. Among his frequent topics:

- Adam, Eve, Jesus, Mary — and you
- Making sense of the Old and New Testament together
- The Six Great "Shaliachs" of Sacred Scripture
- Unlocking The Mystery of the Book of Revelation
- Jesus and the Four Gospels (especially the Gospel of John)
- Pope Benedict XVI's Biblical Vision (*Jesus of Nazareth*)
- Understanding and Believing the *Catechism of the Catholic Church*

And of course …
- The Seven Principles of Catholic Biblical Interpretation

Dr. Smith's schedule can fill up quickly! Yet, he is interested to learn about your upcoming event and how he may be of service. To invite him to your event, or to learn more about this book and other exciting projects, go to:

WWW.THEGODWHOSPEAKS.COM

You may also contact Dr. Smith directly at: scsmith@msmary.edu. Dr. Smith's website, www.thegodwhospeaks.com, has more up-to-date information. Help us spread the word about *The Word of the Lord!*